RECIPES FROM
GOLD MEDAL
WINERIES

Designed by Marilyn Appleby Design
Edited by Carlene M. Przykucki and Anne E. Przykucki

Library of Congress Control Number: 2004115933
ISBN 1-881892-07-7
Printed and bound in the United States of America.

Published by Spradlin & Associates
PO Box 863, Lapeer, MI 48446. Telephone 810.664.8406.
First Edition.

RAPTOR PRESS

Raptor Press is an imprint of Spradlin & Associates.

RECIPES

FROM

GOLD MEDAL
WINERIES

JOE BORRELLO

DEDICATION

■

TO JOE AND BETTY SCHAGRIN
FOR THEIR ENDLESS EFFORTS TO EDUCATE
AND PROMOTE A RESPONSIBLE APPRECIATION
FOR WINE WITH FOOD.

CONTENTS

RECIPES FROM GOLD MEDAL WINERIES

COMPILED AND EDITED BY JOE BORRELLO

Long before there were North American wineries, and indeed before there was even a land known as America, Europeans were enjoying the "fermented" fruits of their labor along with the preparation of other food gifts from the earth. Wine has been a part of the civilized dining table for centuries.

One of the greatest gifts early settlers brought to America was their knowledge and love of wine and food. This knowledge was propagated by homesteaders, missionaries and later by immigrant farmers from the great culinary countries of Europe and Asia. Many of these early migrants settled on farms and planted vineyards alongside their other crops. Harvest time included the making of wine and the celebration of another bountiful winter of provisions.

The uniqueness of America's wine development is the influence of a variety of gifted grape growers and winemakers. From Germany, Switzerland, France, Portugal, Spain, Italy, Hungary and Russia they brought their family's generations-old trade to work the promising fertile ground of the New World. Today, we find the ethnic influences of all these countries, and many more, in America's great agricultural evolu-

tion. These early pioneers, and indeed even more recent immigrants, also brought with them developed skill in the kitchen.

Throughout virtually every family-owned winery in the states and provinces of the U.S. and Canada, you will find some degree of culinary skill woven into the winery's philosophy of wine with food. Even with the corporate expansion of the winery trade around the beginning of the new millennium, recipes and food education together are still a prominent segment of the corporate marketing philosophy, albeit on a more sophisticated culinary level than those of early farm cooks using wood-burning stoves.

The European philosophy of wine, an agricultural product that belongs on the dining table along with all the other foodstuffs grown in the same soil, has withstood the test of time. Although Americans have not adopted local loyalties of wine and cuisine as wholeheartedly as Europeans, there is tremendous growth and interest in North America's local wine production and an adaptation of ethnic cooking in regional America.

Tasters Guild International, a food and wine appreciation society with over 60 chapters throughout the United States, recognized this growth and since 1987 has dedicated itself to the "education and appreciation of the responsible use of wine with food." With thousands of members across the United States, Tasters Guild chapters regularly conduct dinners, wine seminars and various food and wine events for their local members.

On an international level, Tasters Guild conducts two wine judgings annually. One is conducted in the spring with over 2,000 wines entered each year. This wine judging is recognized by the wine trade as one of the top professional wine judgings in the country. The second Tasters Guild Wine Judging is part of the society's educational program for its members and is held in late summer in Washington, D.C. during its national convention. Along with wine and food seminars and demonstrations, members also participate in the Consumers' Wine Judging, where the only qualification to evaluate wines is a consumer's love for wine and food.

In both these competitions, medals are awarded to wines of distinction. When both the professional and the consumers feel a wine is particularly outstanding, it is awarded the coveted Gold Medal. (Current results are viewable at the Tasters Guild web site www.tastersguild.com.)

From over 60 wineries that have earned at least one Gold Medal from one of these wine judgings between 2002-2004, we have collected over 150 recipes. Each of these recipes is representative of the "food with wine" philosophy of the particular winery. Some are quite simple, some require time and patience, but all exemplify the dedication and enthusiasm of combining the joys of wine with an individual taste for food. Just as dedicated as these award-winning wine producers are to growing and bottling the best wine of which they are capable, they also share with us their love of cooking, baking and gracious entertaining. And, of course, a taste of their favorite wines.

Join me, as we take a visitor's tour through the kitchens and dining tables of Gold Medal Wineries — and don't forget a glass of wine for the cook.

Joe Borrello

APPETIZERS

■

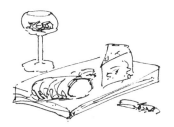

BRIE TOPPED WITH PEAR BUTTER AND TOASTED ALMONDS

FROM LAKE SONOMA WINERY, CALIFORNIA
CHEF ROBIN LEHNHOFF

Serves 8

PEAR BUTTER:
2 pounds fresh pears, unpeeled, cored
  and sliced
1 cup apple cider
3/4 cup light brown sugar
1 teaspoon lemon rind
1 teaspoon cinnamon
1/8 teaspoon ground ginger
1/8 teaspoon ground cloves
pinch salt

BRIE:
2 pounds Brie
1 cup toasted almonds, sliced

NOTES:
SINFULLY DELICIOUS!

PEAR BUTTER:
In saucepan, cook pears and cider until tender. Puree and return to saucepan after straining through china cap. Add remaining ingredients and cook 2 hours or until very thick. Strain to remove lemon rind and refrigerate until ready to serve.

BRIE:
Preheat oven to 350° F. Cut Brie into chunks and place in ovenproof dish. Spoon pear butter on top of cheese and bake 10 minutes. Remove from oven and sprinkle almonds on top. Serve immediately with sliced baguette.

SUGGESTED WINE:
Lake Sonoma Russian River Chardonnay

Per serving: 643 Calories; 41g Fat (56% calories from fat); 28g Protein; 46g Carbohydrate; 114mg Cholesterol; 725mg Sodium
Food Exchanges: 1/2 Starch/Bread; 3 Lean Meat; 1 1/2 Fruit; 5 Fat; 1 1/2 Other Carbohydrates

CABERNET BLUE CHEESE WALNUT SPREAD

FROM CEDAR MOUNTAIN WINERY, CALIFORNIA

Serves 8

4 ounces blue cheese
1 tablespoon Cabernet Sauvignon
4 tablespoons walnuts, finely chopped

Process blue cheese and wine in food processor until smooth and about the consistency of soft butter. Add walnuts as suggested.

NOTES:
VERSATILE AND EASY TO MAKE ON A MOMENT'S NOTICE.

SERVING SUGGESTIONS:

Spread on toast points, sprinkle with chopped walnuts and serve as an accompaniment to a tossed green salad.

As an appetizer or a light dessert, spread on sliced pears or apples and sprinkle with chopped walnuts.

As an hors d'oeuvre, bake a 5-pound bag of chicken wings in oven until golden brown. Put Cabernet Blue Cheese Walnut Spread in bowl on serving platter; surround with baked chicken wings. Have guests dip wings in spread and enjoy this truly unique treat.

SUGGESTED WINE:
Cedar Mountain Winery Estate Cabernet Sauvignon

Per serving: 75 Calories; 6g Fat (75% calories from fat); 4g Protein; 1g Carbohydrate; 11mg Cholesterol; 199mg Sodium
Food Exchanges: 1/2 Lean Meat; 1 Fat

QUICHE WITHOUT A CRUST

FROM CHATEAU CHANTAL WINERY/BED & BREAKFAST, MICHIGAN
CHEF NADINE BEGIN

Serves 10

1 tablespoon butter
1 cup onions, chopped
1 cup mushrooms, chopped
2 cups fresh spinach, chopped
1 cup Feta cheese, crumbled
12 large eggs
$^1/_2$ cup all-purpose flour
dash sea salt
dash thyme
dash dry mustard
dash cayenne pepper
$^3/_4$ cup half and half
dash paprika
dash black pepper
dash parsley
$^1/_8$ cup Parmesan cheese, freshly grated

Preheat oven to 350° F. Generously coat quiche or pie pan with cooking spray. Add butter and sauté onions, mushrooms and spinach for a few minutes. Add crumbled Feta cheese. In separate bowl, beat eggs until light and fluffy. Add flour and a little salt; continue to beat. Add other seasonings. Add half and half; continue to beat. Pour over prepared vegetables and cheese. Sprinkle with paprika, pepper, parsley and Parmesan cheese. Add additional toppings such as sliced tomatoes, olives, etc. if desired. Place pan on baking sheet and bake 30 minutes or until quiche is high and eggs are firm — it will sink afterwards. Remove from oven and let set for a few minutes. Slice into "finger food" pieces.

SUGGESTED WINE:
Chateau Chantal Sparkling Wine

Per serving: 200 Calories; 13g Fat (58% calories from fat); 12g Protein; 9g Carbohydrate; 282mg Cholesterol; 290mg Sodium
Food Exchanges: 1/2 Starch/Bread; 1 1/2 Lean Meat; 1/2 Vegetable; 1 1/2 Fat

NOTES:
BE SURE TO MAKE PLENTY — THESE TASTY LITTLE MORSELS ARE THE FIRST TO DISAPPEAR FROM THE BUFFET TABLE.

RAINBOW OF COUSCOUS

FROM CEDAR MOUNTAIN WINERY, CALIFORNIA

Serves 15

10 ounces uncooked couscous, divided
1 pinch saffron
2 cloves garlic, finely minced
3 medium red bell peppers, seeded and diced
4 ounces smoked salmon, finely chopped
2 $^1/_4$ ounces capers, drained
2 large eggs, hard-boiled and finely chopped
$^1/_4$ cup parsley, finely chopped
1 medium yellow bell pepper, seeded and diced

NOTES:
ALL IN ONE — ATTRACTIVE, TASTY, LOW-CAL AND LOW-CARB.

Cook $^1/_2$ of couscous with saffron; cook other $^1/_2$ of couscous with finely minced garlic (follow cooking directions on package of couscous). Let each cool to room temperature.

ASSEMBLE THE RAINBOW:
Starting with red bell peppers, form a 10- to 12-inch diameter semi-circular strip on serving platter. Place a strip of saffron couscous inside bell peppers. Continue this procedure with smoked salmon, capers, eggs, garlic couscous, parsley and ending with yellow bell peppers. The result should look like a rainbow, with the top of the rainbow being red bell peppers and the bottom of the rainbow being yellow bell peppers.

To eat the rainbow, scoop up a portion with crackers and enjoy the variety of colors and flavors.

SUGGESTED WINE:
Cedar Mountain Merlot

Per serving: 100 Calories; 1g Fat (11% calories from fat); 5g Protein; 17g Carbohydrate; 30mg Cholesterol; 165mg Sodium
Food Exchanges: 1 Starch/Bread; 1/2 Lean Meat; 1/2 Vegetable

ROASTED RED PEPPERS WITH ANCHOVIES

FROM SHARPE HILL VINEYARD, CONNECTICUT

Serves 8

10 medium red bell peppers
1 clove garlic
3 tablespoons extra virgin olive oil
4 ounces canned anchovies, drained

Roast red peppers over wood fire, outdoor grill, gas stovetop burner or broiler until skin is charred. Put peppers into brown paper bag for 1 hour.

Remove peppers, cut in half and remove blackened skins, seeds and interior membranes; cut in wide slices and set aside.

Thinly slice garlic clove. Brush serving platter with oil, then evenly distribute garlic slices on platter. Place peppers on platter and arrange anchovies on top. Drizzle with olive oil and marinate 1 hour before serving.

SUGGESTED WINE:
Sharpe Hill Chardonnay

Per serving: 100 Calories; 7g Fat (57% calories from fat); 5g Protein; 6g Carbohydrate; 12mg Cholesterol; 522mg Sodium
Food Exchanges: 1/2 Lean Meat; 1 Vegetable; 1 Fat

NOTES:
ANYBODY FOR ANTIPASTO?

SMOKED BACON AND GOAT CHEESE TART

FROM VALLEY OF THE MOON WINERY, CALIFORNIA
CHEF LAURIE SOUZA

Serves 8

6 medium leeks
6 tablespoons unsalted butter, divided
salt and white pepper, freshly ground
$^1/_2$ pound thick-sliced bacon, diced
2 large eggs
1 cup heavy cream
1 teaspoon Dijon mustard
puff pastry dough, 10-inches round,
   $^1/_8$-inch thick
5 ounces goat cheese
$^1/_2$ cup fresh bread crumbs, toasted
   and ground

Preheat oven to 400° F. Trim leeks, leaving just a small amount of the green. Wash and julienne leeks very carefully in several changes of water. Drain and pat dry.

NOTES:
THE AROMAS AND FLAVORS ALONE ARE
WORTH THE EFFORT, NOT TO MENTION
THE RAVES FROM YOUR GUESTS.

Heat 4 tablespoons butter in medium skillet over low heat. Add leeks and cook for about 15 minutes, until wilted. Sprinkle with salt and pepper and cover. Continue cooking another 10 minutes, shaking pan occasionally. Drain and set aside to cool slightly.

Meanwhile, fry diced bacon until crispy and drain off fat. Beat eggs and cream together, then add mustard. Place rolled-out puff pastry into 9-inch tart pan. Fit to pan and roll a rolling pin over top of tart pan; trim excess dough. Prick sides and bottom of pastry. Place cooled and drained leeks into bottom of tart pan. Sprinkle cooked bacon over top. Crumble cheese over bacon. Fill shell with egg and cream mixture to just below top of shell. Sprinkle bread crumbs over top. Melt and drizzle remaining 2 tablespoons butter over top. Bake 15 minutes. Reduce heat to 350° F and continue baking until nicely browned, about 30 minutes.

SUGGESTED WINE:
Valley of the Moon Sangiovese

Per serving: 510 Calories; 42g Fat (74% calories from fat); 18g Protein; 16g Carbohydrate; 162mg Cholesterol; 583mg Sodium
Food Exchanges: 2 Lean Meat; 2 Vegetable; 7 Fat

SPAM LORRAINE

FROM CEDAR MOUNTAIN WINERY, CALIFORNIA

Serves 6

1 large onion, diced
1 tablespoon butter, margarine or oil
12 ounces canned SPAM luncheon meat
3 large eggs
1 cup cream or milk
pinch nutmeg
pinch cayenne pepper
$1/8$ teaspoon black pepper, freshly ground
1 pie crust, 9-inches, unbaked and chilled
1 cup Swiss cheese, shredded

Preheat oven to 350° F.

Sauté onion in butter, margarine or oil until lightly browned. Set aside. Cut SPAM luncheon meat into 1/4-inch cubes and sauté until lightly browned. Drain on paper towel and set aside.

Combine eggs, cream or milk, nutmeg, cayenne and black pepper. Beat with whisk or rotary beater until well mixed.

Sprinkle pie shell with SPAM luncheon meat and spread sautéed onions on top. Cover with shredded Swiss cheese. Pour in egg mixture carefully. Bake 10 minutes. Reduce heat to 300° F and bake 40 minutes or until knife inserted in center comes out clean. Serve either hot or cold.

NOTES:
HERE IS A VERY DIFFERENT QUICHE RECIPE THAT WORKS WELL FOR BUFFET ENTERTAINING.

■

SUGGESTED WINE:
Cedar Mountain Cabernet Sauvignon

Per serving: 500 Calories; 38g Fat (69% calories from fat); 21g Protein; 18g Carbohydrate; 192mg Cholesterol; 1057mg Sodium
Food Exchanges: 1 Starch/Bread; 1/2 Vegetable; 6 Fat

SUN-DRIED TOMATO DIP

FROM ST. JULIAN WINE COMPANY, MICHIGAN

Serves 8

1 cup sun-dried tomatoes
1/4 cup sour cream
1 scallion, chopped
1/2 cup Hellmann's mayonnaise
6 ounces cream cheese
1/2 cup carrots, chopped
2 teaspoons fresh parsley, chopped
1 teaspoon fresh basil, chopped
1/2 teaspoon black pepper, freshly ground
2 tablespoons St. Julian Italian
   Salad Dressing
1/4 cup St. Julian Pinot Grigio

Chop tomatoes in food processor. Add remaining ingredients. Process until well blended.

Serve with veggies, bagel chips, pita triangles or crackers.

SUGGESTED WINE:
St. Julian Blue Heron

Per serving: 232 Calories; 23g Fat (85% calories from fat); 3g Protein; 6g Carbohydrate; 31mg Cholesterol; 319mg Sodium
Food Exchanges: 1/2 Starch/Bread; 1/2 Lean Meat; 3 Fat

NOTES:
THIS IS NOT YOUR ORDINARY CHIP DIP—
IT GOES WAY BEYOND.

TOMATO BASIL BRUSCHETTA

FROM MARTINI & ROSSI, ITALY

Serves 8

6 ripe Roma tomatoes, seeded and diced
15 basil leaves, chopped
$1/_4$ medium red onion, finely diced
$1/_2$ cup Martini & Rossi Rosso
   Sweet Vermouth
2 tablespoons extra virgin olive oil,
   divided
$1/_2$ teaspoon sea salt
black pepper, freshly ground, to taste
1 loaf Italian bread
2 cloves garlic, cut in half

NOTES:
ALWAYS A POPULAR APPETIZER, BUT
EVEN BETTER WITH THE ADDITION OF
MARTINI & ROSSI ROSSO SWEET
VERMOUTH.

Prepare topping by combining tomatoes, basil, red onion, vermouth and 1 tablespoon olive oil. Add salt and pepper to taste. Let flavors marinate in refrigerator at least 2 hours.

Slice bread into 16 slices. Toast bread on barbeque, indoor grill or in toaster. Rub with cut garlic and brush lightly with remaining olive oil.

To assemble, drain topping to remove excess liquid. Place 2 tablespoons topping on each slice of toast. Garnish with small basil leaf, if desired.

SUGGESTED WINE:
Martini & Rossi Prosecco

Per serving: 88 Calories; 4g Fat (46% calories from fat); 1g Protein; 9g Carbohydrate; 0mg Cholesterol; 150mg Sodium
Food Exchanges: 1 Vegetable; 1/2 Fat

WARM CRAB APPETIZER

FROM BYINGTON VINEYARD & WINERY, CALIFORNIA

Serves 16

8 ounces cream cheese, softened
3 tablespoons Byington Chardonnay
8 ounces crab meat
2 tablespoons green onions,
  finely chopped
1 teaspoon horseradish sauce
$1/2$ teaspoon Old Bay seasoned salt
$1/4$ cup toasted pistachios, finely chopped

Preheat oven to 375º F.

Place softened cream cheese in bowl and mix in wine. Add remaining ingredients except pistachios; mix until just blended.

Put mixture into 3-cup ovenproof baking dish. Sprinkle chopped pistachios on top and bake in oven until bubbly, about 20 minutes.

Let dip cool about 5 minutes before serving. Accompany with pita wedges, crackers or sliced baguette.

SUGGESTED WINE:
Byington Winery Chardonnay

Per serving: 79 Calories; 6g Fat (72% calories from fat); 4g Protein; 1g Carbohydrate; 28mg Cholesterol; 135mg Sodium
Food Exchanges: 1/2 Lean Meat; 1 Fat

NOTES:
GREAT FOR COCKTAIL PARTIES OR A DAY ON THE SOFA WATCHING FOOTBALL.

WILD RICE FRITTATA

FROM BARGETTO WINERY, CALIFORNIA

Serves 8

2 tablespoons olive oil
$^1/_2$ cup scallions, sliced
2 cloves garlic, minced
2 ounces shiitake mushrooms,
   coarsely chopped
1 cup Canadian bacon or ham, diced
$^1/_3$ cup fresh parsley, chopped
12 medium eggs
$^1/_2$ cup heavy cream
1 cup wild rice, cooked
1 cup Swiss cheese, grated
$^1/_2$ cup Parmesan cheese, grated

Heat oil in ovenproof pan or iron skillet, then add scallions and garlic and sauté for 2 minutes. Add mushrooms, bacon or ham and cook 3 minutes, stirring constantly. Add parsley and remove from heat. Beat eggs with cream and combine with wild rice. Mix together egg, mushroom mixture and Swiss cheese. Cook slowly 10 minutes (about 80% done). Sprinkle with Parmesan cheese and finish under broiler, about 2 $^1/_2$ minutes.

NOTE: The frittata mixture can be finished in oven at 350º F, about 12 $^1/_2$ minutes, instead of cooking slowly on stovetop.

NOTES:
PERFECT WARM OR AT ROOM TEMPERATURE FOR A SUMMER BRUNCH OR OUTDOOR WINE PARTY.

SUGGESTED WINE:
Bargetto Pinot Grigio

Per serving: 361 Calories; 24g Fat (60% calories from fat); 24g Protein; 13g Carbohydrate; 375mg Cholesterol; 651mg Sodium
Food Exchanges: 1/8 Starch/Bread; 3 Lean Meat; 1 Vegetable; 3 Fat

NOTES:

NOTES:

BEVERAGES

ITALIAN WHITE SANGRIA

FROM MARTINI & ROSSI, ITALY

Serves 7

1 bottle Martini & Rossi Extra
   Dry Vermouth
1 cup orange liqueur
8 ounces fresh orange juice (3 oranges)
4 ounces fresh lemon juice (2 lemons)
2 ounces fresh lime juice (1 lime)
$1/2$ cup sugar
1 medium orange, thinly sliced
1 medium lemon, thinly sliced
1 medium lime, thinly sliced
1 medium apple, cored and thinly sliced
1 cup sparkling water, chilled

Combine vermouth, orange liqueur, fruit juices and sugar in large pitcher. Stir until sugar is dissolved. Chill until ready to serve. Stir in sliced fruit and sparkling water. Serve over ice.

Per serving: 230 Calories; less than 1g Fat (1% calories from fat); 1g Protein; 39g Carbohydrate; 0mg Cholesterol; 4mg Sodium
Food Exchanges: 2 Fruit; 1 Other Carbohydrates

NOTES:
COOL, REFRESHING AND DELICIOSO!

PROSECCO MARTINI

FROM MARTINI & ROSSI, ITALY

Serves 1

6 ounces Italian lemon ice
1 ounce Grey Goose Vodka
2 ounces Martini & Rossi Prosecco

Place Italian lemon ice into chilled blender and slowly blend in vodka. Add Prosecco at end of blending. Pour into frosted 10- to 12-ounce wine glass and enjoy.

Per serving: unknown

NOTES:
MARTINI & ROSSI PROSECCO "FRIZZANTE" IS THE SECRET INGREDIENT FOR THIS REFRESHING COCKTAIL.

RASPBERRY-INFUSED CHAMPAGNE COCKTAIL

FROM ST. JULIAN WINE COMPANY, MICHIGAN

Serves 4

4 teaspoons St. Julian Raspberry
  Eau de Vie
3/4 liter St. Julian Michigan White
  Champagne, chilled
fresh raspberries for garnish

NOTES:
A MICHIGAN RENDITION OF EUROPEAN
"KIR ROYALE" — ONLY BETTER.

Pour 1 teaspoon Eau de Vie into each champagne flute, swirling to coat sides.

Top each glass with champagne.

Garnish with fresh raspberries, but lower fruit slowly to avoid overflow.

SUGGESTED WINES:
St. Julian Raspberry Eau de Vie and
Michigan White Champagne

Per serving: 175 Calories; 0g Fat (0% calories from fat); 0g Protein; 7g Carbohydrate; 0mg Cholesterol; 0mg Sodium

NOTES:

NOTES:

DESSERTS

■

BITTERSWEET CHOCOLATE CAKE WITH CINNAMON CRÈME ANGLAISE

FROM ZD WINERY, CALIFORNIA

Serves 8

CAKE:
8 ounces bittersweet chocolate, chopped
3/4 cup unsalted butter
3 large eggs
3 large egg yolks
5 tablespoons granulated sugar
1 1/2 tablespoons all-purpose flour
16 cherries, soaked in brandy

CRÈME ANGLAISE:
1-inch vanilla bean or 1 teaspoon
   vanilla extract
2 cups cream or milk
4 egg yolks
1/3 cup granulated sugar
1/2 teaspoon cinnamon

CAKE:
Preheat oven to 425º F. Generously butter eight 3/4-cup soufflé dishes or custard cups. Sprinkle inside of each dish with sugar, tapping out excess.

Stir chocolate and butter in double boiler until smooth. Remove from heat.

Using electric mixer, beat eggs, egg yolks and sugar in large bowl until thick and pale yellow, about 8 minutes. Fold 1/3 of warm chocolate mixture into egg mixture until well incorporated. Fold in remaining chocolate mixture. Fold in flour. Divide batter among soufflé dishes. Push 2 cherries into center of each soufflé cup. (Can be made 1 day ahead. Cover with plastic; chill. Bring to room temperature before continuing.)

Place soufflé dishes on baking sheet. Bake cakes uncovered about 13 minutes until edges are puffed and slightly cracked, but 1 inch of center of each moves slightly when dishes are shaken gently. Carefully unmold each cake and serve upside down.

CRÈME ANGLAISE:
Place fine mesh strainer inside small bowl and place in larger bowl of ice.

Split about 1 inch of vanilla bean lengthwise and scrape into cream. Put vanilla bean shell in pot with cream and bring to a boil. Let steep for 2 or 3 minutes. Scrape bean again and mix vanilla into cream.

Over double boiler on medium heat, mix egg yolks with sugar until incorporated, about 1 minute. Starting with $^1/_4$ cup, slowly incorporate cream. Slowly stir in remaining cream and keep stirring until mixture coats back of spoon, about 12 to 15 minutes. Strain mixture into bowl sitting in ice. Stir in $^1/_2$ teaspoon of cinnamon. Stir mixture while cooling.

Ladle a pool of crème anglaise onto center of plate and serve warm molten chocolate cakes over it. Sprinkle with powdered sugar if desired.

SUGGESTED WINE:
ZD Cabernet Sauvignon

Per serving: 745 Calories; 57g Fat (59% calories from fat); 12g Protein; 77g Carbohydrate; 368mg Cholesterol; 62mg Sodium
Food Exchanges: 1 Lean Meat; 3 Fruit; 10 1/2 Fat; 1 1/2 Other Carbohydrates

NOTES:
FOR THIS RECIPE, HIGH QUALITY BITTERSWEET CHOCOLATE WILL MAKE ALL THE DIFFERENCE IN THE WORLD.

BLACKBERRY WINE CAKE

FROM ST. JAMES WINERY, MISSOURI

Serves 8

CAKE:
1/2 cup pecans, chopped
1 box white cake mix
3 ounces berry-flavored gelatin
4 large eggs
1/2 cup vegetable oil
1 cup St. James Blackberry Wine

GLAZE:
1 cup powdered sugar
1/2 cup blackberry wine
1 stick butter

NOTES:
IF YOU LIKE FRUIT PASTRIES, YOU ARE GOING TO LOVE THIS CAKE!

CAKE:
Preheat oven to 350º F. Grease and flour bundt pan. Sprinkle pecans on bottom. In large bowl, combine cake mix and gelatin. Add eggs, oil and wine, then blend thoroughly. Pour batter into prepared pan. Bake 50 to 60 minutes or until cake tests done. Turn onto wire rack to cool.

GLAZE:
Combine powdered sugar, wine and butter in saucepan; bring to a boil. Remove from heat. Pour 1/2 of mixture over warm cake and let set for 30 minutes. Pour remaining glaze over cake. (Glaze will have thickened while cooling.)

SUGGESTED WINE:
St. James Blackberry Wine

Per serving: 537 Calories; 27g Fat (47% calories from fat); 6g Protein; 62g Carbohydrate; 112mg Cholesterol; 346mg Sodium
Food Exchanges: 1/2 Lean Meat; 5 Fat; 3 1/2 Other Carbohydrates

BLUEBERRY BUCKLE

FROM CHATEAU CHANTAL WINERY/BED & BREAKFAST, MICHIGAN

Serves 9

TOPPING:
$^1/_3$ cup all-purpose flour
$^1/_3$ cup light brown sugar, packed
$^1/_2$ teaspoon ground cinnamon
4 tablespoons unsalted butter, sliced

BATTER:
6 tablespoons unsalted butter, softened
$^1/_2$ cup granulated sugar
1 large egg
1 teaspoon vanilla extract
$^1/_2$ cup sour cream
1 $^3/_4$ cups all-purpose flour
2 teaspoons baking powder
pinch salt
1 $^1/_2$ cups fresh blueberries,
    rinsed and dried
1 cup heavy cream

NOTES:
A DISH WORTH WAKING UP FOR ON A
SUNNY, SUMMER WEEKEND.

Position rack in center of oven and preheat to 375° F. Butter an 8-inch square pan.

TOPPING:
In small bowl, combine flour, brown sugar and cinnamon. With pastry blender, cut in butter to resemble coarse crumbs. Set aside.

BATTER:
With hand-held mixer, beat butter in large bowl until creamy. Gradually beat in sugar until light and fluffy. Add egg and vanilla; beat until smooth, then beat in sour cream. In medium bowl, stir together flour, baking powder and salt until evenly blended. Quickly stir dry ingredients into butter mixture, just until moistened. Batter will be thick and lumpy. Fold in blueberries and turn into prepared pan.

Crumble reserved topping over batter. Bake 30 to 35 minutes, until toothpick inserted in cake portion emerges clean. Cool on rack 15 to 20 minutes. Cut into 9 squares and serve warm with heavy cream.

Per serving: 441 Calories; 27g Fat (54% calories from fat); 5g Protein; 46g Carbohydrate; 102mg Cholesterol; 112mg Sodium
Food Exchanges: 1 1/2 Starch/Bread; 5 Fat; 1 1/2 Other Carbohydrates

BRANDIED APPLE CAKE

FROM ST. JULIAN WINE COMPANY, MICHIGAN

Serves 8

1 1/2 cups apple slices, peeled, seeded and diced
1/2 cup dates, chopped
1/2 cup St. Julian B&C Brandy
3/4 cup all-purpose flour
3/4 cup sugar
2 teaspoons baking powder
dash salt
1/2 teaspoon cinnamon
1/2 teaspoon nutmeg
1 large egg, slightly beaten
2 tablespoons apple juice
1/2 cup pecans, chopped
powdered sugar for garnish

Preheat oven to 350º F. Marinate apples and dates in brandy. Set aside.

Combine flour, sugar, baking powder, salt, cinnamon, nutmeg and egg. Mix thoroughly and stir in apple juice, apple and date brandy mixture and pecans.

Grease and flour 9-inch cake pan. Pour in complete mixture and bake 20 minutes.

Sprinkle with powdered sugar and serve.

SUGGESTED WINE:
St. Julian Solera Cream Sherry

Per serving: 249 Calories; 5g Fat (22% calories from fat); 3g Protein; 41g Carbohydrate; 27mg Cholesterol; 100mg Sodium
Food Exchanges: 1/2 Starch/Bread; 2 Fruit; 1 Fat; 1 1/2 Other Carbohydrates

NOTES:
AN APPLE CAKE WITH A LITTLE EXTRA KICK.

CABERNET ROYALE CHOCOLATE FRUITCAKE

FROM CEDAR MOUNTAIN WINERY, CALIFORNIA

Serves 6

1 cup dried figs
1 cup dried apricots
$1/_2$ cup dried strawberries
$1/_2$ cup dried cherries
1 cup Cedar Mountain Cabernet Royale Port
$1/_2$ cup butter, softened
$1/_2$ cup sugar
$1/_2$ cup brown sugar
2 teaspoons vanilla
1 teaspoon cinnamon
$1/_2$ teaspoon clove
$1/_2$ teaspoon nutmeg
8 egg yolks
10 ounces semisweet chocolate, melted
2 cups flour plus 6 tablespoons for dried fruit
6 ounces pecans
8 egg whites

Preheat oven to 300º F. In large mixing bowl, macerate dried fruit in wine overnight.

Drain fruit and set aside, saving the liquid. Butter and flour 2 small loaf pans. In electric mixer, cream butter. Gradually add sugars until both are incorporated. Add vanilla, cinnamon, clove, nutmeg and egg yolks. Allow ingredients to mix thoroughly until fluffy.

Add melted chocolate and liquid from drained fruit to egg cream and whip. Gradually add 2 cups flour. Continue mixing until all flour is incorporated. Mix remaining 6 tablespoons flour into dried fruit. Combine dried fruit and pecans and add to batter.

With clean beaters and bowl, beat egg whites until soft peaks form. Gently fold stiff egg whites into batter and pour into 2 loaf pans. Cover batter directly with parchment paper, then tightly cover pan with foil. Place loaf pans in roasting pan and place on rack in oven. Fill roasting pan with water to reach $2/_3$ of the way up loaf pans. Cover each pan with lid or foil and bake fruitcakes 2 $1/_2$ hours.

Fruitcakes are done when cake tester or toothpick comes out clean. Unmold loaves and cool on racks. When cakes are room temperature, wrap tightly in plastic and then in foil. Let stand for at least 8 days at room temperature. Fruitcakes can be prepared up to 3 weeks in advance. The more time they age, the better they taste.

SUGGESTED WINE:
Cedar Mountain Cabernet Royale Port

Per serving: 392 Calories; 15g Fat (35% calories from fat); 7g Protein; 57g Carbohydrate; 106mg Cholesterol; 39mg Sodium
Food Exchanges: 1 Starch/Bread; 1/2 Lean Meat; 1 1/2 Fruit; 3 Fat; 1 1/2 Other Carbohydrates

CHERRY BRANDY TRUFFLES

FROM CHATEAU CHANTAL WINERY/BED AND BREAKFAST,
MICHIGAN

Serves 10

1 pound milk chocolate chips
4 tablespoons unsalted butter
$1/2$ cup Chateau Chantal Cerise
1 cup whipping cream
$1/2$ pound bittersweet chocolate, melted

Melt milk chocolate in double boiler over simmering water. Add butter, wine and whipping cream. Finely chopped nuts can be added if desired. Chill until firm enough to roll into 1-inch balls. Freeze.

Dip into melted bittersweet chocolate. Can be drizzled with white chocolate or decorated with nuts.

NOTES:
THERE IS NO BETTER WAY TO TOP OFF A DELICIOUS MEAL THAN WITH THESE DELECTABLE TIDBITS.

SUGGESTED WINE:
Chateau Chantal Cerise

Per serving: 504 Calories; 40g Fat (69% calories from fat); 6g Protein; 34g Carbohydrate; 56mg Cholesterol; 50mg Sodium
Food Exchanges: 8 Fat; 2 Other Carbohydrates

CHOCOLATE ALMOND RASPBERRY CAKE

FROM ALBA VINEYARD, NEW JERSEY

Serves 10

CAKE:
4 ounces semisweet chocolate, chopped
$1/4$ cup unsalted butter
$1/2$ cup blanched almonds
$2/3$ cup sugar, divided
$1/3$ tablespoon cornstarch
3 medium eggs, separated
1 tablespoon Alba Red Raspberry Wine
$1/4$ teaspoon cream of tartar

FROSTING:
$3/4$ cup whipping cream, well chilled
$1\,1/2$ teaspoons sugar
$1\,1/2$ teaspoons Alba Red Raspberry Wine
$1/2$ ounce semisweet chocolate

CAKE:
Position rack in center of oven. Preheat oven to 350° F. Butter 9x1 $1/2$-inch round cake pan. Line bottom with parchment or foil; butter lightly.

Melt chocolate and butter in large heat-proof bowl set in pan of hot water over low heat; stir until smooth. Cool about 10 minutes.

Grind nuts with 3 tablespoons sugar in food processor until as smooth as possible; transfer to small bowl. Thoroughly mix in 4 tablespoons sugar and cornstarch. Stir into chocolate. Beat in egg yolks with wooden spoon until mixture is smooth and thick. Stir in wine.

Using clean beaters, beat egg whites with cream of tartar in large bowl until soft peaks form. Beat in remaining $1/4$ cup sugar, 1 tablespoon at a time. Continue beating until whites are stiff but not dry. Fold $1/3$ of whites into chocolate mixture. Spoon chocolate mixture back into whites. Fold until blended and no white streaks remain. Pour batter into prepared pan.

Bake 25 minutes. Let cool 10 minutes then run thin-bladed knife around sides of cake. Invert onto wire rack and remove paper. Turn right side up and cool completely. Refrigerate at least 1 hour before frosting.

FROSTING:
Beat cream with sugar and wine in chilled bowl until soft peaks form. Spread on sides and top of cake. Grate chocolate on top. Serve at room temperature.

SUGGESTED WINE:
Alba Red Raspberry Wine

Per serving: 286 Calories; 20g Fat (61% calories from fat); 4g Protein; 25g Carbohydrate; 101mg Cholesterol; 74mg Sodium
Food Exchanges: 1/2 Lean Meat; 1 Fruit; 4 Fat; 1 1/2 Other Carbohydrates

DOUBLE CHOCOLATE CHEESECAKE

FROM BEAULIEU VINEYARD, CALIFORNIA

Serves 16

CRUST:
$^3/_4$ cup graham cracker crumbs, finely crushed
$^1/_4$ cup butter, melted
$^1/_3$ cup sugar
$^1/_4$ cup cocoa
$^1/_2$ cup pecans or walnuts, finely chopped

CHEESECAKE FILLING:
24 ounces cream cheese, room temperature
10 ounces white chocolate, melted
1 can sweetened condensed milk
4 large eggs
1 cup milk chocolate chips

CRUST:
Preheat oven to 350º F. Butter round, 9-inch springform pan on bottom and sides. Mix together ingredients and press firmly into bottom and $^1/_3$ of way up side of pan. Bake crust 10 to 15 minutes or until lightly browned. Remove from oven and cool on rack. Reduce heat to 300º F.

NOTES:
IF THIS IS "DEATH BY CHOCOLATE" — WHAT A WAY TO GO!

CHEESECAKE FILLING:
In large electric mixing bowl, whip cream cheese until fluffy. Gently melt white chocolate in top of double boiler over simmering water, or microwave on 50% power for about 2 to 3 minutes. Mix into cream cheese on medium speed. Continuing to mix on medium speed, pour in sweetened condensed milk slowly, scraping down sides several times.

Still mixing on medium speed, add eggs 1 at a time. Stop mixer and stir in chocolate chips with wooden spoon. Pour filling into prepared crust and bake about 1 hour and 15 minutes. Cake should be firm, but not browned or cracking, with only a moderate jiggle in middle when gently shaken. Remove from oven and cool on rack. Refrigerate until cold before removing from pan. Serve with chocolate sauce, if desired, or decorate with chocolate chips or walnut halves.

SUGGESTED WINE:
Beaulieu Vineyard Signet Napa Valley Port

Per serving: 456 Calories; 33g Fat (62% calories from fat); 9g Protein; 37g Carbohydrate; 117mg Cholesterol; 230mg Sodium
Food Exchanges: 1/2 Starch/Bread; 1/2 Lean Meat; 1/2 Fruit; 6 Fat; 2 Other Carbohydrates

HAZELNUT BISCOTTI

FROM FENN VALLEY VINEYARDS, MICHIGAN

Serves 36

2 cups flour
1 cup sugar
$3/4$ teaspoon baking powder
$1/4$ teaspoon salt
2 large eggs, lightly beaten
$1/4$ cup Franjelico hazelnut liqueur
1 teaspoon vanilla extract
$3/4$ cup hazelnuts, toasted and chopped

NOTES:
ALMONDS AND AMARETTO MAY BE
SUBSTITUTED IF DESIRED. BECAUSE THEY
HAVE NO SHORTENING, THESE COOKIES
GET HARD AS THEY AGE. GREAT DUNKERS!

Preheat oven to 350° F.

Combine dry ingredients. Combine eggs, liqueur and vanilla. Add to dry ingredients and mix. Add nuts.

Turn dough out on floured surface and knead lightly until it holds together and can be formed into a roll. Place on greased cookie sheet and flatten to about 1-inch thick.

Bake 30 minutes. Cool slightly. Reduce heat to 325° F. Cut dough on diagonal, about 36 slices. Place slices on edge on cookie sheet. Return to oven 10 minutes. Cool. Biscotti will harden while cooling.

SUGGESTED WINE:
Fenn Valley Late Harvest Vignoles

Per serving: 83 Calories; 4g Fat (39% calories from fat); 1g Protein; 11g Carbohydrate; 12mg Cholesterol; 26mg Sodium
Food Exchanges: 1/2 Starch/Bread; 1/2 Fruit; 1/2 Fat; 1/2 Other Carbohydrates

INFUSED CHOCOLATE SAUCE

FROM ST. JULIAN WINE COMPANY, MICHIGAN

Serves 8

2 cups semisweet chocolate chips
$1/2$ cup half and half
$1/4$ cup St. Julian Raspberry or
   Cherry Infusion (port-style wine)

Microwave semisweet chips and half and half in 4-cup microwave-safe container for 2 minutes. Remove from microwave and stir until chocolate is melted. Add infused port wine and stir until blended.

Serve on cream puffs, as an ice cream topping, or as a glaze for cookies, cupcakes, cake and cheesecake.

NOTES:
A DISH OF FRENCH VANILLA ICE CREAM WILL NEVER BE THE SAME.

SUGGESTED WINE:
St. Julian Raspberry Infusion

Per serving: 298 Calories; 18g Fat (51% calories from fat); 3g Protein; 37g Carbohydrate; 6mg Cholesterol; 13mg Sodium
Food Exchanges: 3 1/2 Fat; 2 1/2 Other Carbohydrates

MINIATURE CHEESECAKES

FROM GRAY GHOST VINEYARDS, VIRGINIA

Serves 70

1 box vanilla wafer cookies, crushed
4 large eggs
32 ounces cream cheese
1 cup sugar
1 teaspoon vanilla extract

NOTES:
GREAT FOR NIBBLES WITH A HOUSE FULL
OF GUESTS.

Preheat oven to 350° F.

Put 1 teaspoon wafer crumbs in each of 70 mini-size baking cups.

Beat eggs, then add cream cheese, sugar and vanilla until well blended.

Put about 1 tablespoon batter into each cup. Bake 12 minutes.

◼

SUGGESTED WINE:
Gray Ghost "Adieu"

Per serving: 61 Calories; 5g Fat (70% calories from fat); 1g Protein; 3g Carbohydrate; 27mg Cholesterol; 42mg Sodium
Food Exchanges: 1 Fat

NEW YORK CHEESECAKE (CRUSTLESS STYLE)

FROM DR. KONSTANTIN FRANK VINIFERA WINE CELLARS, NEW YORK

Serves 16

32 ounces whipped cream cheese, not blocks
16 ounces sour cream
$1/4$ pound sweet cream butter
5 large eggs
2 tablespoons cornstarch
1 $1/4$ cups sugar
1 $1/4$ teaspoons vanilla
1 teaspoon lemon juice

NOTES:
DRIZZLE THIS CHEESECAKE WITH YOUR FAVORITE FRUIT TOPPING, WHITE CHOCOLATE OR CARAMEL AND SEE HOW QUICKLY IT DISAPPEARS.

Let cream cheese, sour cream, butter and eggs stand at room temperature approximately 1 hour.

Preheat oven to 375° F. Blend cream cheese, sour cream and butter together then add cornstarch, sugar, vanilla and lemon juice. Beat in eggs 1 at a time until very smooth.

Pour into 9 $1/2$-inch greased springform pan. Place springform pan in another pan and fill with warm water halfway up springform pan. Bake 1 hour or until top is golden brown. Turn off oven. Let cake cool in oven with door open 1 hour. Remove and let stand 2 hours on counter. Cover and refrigerate at least 6 hours before serving.

SUGGESTED WINES:
Dr. Frank's Semi-Dry Riesling or Salmon Run Rainbow Rosé

Per serving: 398 Calories; 33g Fat (74% calories from fat); 7g Protein; 20g Carbohydrate; 158mg Cholesterol; 261mg Sodium
Food Exchanges: 1 Lean Meat; 1 Fruit; 6 Fat; 1 Other Carbohydrates

NEW YORK-STYLE CHEESECAKE WITH WARM BERRY SAUCE

FROM STONE HILL WINERY, MISSOURI

Serves 12

CRUST:
4 tablespoons butter or margarine
1 $^{1}/_{2}$ cups graham cracker crumbs

CHEESECAKE FILLING:
24 ounces cream cheese
$^{1}/_{4}$ cup butter, softened
1 cup sugar
1 teaspoon lemon zest
1 teaspoon vanilla extract
3 large eggs
1 cup sour cream for topping

BERRY SAUCE:
2 cups fresh or frozen berries,
    cleaned and sliced
$^{1}/_{3}$ cup granulated sugar
1 $^{1}/_{2}$ tablespoons fresh lemon juice
1 $^{1}/_{2}$ teaspoons lemon zest
$^{1}/_{2}$ cup water
1 teaspoon cornstarch,
    dissolved in 2 tablespoons cold water

CRUST:
Preheat oven to 375º F. Melt butter and mix thoroughly with graham cracker crumbs. Spread evenly over bottom of 9-inch springform pan, patting firmly to pack. Bake 10 minutes. Remove from oven and set pan aside. Reduce oven temperature to 275º F.

CHEESECAKE FILLING:
In large mixing bowl, beat cream cheese and butter until smooth. Slowly add sugar and mix, scraping down sides of bowl while mixing. Add lemon zest, vanilla and eggs, 1 at a time, beating well after each addition. Scrape down sides of bowl and mix until smooth. Pour batter into springform pan. Bake in 275º F oven 1 hour or until cheesecake tests done. Cool completely before topping with sour cream.

BERRY SAUCE:
In saucepan combine berries, sugar, lemon juice, lemon zest, water and cornstarch. Warm over moderate heat. Stir gently and bring to a gentle boil. Stir until sauce is clear and thickened. Remove from heat. Reheat sauce just before serving. Drizzle $^{1}/_{4}$ cup sauce over top of individual cheesecake portions.

SUGGESTED WINE:
Stone Hill Winery Late Harvest Vignoles

Per serving: 465 Calories; 34g Fat (64% calories from fat); 7g Protein; 35g Carbohydrate; 145mg Cholesterol; 335mg Sodium
Food Exchanges: 1/2 Starch/Bread; 1 Lean Meat; 1 Fruit; 6 Fat; 1 1/2 Other Carbohydrates

NOTES:
PICK YOUR FAVORITE FRESH BERRY TO TOP THIS CLASSIC CHEESECAKE.

OLALLIEBERRY WINE CHEESECAKE WITH CARMEL SAUCE

FROM BARGETTO WINERY, CALIFORNIA

Serves 12

CRUST:
1 cup graham cracker crumbs
2 tablespoons sugar
1 ounce butter, melted
2 tablespoons olallieberry or blackberry wine

CHEESECAKE FILLING:
32 ounces cream cheese
1 1/3 cups sugar
1/2 cup heavy whipping cream
5 large eggs
1/2 cup olallieberry or blackberry wine
1 teaspoon vanilla

SAUCE:
1 1/4 cups olallieberry or blackberry wine
3/4 cup sugar

Preheat oven to 325° F. Grease 10-inch round cake pan.

CRUST:
Mix together graham cracker crumbs, sugar, butter and wine. Coat bottom of cake pan evenly with graham cracker crumb mixture. Pat crumbs down to adhere to cake pan.

CHEESECAKE FILLING:
Cream together cream cheese and sugar until smooth. Scrape down sides of bowl and mix in heavy cream until smooth. Mix in eggs, wine and vanilla until smooth. Pour batter into prepared cake pan. Bake 1 1/2 hours. To check if cheesecake is done, tap edge of pan. It should move as 1 unit. When cheesecake is done, turn off oven and let cheesecake cool in oven 30 minutes. Remove from oven and chill overnight before cutting. When removing cheesecake from pan, run hot knife around edge of pan, then flip over and gently shake out.

SAUCE:
In saucepan, mix wine and sugar. Bring to a boil and reduce heat to medium. Cook about 15 minutes. Cool about 10 minutes before serving over cheesecake.

SUGGESTED WINE:
Chaucer's Olallieberry Wine

Per serving: 577 Calories; 35g Fat (57% calories from fat); 9g Protein; 49g Carbohydrate; 192mg Cholesterol; 319mg Sodium
Food Exchanges: 1/2 Starch/Bread; 1 Lean Meat; 2 1/2 Fruit; 6 1/2 Fat; 2 1/2 Other Carbohydrates

NOTES:
OLALLIEBERRY IS SIMILAR TO LOGANBERRY AND BLACKBERRY. WE PREFER THE OLALLIEBERRY WINE FOR THIS RECIPE, BUT YOU COULD SUBSTITUTE, IF YOU MUST.

PEACHES IN
LATE HARVEST VIDAL

FROM MAGNOTTA WINERY, ONTARIO, CANADA

Serves 8

12 ripe peaches
1 lemon, juiced
$1/_2$ bottle Magnotta Late Harvest
   Vidal Wine

Peel, core and slice peaches. Place in glass bowl, pour lemon juice over fruit and toss to coat.

Pour wine over peaches and cover with plastic wrap. Refrigerate 2 hours.

Arrange artistically on dessert plates and serve. Top with fresh whipped cream for an extra treat.

SUGGESTED WINE:
Magnotta Vidal Select Late Harvest

NOTES:
SIMPLE, DELICIOUS AND IMPRESSIVE.

Per serving: 62 Calories; less than 1g Fat (2% calories from fat); 1g Protein; 16g Carbohydrate; 0mg Cholesterol; 1mg Sodium
Food Exchanges: 1 Fruit

PEAR-INFUSED PEAR CAKE

FROM ST. JULIAN WINE COMPANY, MICHIGAN

Serves 10

2 tablespoons butter
4 cups pears, peeled, cored and cubed
3 tablespoons St. Julian Pear Infusion
  (port-style wine)
1 $1/2$ cups packed brown sugar
2 teaspoons cinnamon
$1/2$ teaspoon nutmeg
1 tablespoon vanilla
1 cup plain nonfat yogurt
2 $1/2$ cups flour
2 teaspoons baking soda
$1/2$ cup vegetable oil
3 large eggs, beaten

Preheat oven to 350º F. Grease 9x12-inch pan with butter. In medium skillet, melt butter over medium heat. Add pears and stir about 5 minutes. Turn off heat and add wine. Set aside.

In large mixing bowl, combine remaining ingredients. Stir until blended. Add pear mixture and blend into batter. Pour batter into prepared pan. Bake 45 to 50 minutes or until toothpick inserted in center comes out clean. Cool on wire rack.

Top with whipped cream or sprinkle with confectioners' sugar, if desired.

NOTES:
IT TASTES AS DELICIOUS AS IT SOUNDS.

SUGGESTED WINE:
St. Julian Pear Infusion

Per serving: 446 Calories; 15g Fat (31% calories from fat); 7g Protein; 69g Carbohydrate; 71mg Cholesterol; 325mg Sodium
Food Exchanges: 1 1/2 Starch/Bread; 1/2 Lean Meat; 1/2 Fruit; 3 Fat; 2 Other Carbohydrates

PLUM AND PINOT GRIS SORBET

FROM KING ESTATE WINERY, WASHINGTON STATE

Serves 4

2 cups dark plums, peeled,
   pitted and cubed
1 cup dry white wine,
   similar to Pinot Gris
3/4 cup sugar

Place all ingredients in medium saucepan and bring to a boil, stirring occasionally. Simmer for 5 to 8 minutes, then remove from heat and let cool. Place saucepan in bowl of ice water and chill mixture to 40° F, stirring constantly.

Place mixture in ice cream freezer and churn until frozen.

Scoop into freezer-safe container and freeze until set, about 2 hours.

NOTES:
A REFRESHING "INTERMEZZO" OR DESSERT. BEST IF ENJOYED WITHIN 3 DAYS.

SUGGESTED WINE:
King Estate Winery Pinot Gris

Per serving: 266 Calories; 1g Fat (3% calories from fat); 1g Protein; 57g Carbohydrate; 0mg Cholesterol; 3mg Sodium
Food Exchanges: 3 1/2 Fruit; 2 1/2 Other Carbohydrates

POACHED PEARS

FROM QUADY WINERY, CALIFORNIA
SQUARE ONE RESTAURANT

Serves 8

4 Bosc or Winterized pears
3 tablespoons lemon juice
$1/2$ cup sugar
$1/2$ cup water
2 teaspoons lemon rind, grated
6 tablespoons orange peel
1 stick cinnamon
1 bottle Quady Elysium Dessert Wine

NOTES:
A SWEET TAKE ON POACHED PEARS THAT
AIMS TO PLEASE.

Peel pears and remove stem tops. Cut pears in half and remove seeds with melon baller. Place pear halves in bowl of water mixed with lemon juice to prevent discoloration.

Combine sugar, $1/2$ cup water, lemon rind, orange peel, cinnamon stick and wine in large pot. Bring to a boil. Add pears, cover pan and simmer until pears are cooked through, about 30 minutes. A toothpick inserted in pears should penetrate easily. Remove pears from poaching liquid. Cool liquid to room temperature. Store pears in cooled liquid in refrigerator overnight.

SUGGESTED WINE:
Quady Elysium

Per serving: 115 Calories; less than 1g Fat (3% calories from fat); 1g Protein; 29g Carbohydrate; 0mg Cholesterol; 2mg Sodium
Food Exchanges: 2 Fruit; 1 Other Carbohydrates

TUTTI FRUTTI BISCOTTI

FROM PEDRONCELLI WINERY, CALIFORNIA

Serves 96

$1/4$ cup dried cranberries, chopped
$1/4$ cup golden raisins
$1/4$ cup dried apricot pieces
$1/4$ cup currants
3 tablespoons Pedroncelli Port Wine
$1/2$ cup vegetable shortening
1 cup sugar
1 $1/2$ teaspoons vanilla
1 teaspoon orange extract
$1/2$ teaspoon almond extract
3 large eggs
2 $1/2$ cups all-purpose flour
1 $1/2$ teaspoons baking powder
1 cup pecans, toasted and chopped

NOTES:
MAKE A BIG BATCH, BECAUSE THEY
DISAPPEAR QUICKLY.

Combine fruit with port in small bowl and set aside 4 hours or overnight.

Cream shortening and sugar. Mix in vanilla, orange and almond extracts. Beat in eggs, 1 at a time. Mix flour and baking powder and gradually add to creamed mixture. Stir in fruit and chopped pecans. Chill at least 4 hours or overnight (overnight is better).

Preheat oven to 375º F. Dough will be sticky, so flour hands and work surface. Divide dough in quarters and form into loaves approximately 14-x2-inches. Place 2 loaves about 3 inches apart on lightly sprayed baking sheet. Gently flatten logs with spatula or by hand.

Bake 15 to 18 minutes until light golden brown. Reduce oven temperature to 325º F. Cool loaves and then cut into $1/3$-inch slices. Place cut side down, return to oven and bake 15 minutes longer or until lightly toasted, turning over halfway through baking time.

Cool and store in airtight container

SUGGESTED WINES:
Pedroncelli Mother Clone Zinfandel or Port

Per serving: 44 Calories; 2g Fat (41% calories from fat); 1g Protein; 6g Carbohydrate; 7mg Cholesterol; 8mg Sodium

VIDAL ICE WINE EGGNOG CHEESECAKE

FROM FIRELANDS WINERY, OHIO

Serves 16

CRUST:
1 cup cashews, finely ground
1 cup graham cracker crumbs, finely crushed
$1/2$ cup sugar
$1/2$ cup butter, melted

FILLING:
8 ounces nonfat cream cheese
1 cup sugar
1 tablespoon Firelands Vidal Ice Wine
1 teaspoon vanilla
$1/2$ teaspoon ground nutmeg
3 large eggs
1 $1/2$ cups eggnog

Preheat oven to 350º F.

CRUST:
In medium bowl, stir together ground cashews, graham cracker crumbs and sugar. Drizzle melted butter over cashew mixture. Mix well then press in bottom and about 1 $1/2$ inches up sides of 10-inch springform pan.

NOTES:
RICH AND DELICIOUS. A LUSCIOUS TREASURE FOR THE HOLIDAY TABLE.

FILLING:
In large mixing bowl, beat cream cheese with electric mixer on medium-high speed 3 to 4 minutes or until light and fluffy. Gradually add sugar, beating 2 to 3 minutes or until mixture is completely smooth, scraping sides of bowl. Reduce speed to medium. Mix in wine, vanilla and nutmeg. Add eggs all at once. Beat on low speed until just combined. Stir in eggnog.

Pour filling into crust-lined pan. Place springform pan into shallow roasting pan. Bake 45 to 50 minutes or until center appears nearly set when shaken. Carefully remove pan and transfer to wire rack. Cool 15 minutes, loosen crust from sides and cool 30 minutes. Remove side of pan and let cool completely.

Cover with plastic wrap and refrigerate up to 2 days.

SUGGESTED WINE:
Firelands Winery Vidal Ice Wine

Per serving: 254 Calories; 13g Fat (45% calories from fat); 6g Protein; 29g Carbohydrate; 71mg Cholesterol; 195mg Sodium
Food Exchanges: 1/2 Starch/Bread; 1/2 Lean Meat; 1 Fruit; 2 1/2 Fat; 1 1/2 Other Carbohydrates

WINE CAKE

FROM SEBASTIANI VINEYARDS, CALIFORNIA

Serves 12

CAKE:
1 package yellow cake mix
$^3/_4$ cup vegetable oil
$^3/_4$ cup Sebastiani Symphony White Wine
4 large eggs
1 package vanilla pudding mix
$^1/_4$ tablespoon nutmeg

FROSTING:
$^1/_2$ cup butter
1 package powdered sugar
$^1/_4$ cup cream sherry

NOTES:
DELICIOUS CAKE FOR ALL BIRTHDAYS
AND ANNIVERSARIES.

CAKE:
Preheat oven to 350° F. Grease and flour tube pan. In mixing bowl, combine cake mix, oil and wine. Blend well then add eggs, 1 at a time, mixing well after each addition. Add vanilla pudding mix and nutmeg and beat 4 minutes at medium speed. Bake 45 minutes in prepared pan.

FROSTING:
Cream butter and add sugar gradually. Add sherry and blend well. Spread over cooled cake and serve.

SUGGESTED WINE:
Sebastiani "Sylvia's Symphony"

Per serving: 486 Calories; 28g Fat (53% calories from fat); 4g Protein; 52g Carbohydrate; 93mg Cholesterol; 447mg Sodium
Food Exchanges: 1/2 Lean Meat; 5 1/2 Fat; 3 1/2 Other Carbohydrates

ZINFANDEL PORT BALLS

FROM EOS ESTATE WINERY, CALIFORNIA

Serves 24

1 cup walnuts, finely chopped
2 cups vanilla wafers, finely chopped
2 tablespoons corn syrup
1/4 cup EOS Zinfandel Port
powdered sugar for rolling

Mix all ingredients, except powdered sugar, together in mixer. Refrigerate dough 1 hour. Roll into 1-inch balls and roll in powdered sugar. Store in airtight container up to 2 weeks.

Hint: Use a food processor or spice grinder to finely chop nuts. A food processor also works well for making extra fine vanilla wafer crumbs.

SUGGESTED WINE:
EOS Zinfandel Port

Per serving: 134 Calories; 7g Fat (45% calories from fat); 2g Protein; 16g Carbohydrate; 0mg Cholesterol; 62mg Sodium
Food Exchanges: 1 1/2 Fat; 1 Other Carbohydrates

NOTES:
WATCH THESE LITTLE DESSERT MUNCHIES DISAPPEAR QUICKER THAN YOU CAN NAME SANTA'S EIGHT REINDEER.

ZING! ROSÉ FRUIT COMPOTE

FROM PEDRONCELLI WINERY, CALIFORNIA

Serves 6

3 cups assorted fruit, fresh,
  dried or frozen
1 cup sugar
1 cup Zinfandel Rosé Wine
2 strips lemon peel, 1 inch long
1 teaspoon vanilla extract or 1 vanilla bean

Rinse, pit, core and skin fruit as desired. Place all ingredients in non-reactive, heavy saucepan and bring to a gentle boil. Simmer 15 minutes or until fruit is softened. If using vanilla bean, put in with ingredients. If using vanilla extract, add during last few minutes. Remove and discard lemon peel. Serve warm or chilled over plain vanilla ice cream, pound or angel food cake.

NOTES:
A SWEET TREAT OF SEASONAL FRUIT ALL YEAR LONG.

Per serving: 218 Calories; 0g Fat (0% calories from fat); 1g Protein; 49g Carbohydrate; 0mg Cholesterol; 7mg Sodium
Food Exchanges: 3 Fruit; 2 Other Carbohydrates

NOTES:

FISH
&
SEAFOOD

■

BAKED WALLEYE

FROM FIRELANDS WINERY, OHIO

Serves 6

2 pounds walleye filets
4 shallots, roasted
3 tablespoons butter
salt and pepper to taste
1 cup Firelands Riesling Wine, heated

NOTES:
THERE'S NOTHING BETTER THAN GREAT
LAKES FISH WITH GREAT LAKES RIESLING.

Preheat oven to 400º F. Place filets in buttered baking dish. Add shallots and dot with butter. Season with salt and pepper. Cover fish with heated wine and bake 15 minutes or until done.

Remove dish from oven. Place under broiler until lightly browned and bubbly. Serve immediately.

SUGGESTED WINE:
Firelands Winery Riesling

Per serving: 230 Calories; 8g Fat (34% calories from fat); 29g Protein; 3g Carbohydrate; 145mg Cholesterol; 139mg Sodium
Food Exchanges: 4 Lean Meat; 1/2 Vegetable; 1 Fat

CAJUN SHRIMP

FROM GRAY GHOST VINEYARDS, VIRGINIA

Serves 4

1 teaspoon paprika
1 teaspoon cayenne pepper
1 teaspoon black pepper
$1/_2$ teaspoon red pepper, crushed
$1/_2$ teaspoon onion salt
$1/_2$ teaspoon oregano
$1/_2$ teaspoon thyme
2 tablespoons butter
2 cloves garlic, minced
1 pound large shrimp, R-T-C,
    peeled and deveined
$1/_4$ teaspoon Worcestershire sauce
$1/_4$ cup Gray Ghost Vidal Blanc

In small bowl, blend together first 7 ingredients and set aside.

In large, nonstick skillet, heat butter and add garlic. Add shrimp and spice mix. Sauté 2 to 4 minutes until shrimp is slightly opaque. Add Worcestershire sauce and wine. Simmer briefly until hot.

SUGGESTED WINE:
Gray Ghost Vidal Blanc

Per serving: 156 Calories; 7g Fat (42% calories from fat); 19g Protein; 2g Carbohydrate; 190mg Cholesterol; 463mg Sodium
Food Exchanges: 2 1/2 Lean Meat; 1 Fat

NOTES:
R-T-C = READY TO COOK OR UNCOOKED SHRIMP.

CALAMARI ALLA LIVORNESE

FROM PETRONI VINEYARDS, CALIFORNIA
NORTH BEACH RESTAURANT

Serves 4

6 cloves garlic, finely chopped
4 teaspoons extra virgin olive oil
1 medium onion, finely chopped
3 medium leeks, finely chopped
2 pounds calamari, cleaned
$1/4$ cup dry white wine
6 medium tomatoes, chopped
salt and pepper to taste
1 sprig oregano for garnish

Sauté garlic in olive oil until golden brown. Add onion and leeks and cook over medium heat for 5 minutes. Add calamari and sauté 2 to 3 minutes. Add wine and when it has evaporated, add tomatoes. Cook 10 to 15 minutes. Season with salt and pepper.

Garnish with oregano and serve with rice or favorite vegetables.

SUGGESTED WINE:
Petroni Cabernet Sauvignon

Per serving: 388 Calories; 8g Fat (20% calories from fat); 39g Protein; 37g Carbohydrate; 529mg Cholesterol; 138mg Sodium
Food Exchanges: 5 Lean Meat; 4 1/2 Vegetable; 1 Fat

NOTES:
A MEDITERRANEAN
DELICACY – FANTABULOSO!

CIOPPINO

FROM CONCANNON VINEYARD, CALIFORNIA

Serves 8

2 medium yellow onions, chopped
1 cup celery, diced
4 cloves garlic, crushed
2 tablespoons olive oil
2 tablespoons butter
2 tablespoons oregano
1 teaspoon dried thyme
1 bay leaf
1 $1/2$ cups Concannon Petite Sirah
3 cans tomatoes, crushed (28 ounces each)
16 ounces clam juice
16 clams, well scrubbed
16 mussels, well scrubbed
1 cooked Dungeness crab,
  cleaned and cracked
16 large shrimp, peeled and deveined
1 pound swordfish or other firm white fish
salt and pepper to taste
$1/4$ cup fresh basil, chopped

NOTES:
"TIS THE SEASON FOR CIOPPINO" — A
FAVORITE RECIPE FROM HELEN
CONCANNON.

In 8-quart saucepan, sauté onion, celery and garlic in oil and butter over medium heat until soft and translucent. Add oregano, thyme, bay leaf, wine, tomatoes and clam juice. Reduce heat to low simmer, cover and cook for 30 minutes. Stir occasionally. This can be done the day before serving; store soup in refrigerator.

On day of serving, remove bay leaf and discard. Bring soup to a simmer and add clams, mussels, crab, shrimp and fish. Simmer until shellfish and fish are cooked through, about 8 to 10 minutes. Discard any clams or mussels that fail to open. Season to taste with salt and pepper, then stir in fresh chopped basil.

Ladle into warmed bowls and serve with French bread, green salad and Petite Sirah.

SUGGESTED WINE:
Concannon Petite Sirah, Limited Release

Per serving: 544 Calories; 17g Fat (30% calories from fat); 62g Protein; 27g Carbohydrate; 176mg Cholesterol; 1515mg Sodium
Food Exchanges: 1 Starch/Bread; 7 1/2 Lean Meat; 1 1/2 Vegetable; 1 1/2 Fat; 1/2 Other Carbohydrates

COQUILLE SAINT JACQUES

FROM SHARPE HILL VINEYARD, CONNECTICUT

Serves 8

2 pounds scallops
10 tablespoons butter, divided
$1/_2$ cup Sharpe Hill Chardonnay
$1/_2$ pound mushrooms, sliced
salt and pepper to taste
2 tablespoons flour
2 tablespoons heavy cream
1 cup dry bread crumbs
fresh parsley, chopped

NOTES:
A CLASSIC DISH WITH AN ELEGANT
PRESENTATION.

Wash and drain scallops. In sauté pan large enough to hold scallops, melt 2 tablespoons butter. Add scallops and wine; simmer 5 minutes or until scallops are tender. Drain scallops, reserving liquid. Set both aside.

In same pan, melt 4 tablespoons butter. Add mushrooms, sautéing until golden brown. Add salt and pepper to taste.

Add scallops to mushrooms with 2 tablespoons butter and flour and mix gently. Add reserved liquid and heavy cream, cook and stir over low heat until mixture is thick and smooth.

Fill 8 scallop shells or other serving dishes with mixture; sprinkle with bread crumbs and parsley. Dot with remaining 2 tablespoons butter. Brown in oven until golden. Serve immediately.

SUGGESTED WINE:
Sharpe Hill Vineyard Reserve Chardonnay

Per serving: 317 Calories; 18g Fat (51% calories from fat); 22g Protein; 16g Carbohydrate; 81mg Cholesterol; 425mg Sodium
Food Exchanges: 1/2 Starch/Bread; 2 1/2 Lean Meat; 1/2 Vegetable; 3 Fat

CRAB CAKES WITH CHARDONNAY CREAM SAUCE

FROM WINDSOR VINEYARDS, CALIFORNIA

Serves 8

1 $^3/_4$ cups Windsor Chardonnay
$^1/_3$ cup shallots, chopped
1 cup whipping cream
salt and pepper to taste
1 $^1/_2$ pounds crabmeat
  (about 4 cups drained)
4 cups fresh bread crumbs from French
  bread, divided
7 $^1/_4$ ounces roasted red peppers (1 jar,
  drained and chopped)
$^1/_2$ cup green onions, minced
2 large eggs
1 teaspoon lemon juice
2 tablespoons fresh dill, chopped
1 tablespoon Dijon mustard
1 tablespoon whole grain mustard
2 tablespoons mayonnaise
$^1/_4$ cup vegetable oil

Boil wine and shallots in heavy medium saucepan until mixture is reduced to $^1/_2$ cup, about 10 minutes. Add whipping cream and boil until liquid is reduced to sauce consistency, about 10 minutes. Season to taste with salt and pepper.

NOTES:
A CLASSIC DISH WITH AN INTRIGUING CREAM SAUCE.

Mix crabmeat, 2 cups bread crumbs and remaining ingredients, except oil, in large bowl until well blended. Form mixture into sixteen 2x2-inch diameter cakes, using $^1/_4$ cup crab mixture for each cake. (Can be prepared 6 hours ahead. Cover sauce and crab cakes separately and refrigerate. Before serving re-warm sauce over medium-low heat, stirring occasionally.) Place remaining bread crumbs in shallow dish. Press each cake into bread crumbs, turning to coat evenly.

Heat 2 tablespoons oil in heavy large skillet over medium-high heat. Working in batches, add crab cakes to skillet and cook until golden brown and heated through, about 5 minutes per side. Add oil as necessary. Transfer crab cakes to paper towel-lined plate to drain.

Place 2 crab cakes on each plate; spoon sauce around crab cakes and serve immediately.

SUGGESTED WINE:
Windsor Signature Chardonnay

Per serving: 392 Calories; 24g Fat (60% calories from fat); 20g Protein; 16g Carbohydrate; 162mg Cholesterol; 494mg Sodium
Food Exchanges: 1 Starch/Bread; 2 1/2 Lean Meat; 1/2 Vegetable; 4 Fat

CURRIED SHELLFISH WITH BANANA (OR MANGO) SALSA

FROM CEDAR MOUNTAIN WINERY, CALIFORNIA

Serves 12

BANANA (OR MANGO) SALSA:
2 ripe bananas or mangoes, diced
1 teaspoon Anaheim chili pepper
1 teaspoon walnut oil
1 tablespoon fresh lime juice
1 tablespoon fresh cilantro, minced
1 teaspoon fresh mint, minced
4 tablespoons red bell pepper, diced

CURRY SAUCE:
2 tablespoons butter
2 tablespoons flour
$1/2$ cup chicken broth, warmed
$1/2$ cup Cedar Mountain Chardonnay
1 tablespoon curry powder
$1/3$ cup heavy cream

12 oysters, clams or mussels

NOTES:
PLAN TO MAKE PLENTY OF THESE TASTY
GEMS BECAUSE THEY DISAPPEAR FAST.

BANANA (OR MANGO) SALSA:
Mix ingredients in bowl and set aside.

CURRY SAUCE:
Make roux with butter and flour. Add
warmed chicken broth and wine. Whisk
in curry powder and reduce slightly. Add
cream and continue reducing until sauce
coats back of spoon.

Steam oysters, clams or mussels and shuck.
Place 1 tablespoon salsa on each shell half,
then top with shell meat and curry sauce.
Place under broiler and cook until bubbly.
Do not overcook.

SUGGESTED WINE:
Cedar Mountain Merlot

*Per serving: 87 Calories; 5g Fat (57% calories from fat);
2g Protein; 7g Carbohydrate; 22mg Cholesterol; 123mg
Sodium
Food Exchanges: 1/2 Fruit; 1 Fat*

CURRIED STIR-FRY WITH SHRIMP

FROM OLIVER WINERY, INDIANA

Serves 6

6 cups water, divided
1 $1/2$ cups basmati rice
2 tablespoons olive oil
3 cloves garlic, minced
16 ounces mixed vegetables, fresh or frozen
1 pound frozen cooked shrimp,
  slightly thawed
1 teaspoon ground ginger
1 teaspoon ground black pepper
3 cubes curry sauce mix

In saucepan, bring 3 cups water to a boil. Stir in rice. Reduce heat, cover and simmer for 20 minutes. Remove rice from heat and let stand covered for 5 minutes until all water is absorbed.

While rice is cooking, heat large frying pan over medium heat and add olive oil. Add garlic and sauté until lightly browned. Add mixed vegetables and shrimp. Sprinkle with ginger and black pepper. Stir mixture until vegetables and shrimp are done, about 8 to 10 minutes.

In another saucepan, heat remaining 3 cups water and add curry sauce mix, stirring until completely dissolved. Stir mix into vegetable and shrimp stir-fry and serve over rice.

NOTES:
GEWÜRZTRAMINER IS AN IDEAL WINE FOR CHINESE AND INDIAN DISHES.

SUGGESTED WINE:
Oliver Winery Gewürztraminer

Per serving: 376 Calories; 11g Fat (26% calories from fat); 23g Protein; 47g Carbohydrate; 148mg Cholesterol; 1099mg Sodium
Food Exchanges: 2 1/2 Starch/Bread; 2 Lean Meat; 1 Vegetable; 1 1/2 Fat

GRILLED GINGER-ORANGE SALMON

FROM FENN VALLEY VINEYARDS, MICHIGAN

Serves 4

$1/_4$ cup dry sherry
$1/_4$ cup soy sauce
$1/_4$ cup Dijon mustard
$1/_4$ cup orange juice
2 tablespoons honey
1 tablespoon ginger root, grated
1 $1/_2$ pounds salmon, cleaned and skinned

Place first 6 ingredients in self-sealing plastic bag. Place fish in bag and marinate several hours. Grill about 5 minutes on each side, basting with marinade.

Marinade also works well with fresh fish, chicken or pork.

SUGGESTED WINE:
Fenn Valley Pinot Noir

NOTES:
THIS IS EXCELLENT AS A HOT ENTREE OR COLD APPETIZER.

Per serving: 276 Calories; 7g Fat (23% calories from fat); 36g Protein; 13g Carbohydrate; 89mg Cholesterol; 1333mg Sodium
Food Exchanges: 4 1/2 Lean Meat; 1/2 Vegetable; 1/2 Other Carbohydrates

LEMON CAPER FISH

FROM FENN VALLEY VINEYARDS, MICHIGAN

Serves 4

1 $1/2$ pounds sole filets or tilapia
$1/4$ cup Italian seasoned bread crumbs
1 tablespoon olive oil
1 lemon, juiced
$1/2$ cup Fenn Valley Pinot Grigio
$1/4$ cup capers

Wash and pat dry fish. Lightly coat fish with bread crumbs.

Heat oil in skillet and sauté fish until done. Pour lemon juice over fish and remove from pan to warmed serving dish. Keep warm.

Deglaze pan with wine, add capers and pour over fish.

SUGGESTED WINE:
Fenn Valley Pinot Grigio

Per serving: 239 Calories; 6g Fat (23% calories from fat); 34g Protein; 8g Carbohydrate; 0mg Cholesterol; 416mg Sodium
Food Exchanges: 1/2 Starch/Bread; 4 1/2 Lean Meat; 1/2 Fat

NOTES:
AS GOOD AS THIS SIMPLE FISH DISH IS, FEEL FREE TO SUBSTITUTE CHICKEN BREASTS.

LOBSTER SPRING ROLLS WITH TANGERINE DIPPING SAUCE

FROM ZD WINERY, CALIFORNIA

Serves 12

1 tablespoon salt
2 pounds whole lobsters (two, 1 pound each)
2 tangerines
$1/4$ cup soy sauce, plus as needed to taste
3 tablespoons sesame oil, plus a few drops
$1/3$ package bean thread noodles
10 whole cilantro leaves, roughly chopped
5 large basil leaves, roughly chopped
5 large mint leaves, roughly chopped
$1/2$ teaspoon ginger root, grated
1 cup coconut milk
2 tablespoons sesame seeds, toasted
1 package rice paper wrappers
2 medium avocados, peeled and thinly sliced
salt and pepper to taste

Put 2 large pots of water on stove to boil. In 1 pot add salt. Drop lobsters into boiling, salted water and set timer for 7 minutes. After 7 minutes, remove lobsters and let cool at room temperature.

Meanwhile, make dipping sauce by juicing tangerines in small bowl. Add soy sauce to taste and a few drops of sesame oil. Set aside.

Place bean thread noodles in large bowl. Pour second pot of boiling water over noodles. Cover and let stand 20 minutes, then drain.

While noodles are softening, prepare marinade for lobsters and noodles. Place herbs in mixing bowl. Add grated ginger, coconut milk, $1/4$ cup soy sauce, 3 tablespoons of sesame oil and toasted sesame seeds. Mix all ingredients and marinate noodles with half of mixture.

Break down lobsters, cutting into medium-size pieces. Marinate lobster with other half of marinade.

To soften wrappers, let soak in bowl of water 3 to 5 minutes. When wrappers are soft, take 1 out and place on clean towel. Put 1 thin slice avocado near bottom of wrapper. Sprinkle with a little salt. Put a little of marinated bean thread noodles on top, then put some lobster meat on top of that. Roll bottom part of wrapper up 1 turn. Then tightly fold in sides and roll rest of the way. Repeat until lobster meat is gone. If not serving right away, store with wet towel over spring rolls to retain moisture. Serve with dipping sauce.

SUGGESTED WINE:
ZD California Chardonnay

Per serving (excluding unknown items): 230 Calories; 15g Fat (56% calories from fat); 16g Protein; 9g Carbohydrate; 72mg Cholesterol; 318mg Sodium Food Exchanges: 1/2 Starch/Bread; 2 Lean Meat; 1/2 Vegetable; 3 Fat

NOTES: MOST OF THE INGREDIENTS CAN BE FOUND AT AN ASIAN GROCERY.

PAN-SEARED HALIBUT WITH ONION MARMALADE & CILANTRO PESTO

FROM KENWOOD VINEYARDS, CALIFORNIA, EXECUTIVE CHEF PHIL MCGAULEY

Serves 6

MARMALADE:
1/2 orange, juiced
1/2 cup Kenwood Sauvignon Blanc
1/4 cup sugar
1/4 cup red wine vinegar
2 cups thin sliced red onions
2 teaspoons minced orange zest
1 teaspoon salt
1/4 teaspoon white pepper

PESTO:
1 bunch cilantro, chopped
1/2 cup almonds, toasted and slivered
5 tablespoons lime juice
3 tablespoons water
1 tablespoon honey
1/2 teaspoon cumin
1 teaspoon salt
1/4 teaspoon white pepper
1 clove garlic, chopped

HALIBUT:
30 ounces halibut filets (six 5-ounce filets)
salt and white pepper to taste
3 tablespoons flour
1/4 cup olive oil, divided
1/4 cup almonds, toasted and sliced

NOTES:
FULL OF FLAVOR AND LOOKS GOOD, TOO.
SERVE WITH SAUTÉED FRESH VEGGIES.

MARMALADE:
Combine orange juice, wine, sugar and vinegar in saucepan and reduce to 1 cup. Add onions and zest and cook until onions are soft. Season with salt and pepper; set aside.

PESTO:
Place all ingredients in blender and process until smooth. Season with salt and pepper; set aside.

HALIBUT:
Working in 2 batches, season halibut with salt and pepper and then dredge through flour. Place large sauté pan over medium-high heat and add half of olive oil. Shake off excess flour from halibut and sauté until golden brown. Turn over and sauté until just done, about 2 to 3 minutes. Repeat with remaining halibut. Serve with onion marmalade, cilantro pesto and garnish with sliced almonds.

SUGGESTED WINE:
Kenwood Reserve Sauvignon Blanc

Per serving: 434 Calories; 21g Fat (43% calories from fat); 34g Protein; 26g Carbohydrate; 45mg Cholesterol; 794mg Sodium
Food Exchanges: 1/2 Starch/Bread; 4 1/2 Lean Meat; 1 Vegetable; 1/2 Fruit; 3 Fat; 1 Other Carbohydrates

PRAWN NECTAR

FROM RODNEY STRONG VINEYARDS, CALIFORNIA

Serves 6

30 large jumbo shrimp, cleaned and shelled
$1/4$ cup lime juice, freshly squeezed
2 tablespoons fresh basil, roughly chopped
$1/4$ teaspoon crushed red pepper
2 tablespoons olive oil
1 cantaloupe
3 peaches
6 apricots
salt and pepper to taste

NOTES:
JUST SIT BACK ON A LAZY AFTERNOON
WITH A GLASS OF SAUVIGNON BLANC
AND A BOWL FULL OF THESE DELIGHTS.

Marinate prawns with fresh lime juice, basil, red pepper and olive oil for 1 hour.

Peel fruit and slice into thin wedges.

Grill prawns and lightly toss with fruit.

SUGGESTED WINE:
Rodney Strong "Charlotte's Home" Sauvignon Blanc

Per serving: 283 Calories; 12g Fat (36% calories from fat); 27g Protein; 18g Carbohydrate; 192mg Cholesterol; 195mg Sodium
Food Exchanges: 3 1/2 Lean Meat; 1 Fruit; 2 Fat

ROASTED SALMON WITH SUN-DRIED TOMATO CRUST

FROM VALLEY OF THE MOON WINERY, CALIFORNIA
CHEF LAURIE SOUZA

Serves 4

1 $1/2$ pounds salmon filet
$1/2$ cup Valley of the Moon Pinot Noir
$1/4$ cup balsamic vinegar
$1/2$ cup olive oil or more if needed
$1/2$ cup sun-dried tomato paste
2 tablespoons dark brown sugar
5 cloves garlic, minced
2 tablespoons fresh thyme
2 tablespoons fresh parsley, minced
1 tablespoon fennel seeds
2 teaspoons dried basil
1 bay leaf, crumbled
$1/2$ teaspoon dry mustard
1 teaspoon Worcestershire sauce
$1/2$ teaspoon Tabasco sauce
1 teaspoon salt
$1/2$ teaspoon fresh ground black pepper

Portion salmon into 4 pieces. Combine remaining ingredients to create marinade. Marinate fish overnight.

Preheat oven to 425º F. Dry salmon on screen or pat dry before cooking. Boil marinade for several minutes. Place salmon on baking sheet and cook salmon in oven until done, about 8 to 10 minutes depending on thickness. While fish is cooking baste with reduced marinade.

SUGGESTED WINE:
Valley of the Moon Zinfandel

Per serving: 336 Calories; 22g Fat (62% calories from fat); 24g Protein; 7g Carbohydrate; 59mg Cholesterol; 551mg Sodium
Food Exchanges: 3 Lean Meat; 1/2 Vegetable; 3 1/2 Fat

NOTES:
FRESH SALMON NEVER TASTED SO GOOD WITH THIS MARINADE.

SALMON WITH GREEN SAUCE

FROM ST. JULIAN WINE COMPANY, MICHIGAN

Serves 4

MARINADE:
1/3 cup St. Julian Chardonnay
1/2 cup pineapple juice
1/3 cup soy sauce
2 pounds salmon filets, skin on

GREEN SAUCE:
2 scallions, cleaned
3 teaspoons chives
1 cup fresh baby leaf spinach
3 tablespoons mayonnaise
3/4 cup sour cream
1 teaspoon garlic powder
1 teaspoon fresh dill

NOTES:
THIS DISH LOOKS GREAT PRESENTED ON A
BED OF FRESH SPINACH LEAVES AND IT
TASTES EVEN BETTER.

MARINADE:
Mix wine, juice and soy sauce in 12x9-inch glass pan. Place salmon in pan, cover with wax paper or plastic wrap and place in refrigerator. Marinate 2 to 4 hours, turning at least twice.

GREEN SAUCE:
In food processor, chop scallions, chives and spinach leaves until fine. Next add mayonnaise, sour cream, garlic powder and dill. Sauce can be made and refrigerated while salmon is marinating.

Preheat oven to 450° F. Coat baking sheet with olive oil. Place salmon, flesh side up, on baking sheet. Roast about 12 to 15 minutes. Place on serving tray and top with green sauce.

SUGGESTED WINE:
St. Julian Pinot Grigio or Chardonnay

Per serving: 482 Calories; 26g Fat (50% calories from fat); 49g Protein; 10g Carbohydrate; 141mg Cholesterol; 1619mg Sodium
Food Exchanges: 6 1/2 Lean Meat; 1/2 Vegetable; 1/2 Fruit; 2 1/2 Fat

SALMON WITH PROSECCO-CAPER SAUCE

FROM MARTINI & ROSSI, ITALY

Serves 4

1 ¹/₂ pounds salmon filet, cut into 4 pieces
¹/₂ cup Martini & Rossi Prosecco
2 tablespoons capers, drained
1 teaspoon lemon rind, grated
4 tablespoons butter, cut in small pieces
1 teaspoon chopped parsley

NOTES:
ALTHOUGH THIS IS A GREAT SAUCE ON SALMON, ANY THICK WHITE FISH FILETS WILL ALSO BENEFIT FROM THIS SAUCE MADE WITH ITALIAN PROSECCO.

Preheat oven to 450º F. Put each salmon filet in center of 12-inch square of aluminum foil. Gather foil around filet and drizzle with wine. Fold edges of foil to make sealed packages. Place on baking sheet and bake 12 minutes.

Open 1 end of packages and drain juices into small saucepan. Add capers and lemon rind. Boil over high heat until liquid is reduced to a syrupy consistence. Remove pan from heat and whisk in butter and parsley until butter melts and thickens sauce.

Slide spatula between cooked salmon and skin to serve salmon skinless. Top with sauce.

SUGGESTED WINE:
Martini & Rossi Prosecco

Per serving: 319 Calories; 17g Fat (53% calories from fat); 34g Protein; 0g Carbohydrate; 119mg Cholesterol; 270mg Sodium
Food Exchanges: 5 Lean Meat; 2 Fat

SEAFOOD BEGGAR'S PURSE

FROM ZD WINERY, CALIFORNIA

Serves 4

4 ounces whitefish or similar
4 ounces salmon filet
6 bay scallops
3 ounces shrimp
3 tablespoons ZD Chardonnay
3 tablespoons fresh lemon juice (1 lemon)
6 tablespoons fresh orange juice (1 orange)
$1/2$ bunch chives, finely chopped
$1/4$ cup mascarpone cheese
salt and pepper to taste
1 package phyllo dough
1 stick butter

Preheat oven to 375° F. Cut fish into 1-inch cubes. Dice scallops into small cubes. Split shrimp in half lengthwise. Mix together remaining ingredients, except phyllo and butter, and marinate fish at least 20 minutes.

Melt butter in small saucepan. Brush single sheet of phyllo with butter. Place another sheet of phyllo on top and brush with butter. Repeat until 4 layers are formed. Then cut four 6-inch squares out of dough.

Put a generous spoonful of fish mixture into dough and pull sides up around it. Secure with small strip of aluminum and bake until dough becomes golden brown.

■

NOTES:
A UNIQUE PRESENTATION OF A ZESTY SEAFOOD MEDLEY.

SUGGESTED WINE:
ZD California Chardonnay

Per serving: 225 Calories; 10g Fat (41% calories from fat); 24g Protein; 8g Carbohydrate; 96mg Cholesterol; 201mg Sodium
Food Exchanges: 3 Lean Meat; 1 Fat

SHRIMP SCAMPI

FROM MARTINI & ROSSI, ITALY

Serves 2

2 teaspoons olive oil
6 cloves garlic, crushed
$1/2$ cup Martini & Rossi Rosso
  Sweet Vermouth
1 cup diced tomatoes
$3/4$ pound jumbo shrimp, shelled
  and deveined
$1/2$ cup fresh parsley, chopped
$1/8$ teaspoon hot pepper sauce
salt and pepper to taste

Heat olive oil in medium-size nonstick skillet on medium-high heat. Sauté garlic for a few seconds, then add vermouth and tomatoes.

Cook 5 minutes. Add shrimp and parsley; cook 2 to 3 minutes until shrimp are pink.

Season with hot pepper sauce, salt and pepper to taste. Divide between 2 plates and serve.

SUGGESTED WINE:
Martini & Rossi Prosecco

Per serving: 357 Calories; 8g Fat (25% calories from fat); 36g Protein; 17g Carbohydrate; 259mg Cholesterol; 283mg Sodium
Food Exchanges: 5 Lean Meat; 1 1/2 Vegetable; 1 Fat

NOTES:
IT'S WONDERFUL ON A BED OF RISOTTO OR AS PART OF THE PICNIC FARE.

SMOKED SALMON CARPACCIO

FROM STONE HILL WINERY, MISSOURI

Serves 4

16 ounces smoked salmon, thinly sliced
2 tablespoons olive oil
1 tablespoon vegetable oil
1 tablespoon Stone Hill Chardonel
1 $1/4$ teaspoons gin
2 teaspoons fresh lemon juice
$1/2$ shallot, chopped
1 teaspoon fresh parsley, chopped
1 teaspoon fresh dill, chopped
$1/2$ teaspoon fresh basil, chopped
salt to taste
black pepper, freshly ground, to taste

NOTES:
A WONDERFUL APPETIZER COURSE FOR
YOUR SPECIAL DINNER PARTY.

Divide salmon filet among 4 chilled plates, arranging in an even layer. Cover plates with plastic wrap and refrigerate until well chilled.

In medium bowl, mix together olive and vegetable oils, wine, gin, lemon juice, shallot, parsley, dill and basil. Salt and pepper to taste.

Remove plates from refrigerator, uncover, drizzle dressing mixture over salmon and serve.

SUGGESTED WINE:
Stone Hill Winery Seyval

Per serving: 231 Calories; 15g Fat (61% calories from fat); 21g Protein; 1g Carbohydrate; 26mg Cholesterol; 890mg Sodium
Food Exchanges: 3 Lean Meat; 2 Fat

SOUSED SHRIMP

FROM SHARPE HILL VINEYARD, CONNECTICUT

Serves 8

1 ¹/₂ pounds shrimp, uncooked and shelled
10 whole black peppercorns
1 bay leaf
¹/₂ teaspoon salt
8 lemons
6 large Vidalia onions, thinly sliced
¹/₂ cup fresh tarragon, minced
2 tablespoons peanut oil
1 tablespoon tarragon vinegar
1 lemon, juiced
salt and pepper to taste

Devein and clean shrimp. Place in pot with water, peppercorns, bay leaf and salt. Bring to a boil and simmer until shrimp are just tender. Drain and set aside to cool.

With sharp knife, thinly peel lemons, removing white pith from skins; julienne lemon peels. Combine cooked shrimp, onions, lemon peel and tarragon leaves. Toss with oil, vinegar and lemon juice. Salt and pepper to taste. Marinate 2 hours before serving.

SUGGESTED WINE:
Sharpe Hill Ballet of Angels

NOTES:
A UNIQUE MIXTURE OF SHRIMP THAT COMBINES WONDERFULLY WITH RICE.

Per serving: 189 Calories; 5g Fat (23% calories from fat); 20g Protein; 21g Carbohydrate; 129mg Cholesterol; 268mg Sodium
Food Exchanges: 1/2 Starch/Bread; 2 Lean Meat; 1 Vegetable; 1/2 Fruit; 1/2 Fat

SPICY LOBSTER CAKES

FROM HARMONY CELLARS, CALIFORNIA

Serves 6

2 $1/2$ tablespoons chili sauce,
  any brand, divided
$1/2$ cup mayonnaise, divided
2 tablespoons chives, chopped and divided
$1/2$ ripe mango
2 tablespoons cilantro, chopped
salt and pepper to taste
2 limes, juiced and divided
1 teaspoon honey
1 pound lobster meat
1 cup all-purpose flour
3 extra large eggs, lightly beaten
1 cup bread crumbs, panko, if available
2 tablespoons vegetable oil
8 ounces greens for garnish
2 limes, cut in $1/4$-inch cubes

Mix 1 tablespoon chili sauce, $1/4$ cup mayonnaise and 1 tablespoon chives. Set aside for garnishing.

Cut mango into cubes then mix in cilantro, $1/2$ tablespoon chili sauce, salt, pepper and lime juice to taste. Set aside.

NOTES:
IT'S WORTH THE EFFORT FOR THIS
DELICIOUS DISH.

In another bowl combine 1 tablespoon chili sauce, $1/4$ cup mayonnaise and 1 tablespoon chives with honey, juice of 1 lime and lobster meat. Season to taste with salt and pepper. Divide mixture into 12 equal parts. With wet hands, form portions into plump, tightly packed cakes.

In 3 separate dishes place flour, eggs and bread crumbs. Start by dusting cakes with flour. Then coat in egg wash and finally roll in bread crumbs.

Coat large sauté pan with oil and bring to high heat. Place lobster cakes in pan so they do not touch each other. Sear until brown and crispy on both sides, about 2 to 3 minutes per side. Place on paper towel to drain.

Lightly sauté greens and place on plate. Lean 2 lobster cakes against greens, top with mango mixture and put dollop of chili-mayonnaise mixture to side with cube of lime.

SUGGESTED WINE:
Harmony Cellars Reserve Chardonnay

Per serving: 468 Calories; 25g Fat (46% calories from fat); 23g Protein; 42g Carbohydrate; 186mg Cholesterol; 528mg Sodium
Food Exchanges: 2 Starch/Bread; 3 Lean Meat; 1/2 Fruit; 2 1/2 Fat

NOTES:

NOTES:

MEAT

■

"BUSY DAY" OVEN STEW

FROM FENN VALLEY VINEYARDS, MICHIGAN

Serves 8

1 pound rump roast, trimmed and cubed
1 pound pork tenderloin, cubed
8 medium red potatoes, quartered
16 baby carrots
2 medium onions, sliced
4 stalks celery, chopped
1 cup Fenn Valley Meritage
1 bay leaf
16 ounces canned tomatoes, diced
1 tablespoon sugar
3 tablespoons flour
14 ounces beef broth

Preheat oven to 300º F. Combine first 9 ingredients in Dutch oven. Add sugar and flour to beef broth, blend and pour over rest of ingredients. Cover and bake 4 hours undisturbed.

HINT: A package of frozen peas and a cup of sliced mushrooms can be added 45 minutes before completion, if desired.

SUGGESTED WINE:
Fenn Valley Lakeshore Meritage

Per serving: 322 Calories; 5g Fat (15% calories from fat); 31g Protein; 33g Carbohydrate; 70mg Cholesterol; 491mg Sodium
Food Exchanges: 1 1/2 Starch/Bread; 3 1/2 Lean Meat; 1 1/2 Vegetable

NOTES:
SERVE WITH A SALAD AND FRENCH BREAD; IT MAKES A GOOD, HEALTHY MEAL.

BEEF BARBECUE

FROM FENN VALLEY VINEYARDS, MICHIGAN

Serves 12

3 pounds rump roast, trimmed
1 can consommé
1 medium onion, thinly sliced
1 cup celery, chopped
$1/4$ cup brown sugar, packed
$1/4$ cup Dijon-style mustard
2 tablespoons Worcestershire sauce
2 cups water
$1/2$ cup Fenn Valley Capriccio
1 cup catsup
15 ounces tomato sauce

Combine all ingredients in heavy pot. Simmer 5 to 6 hours. Cool. Shred meat and serve on buns.

SUGGESTED WINE:
Fenn Valley Capriccio

Per serving: 230 Calories; 6g Fat (24% calories from fat); 27g Protein; 15g Carbohydrate; 66mg Cholesterol; 751mg Sodium
Food Exchanges: 3 1/2 Lean Meat; 1/2 Vegetable; 1/2 Other Carbohydrates

NOTES:
A FAVORITE FOR FAMILY GET-TOGETHERS AND WINERY PICNIC GATHERINGS. LEFTOVERS FREEZE WELL, TOO.

BEEF BOURGUIGNON

FROM HOSMER WINERY, NEW YORK

Serves 8

1/3 cup butter, divided
3/4 pound small mushrooms
3 pounds stew meat, cut into 1-inch cubes
1/4 cup all-purpose flour
2 cups beef stock
2 cups Hosmer Cabernet Franc
1 tablespoon tomato paste
4 cloves garlic, minced
1 teaspoon salt
1 teaspoon dried thyme
1 bay leaf
black pepper, freshly ground, to taste
18 small onions, peeled
1/2 teaspoon parsley, chopped, or to taste

NOTES:
A CLASSIC CULINARY DISH OF THE AGES.

Preheat oven to 350° F. In large heavy skillet or Dutch oven, melt 1/2 of butter. Add mushrooms and brown lightly. Remove and set aside.

Add remaining butter to pan. Add beef, browning well on all sides, adding additional butter or oil if needed. Remove beef and set aside. Stir flour into fat remaining in pan. Gradually add stock, wine and tomato paste and bring to a boil, stirring as sauce thickens. Add garlic, salt, thyme, bay leaf and a few grindings of black pepper. Put meat in Dutch oven or heavy casserole. Cover and bake about 2 hours, adding mushrooms and onions for last 30 minutes. Remove bay leaf. Taste and adjust seasoning.

Before serving, sprinkle stew with chopped parsley. Serve with crusty bread and buttered egg noodles.

SUGGESTED WINE:
Hosmer Cabernet Franc

Per serving: 790 Calories; 44g Fat (52% calories from fat); 53g Protein; 36g Carbohydrate; 190mg Cholesterol; 1440mg Sodium
Food Exchanges: 7 Lean Meat; 5 1/2 Vegetable; 4 Fat

BEEF MERLOT

FROM FIRELANDS WINERY, OHIO

Serves 10

3 tablespoons olive oil
$1/4$ pound salt pork
3 pounds stew meat, cut in 1-inch cubes
2 tablespoons flour
salt and pepper to taste
3 medium onions, diced
2 cloves garlic, minced
2 cups Firelands Merlot
1 cup beef broth
1 bay leaf
1 teaspoon thyme
1 tablespoon tarragon vinegar
6 carrots, sliced
$1/2$ pound fresh mushrooms, sliced
1 teaspoon butter
3 tablespoons fresh parsley, chopped

Heat olive oil in heavy Dutch oven. Add salt pork. Sprinkle beef cubes with flour, salt and pepper. Brown meat thoroughly. Add onions and garlic. Cook until onions start to turn transparent. Add wine, beef broth, bay leaf, thyme and vinegar. Cover and simmer 1 to 1 $1/2$ hours until meat is tender.

Remove bay leaf and add sliced carrots. Cover and cook an additional 30 minutes. Meanwhile, sauté mushrooms in butter. Add to stew after carrots are tender. Serve with buttered egg noodles. Sprinkle with fresh chopped parsley.

SUGGESTED WINE:
Firelands Winery Merlot

Per serving: 628 Calories; 42g Fat (64% calories from fat); 41g Protein; 12g Carbohydrate; 147mg Cholesterol; 743mg Sodium
Food Exchanges: 5 1/2 Lean Meat; 2 Vegetable; 5 Fat

NOTES:
A HEARTY MEAL, FULL OF FLAVOR.
PERFECT FOR A MIDWEST WINTER.

BLACK FOREST PORK TENDERLOIN

FROM CAMARADERIE CELLARS, WASHINGTON

Serves 4

2 pounds pork tenderloin
2 tablespoons olive oil
2 cups dry red wine
1 cup cherry preserves
salt and pepper to taste

NOTES:
GREAT WHEN ACCOMPANIED WITH
GARLIC-MASHED POTATOES.

In heavy skillet over high heat, sear pork tenderloin in oil on all sides. Reduce heat and continue cooking meat until just pink, about 6 to 8 minutes per side. Remove meat from pan and keep warm.

Add red wine and jam to drippings in pan, scraping all the good bits. Simmer about 5 to 10 minutes to reduce liquid.

Slice tenderloin and serve with red wine sauce.

SUGGESTED WINE:
Camaraderie Cellars Merlot or Cabernet Sauvignon

Per serving: 611 Calories; 15g Fat (24% calories from fat); 48g Protein; 54g Carbohydrate; 148mg Cholesterol; 197mg Sodium
Food Exchanges: 7 Lean Meat; 1 1/2 Fat; 3 1/2 Other Carbohydrates

BLUE CHEESE-CRUSTED BEEF TENDERLOIN

FROM KOVES-NEWLAN VINEYARDS & WINERY, CALIFORNIA

Serves 6

CABERNET SAUVIGNON SAUCE:
1 cup shallots, sliced
2 cloves garlic, chopped
1 tablespoon butter
2 cups Koves-Newlan Cabernet Sauvignon
2 cups cream
1 tablespoon fresh thyme leaves
sea salt to taste
black pepper, freshly ground, to taste

BLUE CHEESE-CRUSTED TENDERLOIN:
4 ounces blue cheese
4 ounces butter, plus 3 tablespoons for searing
1 cup dry bread crumbs
1 tablespoon fresh thyme
6 beef tenderloins, 6 ounces each (filet mignons)
salt and pepper to taste

Preheat oven to 400° F.

CABERNET SAUVIGNON SAUCE:
Sweat shallots and garlic in butter using thick-bottomed saucepot. Stir until fully aromatic. Add wine and cream and bring mixture to a simmer. Continue simmering mixture until it reduces in volume by half, stirring occasionally to prevent sticking or burning. Puree mixture until very smooth in high-speed blender. Strain through fine mesh strainer. Taste and season with thyme, sea salt and black pepper, then reserve.

BLUE CHEESE-CRUSTED BEEF TENDERLOIN:
Combine cheese, 4 ounces butter, bread crumbs and thyme in food processor. Process until smooth paste forms. The paste may be refrigerated and warmed to room temperature later, or used immediately. Season each filet well with freshly ground black pepper.

Sear each face of filet mignons in hot butter. Use thick-bottomed, well-heated skillet and ample butter for best results. Once filets are seared, rest on roasting rack. Season with salt. Divide paste evenly between filets and pat onto top face of each steak, forming a thick topping. Bake steaks until cheese topping browns and meat reaches desired doneness. Times will vary depending on oven and meat; 15 minutes is average.

Serve meat immediately from oven with Cabernet Sauce.

SUGGESTED WINE:
Koves-Newlan Vineyards Cabernet Sauvignon

Per serving: 958 Calories; 76g Fat (75% calories from fat); 34g Protein; 23g Carbohydrate; 230mg Cholesterol; 616mg Sodium
Food Exchanges: 1 Starch/Bread; 4 Lean Meat; 1 Vegetable; 12 1/2 Fat

FABULOUS DRY RUB & SAUCE FOR BARBECUED RIBS

FROM SIERRA VISTA VINEYARDS & WINERY, CALIFORNIA

Serves 4

2 full slabs ribs

DRY RUB:
1 tablespoon cumin
1 tablespoon curry powder
1 teaspoon cinnamon
$1/2$ teaspoon ground cloves
1 tablespoon ground coriander
2 teaspoons kosher salt

BARBECUE SAUCE:
$1/3$ cup yellow onion, finely chopped
4 cloves garlic
2 tablespoons olive oil
$3/4$ cup tomato paste
1 $2/3$ cups water
$1/2$ teaspoon celery seeds
1 teaspoon thyme
3 tablespoons red wine vinegar
2 tablespoons Dijon-style mustard
$1/4$ teaspoon cinnamon
2 tablespoons granulated sugar
2 tablespoons light brown sugar, packed
1 tablespoon instant espresso coffee
salt and pepper to taste

NOTES:
FINGER-LICKING GOOD AND GREAT ON GRILLED CHICKEN, AS WELL!

DRY RUB:
Whisk together dry rub ingredients. Rub spice mixture all over ribs. Refrigerate 24 hours before grilling.

BARBECUE SAUCE:
Sauté chopped onion and minced garlic in olive oil in small saucepan until tender and golden, about 15 minutes. Add tomato paste and water and blend well. Add celery seeds, thyme, vinegar, mustard, cinnamon, sugars and espresso powder. Season with salt and pepper to taste. Simmer 20 minutes, partially covered. Stir occasionally. Taste and correct seasoning, if necessary.

Brush barbecue sauce on ribs toward the end of cooking. Serve extra sauce on the side if desired.

SUGGESTED WINE:
Sierra Vista Cabernet Sauvignon

Per serving: 93 Calories; 4g Fat (37% calories from fat); 2g Protein; 14g Carbohydrate; 0mg Cholesterol; 717mg Sodium
Food Exchanges: 1 Vegetable; 1 Fat; 1/2 Other Carbohydrates

FAGATTO AL FUNGHI
(STUFFED BEEF WITH MUSHROOM SAUCE)

FROM MARTINI & ROSSI, ITALY

Serves 4

24 ounces beef tenderloin
4 tablespoons Dijon mustard
4 ounces mozzarella cheese, shredded
3 tablespoons olive oil, divided
salt and pepper
1 1/2 cups porcini or shiitake mushrooms,
    sliced
1 clove garlic, chopped
1 1/2 tablespoons fresh rosemary
1/2 cup Martini & Rossi Rosso
    Sweet Vermouth

NOTES:
THE WORD "FAGATTO" IS LOOSELY
TRANSLATED TO MEAN "A BUNDLE".

Preheat oven to 400° F. Slice beef tenderloin into 1/4-inch thick slices, approximately square in shape. Flatten slices between 2 pieces of wax paper. Spread mustard onto each beef slice. Next, equally divide shredded mozzarella and sprinkle onto each beef slice. Drizzle each piece with olive oil and add salt and pepper to taste. Fold corners of sliced beef tenderloin together to form pocket with mozzarella inside. Brush each ball with olive oil. Place balls with seams down on greased tray. Bake 8 minutes.

Heat 1 tablespoon olive oil in sauté pan over medium heat. Place balls with seams down in pan. Allow to brown. Add mushrooms, garlic and rosemary. Sauté 2 minutes, then add vermouth. Sauté 3 to 5 minutes until mushrooms are cooked.

Place fagatto on plate. Pour mushroom sauce on top.

SUGGESTED WINE:
Barolo or Barbaresco

Per serving: 730 Calories; 57g Fat (74% calories from fat); 38g Protein; 7g Carbohydrate; 146mg Cholesterol; 391mg Sodium
Food Exchanges: 5 Lean Meat; 1/2 Vegetable; 8 1/2 Fat

FILET MIGNON WITH MUSHROOM SAUCE

FROM STONE HILL WINERY & RESTAURANT, MISSOURI

Serves 4

6 tablespoons butter
2 cloves garlic, chopped
1 teaspoon dried marjoram
24 ounces button mushrooms, quartered
salt and pepper to taste
$2/3$ cup nonfat chicken broth
$2/3$ cup Stone Hill Hermannsberger
6 tablespoons whipping cream
1 tablespoon peanut oil
four 4-inch filet mignons
   (about 6 ounces each)
1 teaspoon truffle oil, divided

NOTES:
PRESSED FOR TIME? NO PROBLEM; THIS
SAUCE CAN BE MADE 3 HOURS AHEAD.
REFRIGERATE IN COVERED SKILLET.

Melt butter in large nonstick skillet over medium heat. Add garlic and marjoram and sauté 30 seconds. Add mushrooms and toss to coat with butter. Sprinkle with salt. Cover and cook until mushrooms release their juices, about 13 minutes. Add chicken broth, wine and whipping cream and bring to a boil. Cook uncovered until mushrooms are tender and sauce coats mushrooms, about 5 minutes. Season mushroom sauce to taste with salt and pepper.

Heat heavy, large skillet over high heat until hot. Add peanut oil and tilt skillet to coat evenly. Sprinkle with salt and pepper. Add meat to skillet and cook to desired doneness, about 4 minutes per side for medium-rare. Transfer steaks to plates. Stirring frequently, re-warm mushroom sauce in skillet over medium heat. Spoon sauce partially over steaks and onto plates. Drizzle $1/4$ teaspoon truffle oil over mushroom sauce on each plate.

■

SUGGESTED WINE:
Stone Hill Norton

Per serving (excluding unknown items): 974 Calories; 81g Fat (76% calories from fat); 46g Protein; 11g Carbohydrate; 238mg Cholesterol; 406mg Sodium Food Exchanges: 5 1/2 Lean Meat; 2 Vegetable; 12 1/2 Fat

GARLIC-ENCRUSTED LAMB SHANKS

FROM CROWN VALLEY WINERY, MISSOURI

Serves 4

6 pounds lamb shank (4 shanks,
   1 $1/2$ pounds each)
$1/8$ cup kosher salt
3 tablespoons olive oil
15 cloves unpeeled garlic
$1/8$ cup parsley, chopped
3 tablespoons black pepper, freshly ground
$1/4$ teaspoon rosemary
$1/4$ teaspoon basil
$1/4$ teaspoon tarragon
1 cup Crown Valley Norton

NOTES:
GARLIC LOVERS REJOICE!

Remove outside fat from lamb shanks and season with salt. In heavy pan with tight-fitting lid, brown lamb shanks in olive oil. Turn shanks over. When second sides begin to brown, toss in garlic cloves. Reduce heat and cook 1 $1/2$ hours. Turn shanks and sprinkle with parsley, pepper, rosemary, basil and tarragon. Cook until almost all liquid has disappeared and begins to sizzle. Add spoonful of water so a touch of liquid remains in bottom of pan.

When liquid has been used and meat begins to sizzle, move to large plate. Pour off fat from pan and deglaze pan with wine, scraping and stirring with wooden spoon to dissolve caramelized pieces of garlic. Pour mixture into sieve to remove garlic hulls. Return mixture to pan and simmer at least 10 minutes or until thick.

Add lamb shanks and coat until lamb is hot. Sprinkle with fresh ground black pepper and fresh parsley and serve.

SUGGESTED WINE:
Crown Valley Norton Wine

Per serving: 1257 Calories; 84g Fat (63% calories from fat); 103g Protein; 8g Carbohydrate; 365mg Cholesterol; 3255mg Sodium
Food Exchanges: 14 1/2 Lean Meat; 1 Vegetable; 7 1/2 Fat

GARLIC ROAST LEG OF LAMB

FROM EOS ESTATE WINERY, CALIFORNIA

Serves 8

$^1/_2$ teaspoon kosher salt
$^1/_2$ teaspoon black pepper, freshly ground
5 pounds leg of lamb, bone in
16 cloves garlic, peeled and quartered
$^1/_4$ cup extra virgin olive oil
$^1/_4$ cup balsamic vinegar
2 sprigs fresh rosemary, chopped

NOTES:
DON'T FORGET TO EAT THE
ROASTED GARLIC . . . IT'S A TREAT!

Sprinkle salt and pepper over lamb. Make small incisions in surface of lamb and insert 1 garlic sliver in each incision.

Combine olive oil, vinegar and rosemary and pour mixture over lamb. Marinate lamb at least 3 hours, preferably overnight, in refrigerator. Allow lamb to reach room temperature before roasting.

Preheat oven to 350° F. Roast lamb 1 $^1/_4$ to 1 $^1/_2$ hours or until meat thermometer registers 135° F. Let roast rest 10 to 15 minutes before carving.

SUGGESTED WINE:
EOS Reserve Petite Sirah

Per serving: 586 Calories; 45g Fat (70% calories from fat); 41g Protein; 3g Carbohydrate; 155mg Cholesterol; 245mg Sodium
Food Exchanges: 6 Lean Meat; 1/2 Vegetable; 5 1/2 Fat

GERMAN SAUERBRATEN

FROM LYNFRED WINERY, ILLINOIS
CHEF CHRIS SMITH

Serves 6

3 $^1/_2$ tablespoons pickling spice
2 $^1/_2$ medium onions, sliced
2 medium carrots, sliced
1 cup water
1 cup Lynfred Syrah
1 cup red wine vinegar
1 tablespoon salt
$^3/_4$ teaspoon black pepper, freshly ground
3 bay leaves
5 pounds sirloin tip roast, trimmed
4 tablespoons vegetable oil
$^1/_4$ cup all-purpose flour
1 tablespoon sugar
$^3/_4$ cup gingersnap cookies
   (about 14 crushed)

Place pickling spice in cheesecloth bag. Put spice bag, onions, carrots, water, wine, red wine vinegar, salt, pepper and bay leaves in shallow dish. Add roast. Cover and chill 8 to 9 hours, turning occasionally.

NOTES:
A GERMAN CLASSIC SERVED
WITH SPAETZLE OR EGG NOODLES AND
RED CABBAGE.

Remove roast from marinade, reserving marinade. In heavy-bottomed pan, brown roast on all sides in hot vegetable oil. Remove roast, reserving drippings in pan. Whisk flour and sugar into drippings. Cook over medium flame 2 to 3 minutes or until browned, whisking constantly. Slowly whisk in marinade.

Return browned roast to pan. Bring sauce to a boil. Cover, reduce heat and simmer 2 $^1/_2$ hours until meat is tender.

Remove spice bag and bay leaves. Remove roast, slice and keep warm. Stir crushed gingersnap cookies into sauce in pan. Simmer sauce 2 minutes, stirring constantly. Pour sauce through colander into bowl. Press vegetables through colander with back of large spoon. Serve sliced meat with gingersnap gravy.

SUGGESTED WINE:
Lynfred Winery Syrah

Per serving: 811 Calories; 30g Fat (35% calories from fat); 84g Protein; 42g Carbohydrate; 227mg Cholesterol; 1533mg Sodium
Food Exchanges: 1/2 Starch/Bread; 11 1/2 Lean Meat; 1 1/2 Vegetable; 2 1/2 Fat; 2 Other Carbohydrates

GRILLED LAMB CHOPS

FROM EAST VALLEY VINEYARDS, CALIFORNIA

Serves 4

4 tablespoons olive oil
4 teaspoons fresh rosemary, chopped
4 teaspoons garlic, minced
2 teaspoons mixed herbs de Provence
8 small lamb loin chops
   (1- to 1$^1/_2$-inches thick)

Mix together first 4 ingredients to make a paste.

Coat both sides of chops with paste.

Barbecue or grill to desired doneness.

SUGGESTED WINE:
East Valley Vineyard Syrah

Per serving: 837 Calories; 75g Fat (81% calories from fat); 38g Protein; 1g Carbohydrate; 170mg Cholesterol; 130mg Sodium
Food Exchanges: 5 1/2 Lean Meat; 12 Fat

NOTES:
A WONDERFUL MEAT ACCENT TO THE MAIN COURSE. WE RECOMMEND COOKING TO THE POINT OF STILL PINK ON THE INSIDE.

GRILLED LAMBURGERS

FROM LAMOREAUX LANDING WINE CELLARS, NEW YORK

Serves 4

2 pounds ground lamb
2 cloves garlic, minced
2 tablespoons fresh rosemary, minced
   or 2 teaspoons dry
1/4 pound crumbled feta cheese
salt and pepper to taste

Mix all ingredients thoroughly, without overly compacting meat. Form into 4 patties.

Oil preheated grill rack and place lamburgers on rack at high heat 3 minutes on each side. Reduce heat to low and cook 5 minutes on each side with grill covered.

Grill or toast hamburger rolls 1 to 2 minutes as lamburgers finish cooking.

Serve with oven-roasted potato fries and cucumber salad with yogurt dressing.

NOTES:
RICH AND SAVORY, A CONNOISSEUR'S BURGER FROM THE GRILL.

SUGGESTED WINE:
Lamoreaux Landing Pinot Noir

Per serving: 718 Calories; 59g Fat (75% calories from fat); 42g Protein; 2g Carbohydrate; 191mg Cholesterol; 451mg Sodium
Food Exchanges: 6 Lean Meat; 8 Fat

GRILLED TRI-TIP BEEF ROAST WITH ZINFANDEL MARINADE

FROM EOS ESTATE WINERY, CALIFORNIA

Serves 8

1/3 cup fresh lime juice
1/3 cup fresh cilantro, chopped
1/3 cup olive oil
1/3 cup soy sauce
1/3 cup EOS Zinfandel
7 cloves garlic, peeled and chopped
2 teaspoons lime rind, grated
2 teaspoons ground cumin
2 teaspoons dried oregano
1 teaspoon coarse ground black pepper
4 pounds beef roast, tri-tip flank or other

Put all ingredients except roast in blender or food processor and process until finely blended.

With small, sharp knife, pierce meat all over. Place meat in large self-sealing plastic bag, add marinade and seal bag. Refrigerate at least 2 hours; overnight is preferable. Turn bag occasionally.

Prepare grill on medium-high heat. Remove meat from marinade and discard marinade. Grill meat to desired doneness, about 10 minutes per side for medium-rare. Transfer to cutting board. Tent with foil and let stand 10 minutes. Cut diagonally across grain.

■

SUGGESTED WINE:
EOS Zinfandel

NOTES:
SERVE THIS LOVELY PIECE OF MEAT WITH FRESH SLICED TOMATOES TOPPED WITH BLUE CHEESE AND BALSAMIC VINEGAR, PLUS SEASONED STEAK FRIES.

Per serving: 577 Calories; 45g Fat (71% calories from fat); 37g Protein; 4g Carbohydrate; 131mg Cholesterol; 808mg Sodium
Food Exchanges: 5 Lean Meat; 1/2 Vegetable; 5 1/2 Fat

HERB-ROASTED RACK OF LAMB WITH SMOKY CABERNET SAUCE

FROM UNIONVILLE VINEYARDS, NEW JERSEY

Serves 4

3 slices thick-sliced bacon, chopped
1 small onion, chopped
1 medium carrot, chopped
1 celery rib, chopped
1 whole plum tomato, chopped
10 black peppercorns
$1/4$ teaspoon dried thyme
1 bay leaf
2 cups Unionville Cabernet Sauvignon
2 cups veal stock or beef broth
3 pounds lamb ribs (two $1\,1/2$-pound racks)
1 tablespoon fresh parsley
1 tablespoon fresh thyme
3 cloves garlic, minced
1 teaspoon olive oil
salt and pepper to taste
3 tablespoons unsalted butter

In large saucepan, cook bacon over moderate heat until crisp. Add onion, carrot and celery and cook until tender. Add tomato, peppercorns, dried thyme, bay leaf and wine. Cook over moderate heat and reduce until almost dry. Add stock and reduce by half. Strain into another saucepan and discard solids. Skim fat from sauce and refrigerate.

Meanwhile, place lamb fat side up in medium roasting pan. Mix parsley, fresh thyme, garlic and oil together in small bowl. Then rub over lamb. Refrigerate at least 30 minutes or up to 3 hours.

Preheat oven to 425° F. Generously season lamb with salt and pepper and roast 30 minutes or until an instant-read thermometer inserted into thickest part of meat registers 140° F (medium-rare). Transfer lamb to cutting board and let rest 10 minutes.

Bring sauce to gentle simmer over moderate heat. Whisk in butter, 1 tablespoon at a time, and season with salt and pepper. Carve racks into single or double chops and transfer to plates. Drizzle sauce over lamb and serve.

NOTES:
A GREAT RECIPE FOR THAT SPECIAL OCCASION OR HOLIDAY OR WHEN YOU JUST WANT TO COOK UP SOMETHING TASTY.

SUGGESTED WINE:
Unionville Vineyards Cabernet Sauvignon

Per serving: 1236 Calories; 101g Fat (78% calories from fat); 43g Protein; 21g Carbohydrate; 222mg Cholesterol; 973mg Sodium
Food Exchanges: 1 Starch/Bread; 5 1/2 Lean Meat; 1 Vegetable; 16 1/2 Fat

JOE'S CHILI-SPICED BURGERS

FROM PEDRONCELLI WINERY, CALIFORNIA

Serves 6

1 ¹/₄ pounds lean ground beef
1 tablespoon chili powder
1 teaspoon ground cumin
¹/₂ teaspoon granulated garlic
2 dashes cayenne pepper
salt and pepper to taste

NOTES:

THERE IS NOTHING LIKE A NICE, SPICY BURGER AND A GLASS OF PEDRONCELLI CALIFORNIA ZINFANDEL.

Place ground meat in medium bowl and sprinkle with spices. Mix with hands until incorporated. Form 6 patties and seal edges, without over-handling meat.

Heat grill to medium-high. Cook patties on grill 3 to 4 minutes per side.

For extra zip, place slice of Pepper Jack cheese on top of meat just before removing from grill.

Toast regular sesame seed or Kaiser buns. Top with desired condiments — avocado would be tasty, too.

SUGGESTED WINE:
Pedroncelli Zinfandel

Per serving: 256 Calories; 20g Fat (71% calories from fat); 17g Protein; 1g Carbohydrate; 71mg Cholesterol; 79mg Sodium
Food Exchanges: 2 1/2 Lean Meat; 2 1/2 Fat

LEG OF LAMB IN A GREEK MARINADE WITH YOGURT & ANISEED

FROM STERLING VINEYARDS, CALIFORNIA

Serves 6

5 pounds leg of lamb, boned and butterflied
1 large onion, chopped
3 cloves garlic, minced
1 tablespoon anise seed or aniseed
1 teaspoon ground cinnamon
1 teaspoon ground coriander
1 teaspoon black pepper, freshly ground
   plus to taste
1 $1/_2$ cups plain yogurt
$1/_4$ cup Ouzo brandy
3 tablespoons olive oil
salt to taste

Trim all excess fat from lamb and place in non-corrosive container. In food processor or blender, puree onion, garlic, spices, yogurt and brandy. Pour marinade over lamb and cover. Refrigerate at least 8 hours, preferably overnight. Turn occasionally.

Bring meat to room temperature. Preheat broiler or make a charcoal fire. Brush meat with olive oil and sprinkle generously with salt and pepper. Grill about 10 to 15 minutes per side or as desired. Meat will be rare to medium, depending on thickness. Slice across grain or cut in larger pieces for rustic country-style presentation.

NOTES:
A GREAT RECIPE FOR AN OUTDOOR BARBECUE PARTY.

SUGGESTED WINE:
Sterling Vineyards Cabernet Sauvignon or Merlot

Per serving: 826 Calories; 60g Fat (68% calories from fat); 56g Protein; 7g Carbohydrate; 214mg Cholesterol; 197mg Sodium
Food Exchanges: 8 Lean Meat; 1/2 Vegetable; 7 Fat

MOUSSAKA

FROM STERLING VINEYARDS, CALIFORNIA

Serves 6

2 medium eggplants
1 $^1/_2$ teaspoons salt, divided plus to taste
$^1/_2$ pound ground beef
1 cup onions, chopped
$^1/_4$ cup Sterling Merlot
$^1/_4$ cup water
2 tablespoons parsley, chopped
2 tablespoons tomato paste
black pepper, freshly ground
$^1/_2$ cup bread crumbs, divided
3 medium eggs, beaten and divided
$^1/_2$ cup cheddar cheese, shredded
   and divided
$^1/_8$ teaspoon cinnamon
$^1/_8$ teaspoon allspice
3 tablespoons butter
3 tablespoons flour
1 $^1/_2$ cups milk
dash nutmeg
2 tablespoons vegetable oil

Preheat oven to 350º F. Cut eggplants in slices $^1/_4$-inch thick. Sprinkle with a little salt and set aside in colander to drain.

In heavy skillet, brown meat and onions. Drain off fat. Add wine, water, parsley, tomato paste, 1 teaspoon salt and dash pepper. Simmer until liquid is nearly absorbed, then cool to room temperature. Stir in $^1/_4$ cup bread crumbs, 2 beaten eggs, $^1/_4$ cup cheese, cinnamon and allspice.

In medium saucepan, melt butter and whisk in flour to make a roux. Cook 1 to 2 minutes and whisk in milk. Cook and stir until smooth and thickened. Add $^1/_2$ teaspoon salt, dash black pepper and nutmeg to beaten egg and mix with roux. Set aside.

In heavy skillet, brown eggplant slices on both sides in heated oil. Sprinkle bottom of 12x7$^1/_2$x2-inch baking dish with remaining $^1/_4$ cup bread crumbs and cover with layer of eggplant slices. Evenly cover with meat mixture. Arrange remaining eggplant over meat and spread white sauce over top. Sprinkle with $^1/_4$ cup shredded cheese and bake about 45 minutes.

SUGGESTED WINES:
Sterling Vineyards Pinot Noir or Merlot

Per serving: 433 Calories; 29g Fat (60% calories from fat); 17g Protein; 26g Carbohydrate; 173mg Cholesterol; 870mg Sodium
Food Exchanges: 1/2 Starch/Bread; 1 1/2 Lean Meat; 2 Vegetable; 4 1/2 Fat

NOTES: A CLASSIC GREEK DISH THAT MUST BE ACCOMPANIED BY A GREEK SALAD.

PAN-BLACKENED SIRLOIN STEAK

FROM STERLING VINEYARDS, CALIFORNIA

Serves 6

$1/2$ teaspoon black pepper, freshly ground
1 teaspoon salt
1 teaspoon garlic powder
1 tablespoon paprika
$1/2$ teaspoon cayenne
1 $1/2$ pounds sirloin steak, boneless
   (1- to 1 $1/2$-inches thick)
3 tablespoons unsalted butter or margarine,
   divided
1 small onion, thinly sliced in rings
2 teaspoons flour
$1/4$ cup Sterling Cabernet Sauvignon
$1/4$ cup chili sauce
2 teaspoons brown mustard
watercress

NOTES:
A HEARTY STEAK TO SERVE WITH
TWICE-BAKED POTATOES!

Mix first 5 ingredients together in small bowl. Press spice mixture firmly into steak on both sides. (Remaining spice may be stored for future use.) Melt 1 tablespoon butter in large, heavy frying pan over medium heat. Cook steak over high heat 3 minutes per side. Continue cooking to desired doneness. Surface of steak will become very dark and crusty.

While steak is cooking, toss onion rings in flour. Melt 2 tablespoons butter in medium skillet over medium heat. Fry onion rings for about 1 minute, until brown and crisp. Remove onions and steak from heat and keep warm. Drain off any fat from large skillet and deglaze pan with wine. Add chili sauce and mustard. Bubble and stir to loosen meat juices and thicken sauce 2 to 3 minutes. Slice steak across grain in thin diagonal slices. To serve, spread sauce on warm platter and lay steak slices on top. Garnish with onions and watercress.

■

SUGGESTED WINES:
Sterling Cabernet Sauvignon or Merlot

Per serving: 316 Calories; 23g Fat (66% calories from fat); 22g Protein; 5g Carbohydrate; 89mg Cholesterol; 446mg Sodium
Food Exchanges: 3 Lean Meat; 1/2 Vegetable; 3 Fat

POACHED TENDERLOIN OF BEEF

FROM RODNEY STRONG VINEYARDS, CALIFORNIA

Serves 8

2 bottles Rodney Strong
   Cabernet Sauvignon
1 bunch fresh rosemary
6 pounds beef tenderloin, trimmed
salt and pepper to taste
6 ounces butter

Put wine and rosemary in pan large enough to hold tenderloin. Bring to a boil.

Season beef with salt and pepper, add to boiling wine and cover. Beef should cook in about 15 minutes. Check with meat thermometer, which should read about 118º F when medium-rare. Remove from pan and let meat rest while making sauce.

Reduce wine until about 2 cups of liquid remain. Remove rosemary and whisk in butter. Slice beef and pour sauce on top.

NOTES:
SIMPLE, BUT FANTASTICALLY GOOD!

SUGGESTED WINE:
Rodney Strong Vineyards Reserve Cabernet Sauvignon

Per serving: 1122 Calories; 96g Fat (78% calories from fat); 61g Protein; 0g Carbohydrate; 288mg Cholesterol; 344mg Sodium
Food Exchanges: 8 Lean Meat; 14 Fat

PORK FILET MIGNON WITH PORT WINE SAUCE

FROM PEDRONCELLI WINERY, CALIFORNIA

Serves 4

2 pounds pork tenderloin, sliced into
  2-inch filets
sea salt to taste
cracked black pepper to taste
1 tablespoon fresh sage, minced
2 tablespoons butter, divided
$^1/_2$ cup shallots, minced
2 cloves garlic, minced
1 cup port wine

Season filets with salt and pepper, sprinkle sage on both sides and gently pat to attach herbs to filets. Melt 1 tablespoon butter over medium-high heat in large sauté pan. Add filets and brown on both sides. Cook until medium-rare. Remove filets to warm platter and cover with an inverted bowl. Meat will continue cooking. Add 1 table-spoon butter, shallots and garlic to pan. Sauté until shallots are tender. Add port wine and simmer until reduced by half. Return pork to sauce and coat on all sides.

Serve pork with chive mashed potatoes and braised Swiss chard. Drizzle sauce on meat and potatoes.

SUGGESTED WINES:
Pedroncelli Pinot Noir or Merlot

Per serving: 432 Calories; 13g Fat (34% calories from fat); 48g Protein; 11g Carbohydrate; 163mg Cholesterol; 176mg Sodium
Food Exchanges: 7 Lean Meat; 1/2 Vegetable; 1 Fat

NOTES:
GREAT "COMFORT FOOD" WITH
A TOUCH OF CLASS.

PORK LOIN WITH CHERRY-CRANBERRY STUFFING

FROM PEDRONCELLI WINERY, CALIFORNIA

Serves 6

3 1/2 pounds pork loin
1/2 cup dried cherries
1/2 cup dried cranberries
3 cups low calorie cranberry juice
1 cup dry-roasted hazelnuts or almonds,
   coarsely chopped
1 lemon (zest of 1 lemon)
2 cups Pedroncelli Zinfandel
8 black peppercorns
2 sticks cinnamon

Trim all extra fat from pork roast. In small pan, mix cherries, cranberries, juice, nuts and lemon zest. Heat through and set aside for 2 hours. Preheat oven to 350° F.

Drain fruit through colander, catching marinade in medium-size pan. Cut pork lengthwise to form pocket. Stuff mixture into center of pork roast and tie with cotton string every 2 inches. Place in roasting pan and place in center of heated oven. Bake 30 minutes.

Meanwhile add wine, black peppercorns and cinnamon sticks to marinade and heat on medium-high until boiling. Reduce heat and cook 30 minutes. Remove pork roast from oven, pour marinade mixture over roast, cover and return to oven. Baste every 15 minutes for 2 hours.

Uncover and bake 30 minutes more to brown, basting every 10 minutes.

Let roast stand 15 minutes covered with foil. Slice and serve with sauce on the side. (Strain sauce to remove cinnamon and peppercorns.)

SUGGESTED WINES:
Pedroncelli Zinfandel or Zinfandel Rosé

Per serving: 618 Calories; 29g Fat (45% calories from fat); 50g Protein; 30g Carbohydrate; 109mg Cholesterol; 166mg Sodium
Food Exchanges: 1/2 Starch/Bread; 6 1/2 Lean Meat; 1 Fruit; 3 Fat

NOTES:
HERE'S A GREAT HOLIDAY TREAT THAT IS DELICIOUS WITH SWEET POTATOES OR CARROT-GARLIC MASHED POTATOES.

PORK LOIN WITH VERJUS AND FENNEL

FROM NAVARRO VINEYARDS, CALIFORNIA

Serves 4

$^1/_2$ cup fennel leaves, packed
$^1/_4$ cup fennel stalks, finely chopped
1 $^1/_4$ cups grape juice ("verjus"), divided
1 cup Navarro Gewürztraminer
2 cloves garlic, minced
$^1/_4$ teaspoon black pepper, freshly ground
4 pounds pork loin
$^1/_2$ cup low-sodium chicken broth

NOTES:
VERJUS IS NON-FERMENTED JUICE FROM UNRIPE GREEN GRAPES WITH HIGH ACIDITY AND A TART APPLE-LIKE FLAVOR. IN THE MIDDLE AGES IT WAS OFTEN PREFERRED OVER VINEGAR AND USED AS A SAUCE INGREDIENT, MEAT TENDERIZER, CONDIMENT AND SALAD DRESSING. WHILE VINEGAR MAY CLASH, VERJUS COMPLEMENTS WINE.

Mix all ingredients except pork, $^1/_4$ cup verjus and chicken broth in large glass bowl or baking dish. Pierce pork so liquid will penetrate. Marinate at room temperature at least 2 hours, or marinate a few hours in refrigerator. Remove loin from refrigerator 2 hours before cooking to bring to room temperature.

Preheat oven to 425º F and bake loin 20 minutes. Reduce heat to 350º F and cook 1 to 1 $^1/_2$ hours, basting every 20 minutes.

Remove pork to carving plate and pour drippings into saucepan, scraping if necessary. Add $^1/_4$ cup verjus and chicken broth and reduce 20 minutes. Slice pork and serve with sauce.

SUGGESTED WINE:
Navarro Gewürztraminer

Per serving: 627 Calories; 23g Fat (35% calories from fat); 80g Protein; 14g Carbohydrate; 188mg Cholesterol; 196mg Sodium
Food Exchanges: 11 Lean Meat; 1 Fruit

SEARED FLANK STEAK WITH CARAMELIZED ONION AND GOLDEN RAISIN COMPOTE

FROM ZD WINERY, CALIFORNIA

Serves 6

MARINADE:
1 whole beef flank
salt and pepper to taste
1 cup ZD Cabernet Sauvignon
6 cloves garlic, smashed
3 sprigs fresh thyme
1 tablespoon olive oil

COMPOTE:
grapeseed oil as needed, plus 1 tablespoon
4 large yellow onions, sliced $1/_8$-inch thick
1 tablespoon balsamic vinegar
salt and pepper to taste
1 tablespoon honey
water as needed
$1/_2$ cup golden raisins
1 large red bell pepper, roasted and diced
2 tablespoons fresh Italian parsley, chopped
$1/_3$ cup toasted pine nuts
1 tablespoon butter

MARINADE:
A day ahead, generously season flank steak with salt and pepper, then marinate in shallow pan with wine, garlic, thyme and olive oil.

COMPOTE:
Heat medium-size sauté pan over high heat. Add a little grapeseed oil and when it begins to smoke, add onions. Stir frequently and reduce heat to medium when onions start to brown. When onions are deep brown, add vinegar and cook 1 minute. Season with salt and pepper. Fold in honey. Barely cover onions with water. Add raisins and bell pepper. Simmer 15 minutes. Add parsley and toasted pine nuts. Set aside. Onion compote may be made up to 2 days in advance.

Bring flank steak to room temperature. Remove from marinade and pat dry. Reserve garlic and thyme. Season generously with salt and pepper.

Preheat oven to 350° F. Heat large skillet over high heat and add grapeseed oil. Cook flank steak on both sides until deep golden brown. Add butter, garlic and thyme. Flip flank over and cook an additional minute, basting with spoon. Roast in oven 10 to 15 minutes, depending on size and desired doneness. Let rest 10 minutes. Slice thin and serve warm compote over top.

SUGGESTED WINE:
ZD Napa Valley Cabernet Sauvignon

Per serving: 260 Calories; 13g Fat (48% calories from fat); 9g Protein; 22g Carbohydrate; 25mg Cholesterol; 77mg Sodium
Food Exchanges: 1 Lean Meat; 1 1/2 Vegetable; 1/2 Fruit; 2 Fat

SIMA
(STUFFED BREAST OF VEAL)

FROM SEBASTIANI VINEYARDS, CALIFORNIA

Serves 8

4 pounds veal breast or shoulder
1 medium onion, chopped
4 tablespoons olive oil
$^1/_3$ cup butter plus 2 tablespoons
2 cloves garlic, pressed and divided
2 packages frozen spinach, finely chopped
$^1/_2$ cup parsley, chopped
5 large eggs
2 cups bread crumbs
$^3/_4$ cup Parmesan cheese, grated
dash dried basil
salt and pepper to taste
1 teaspoon rosemary
1 cup Sebastiani Chardonnay

NOTES:
A SEBASTIANI FAMILY FAVORITE FOR THE CHRISTMAS AND EASTER HOLIDAYS.

Preheat oven to 350° F. Cut pocket into veal. Sauté onion in oil and 2 tablespoons butter, adding 1 clove garlic last. Add spinach, parsley, eggs, bread crumbs, Parmesan cheese, basil, salt and pepper, mixing well with fork.

Stuff mixture into veal pocket and sew with coarse needle and thread, closing completely.

Place veal in roasting pan and rub with 1 clove garlic. Sprinkle with rosemary and baste with wine and $^1/_3$ cup butter. Roast uncovered about 1 hour until brown, basting occasionally.

SUGGESTED WINE:
Sebastiani Chardonnay

Per serving: 621 Calories; 34g Fat (51% calories from fat); 46g Protein; 28g Carbohydrate; 312mg Cholesterol; 808mg Sodium
Food Exchanges: 1 1/2 Starch/Bread; 5 1/2 Lean Meat; 1 1/2 Vegetable; 4 Fat

SLOW-COOKED LAMB WITH POTATOES AND ARTICHOKES

FROM BEAULIEU VINEYARD, CALIFORNIA

Serves 4

1 1/2 pounds potatoes, white or yellow
4 slices thick-sliced bacon
water as needed
2 tablespoons olive oil
4 cloves garlic, sliced
1 1/2 pounds leg of lamb
   (2 slices, about 1/3-inch thick)
1 medium onion, coarsely chopped
2 medium tomatoes, chopped
1 fennel bulb, trimmed and finely chopped
1/2 package frozen artichoke hearts
3/4 teaspoon thyme
3/4 teaspoon marjoram
salt and pepper to taste

Preheat oven to 325° F. Peel potatoes and cut in 1-inch cubes. Put bacon in small saucepan, cover with water and bring to a boil over high heat. Boil 1 minute, drain and let cool. Dice bacon.

Put olive oil in heavy, flat casserole dish and sprinkle with diced bacon and garlic. Lay lamb slices on top and tuck onion, tomatoes, fennel and artichoke hearts around edges. Sprinkle with thyme, marjoram, salt and pepper. Cover and bake 3 1/2 hours or until meat and vegetables are very tender.

■

SUGGESTED WINE:
Beaulieu Vineyard Reserve Tapestry

Per serving: 607 Calories; 36g Fat (54% calories from fat); 33g Protein; 38g Carbohydrate; 104mg Cholesterol; 333mg Sodium
Food Exchanges: 2 Starch/Bread; 4 Lean Meat; 1 1/2 Vegetable; 4 1/2 Fat

NOTES:
THIS DISH GOES TOGETHER QUICKLY AND FILLS THE HOUSE WITH TYPICAL AROMAS FROM THE SOUTH OF FRANCE.

VEAL AND MUSHROOM STEW

FROM CITRA/PALM BAY IMPORTS, ITALY

Serves 6

4 tablespoons olive oil
3 cloves garlic, peeled and crushed
1 $^1/_2$ pounds veal, cut in 1 $^1/_2$-inch cubes
4 tablespoons fresh parsley, chopped
1 pinch salt
$^1/_2$ pound tomatoes, peeled and chopped
1 pound mushrooms, sliced

NOTES:
THIS DISH CAN BE PREPARED A DAY IN ADVANCE, REFRIGERATED AND RE-HEATED.

Heat olive oil and garlic in large skillet over medium heat until garlic turns light brown. Discard garlic from pan. Add veal to skillet and brown thoroughly on all sides, then sprinkle with parsley and pinch of salt. Stir briefly, reduce heat and add tomatoes. Cover and cook at a gentle simmer 15 minutes, stirring occasionally. If extra liquid is needed, add a few tablespoons of water. Add sliced mushrooms, cover and simmer over low heat 30 minutes, stirring occasionally. Serve immediately.

SUGGESTED WINE:
Citra Montepulciano d'Abruzzo

Per serving: 223 Calories; 15g Fat (59% calories from fat); 17g Protein; 6g Carbohydrate; 64mg Cholesterol; 94mg Sodium
Food Exchanges: 2 Lean Meat; 1 Vegetable; 2 Fat

VEAL FRAMBOISE

FROM TOMASELLO WINERY, NEW JERSEY

Serves 6

32 ounces veal cutlet or
   six 6-ounce medallions
3 ounces butter, divided
2 cups flour
10 ounces Tomasello Red Raspberry Wine
10 ounces Tomasello Chardonnay
3 tablespoons shallots, finely chopped
10 ounces heavy cream
salt and pepper to taste
fresh raspberries for garnish

NOTES:
A FRUIT LOVER'S DREAM DISH.

Flatten veal with mallet. In sauté pan, melt 2 ounces butter (clarified is preferable). Flour veal medallions and sauté on both sides until brown. Set aside in covered dish.

Deglaze pan by adding both wines and chopped shallots. Reduce to $^1/_3$ of original volume. Add cream and again reduce to $^1/_3$ over low flame. Salt and pepper to taste. Finish sauce with 1 ounce butter and return veal to pan.

Serve with garnish of fresh raspberries.

SUGGESTED WINE:
Tomasello Chardonnay

Per serving: 740 Calories; 40g Fat (54% calories from fat); 36g Protein; 40g Carbohydrate; 223mg Cholesterol; 296mg Sodium
Food Exchanges: 2 Starch/Bread; 4 1/2 Lean Meat; 6 Fat

VEAL PICCATA

FROM PETRONI VINEYARDS, CALIFORNIA
NORTH BEACH RESTAURANT

Serves 6

12 slices veal cutlet or scaloppini
1/2 cup flour for dredging
2 tablespoons virgin olive oil or as needed
1/2 cup dry white wine
3 tablespoons lemon juice (about 1 lemon)
1 tablespoon butter
2 tablespoons capers

Pound veal slices, if necessary, to about 1/4-inch thick. Lightly flour and sauté in hot olive oil, about 1 minute on each side. Do not overcook. Transfer meat to warm plate. Cover and hold in warm oven.

Discard any excess fat remaining in pan. Pour in wine and deglaze pan, letting liquid nearly evaporate. Add lemon juice, butter and capers. Heat through.

Place veal on serving plates and spoon sauce over meat.

NOTES:
FANTASTIC WITH LEMON RISOTTO OR
BUTTERED FETTUCCINI.

SUGGESTED WINE:
California Sauvignon Blanc

Per serving: 759 Calories; 37g Fat (45% calories from fat); 93g Protein; 9g Carbohydrate; 386mg Cholesterol; 423mg Sodium
Food Exchanges: 1/2 Starch/Bread; 13 1/2 Lean Meat; 1 1/2 Fat

VEAL SAUTÉED WITH OLIVES

FROM SEBASTIANI VINEYARDS, CALIFORNIA

Serves 4

1 ¹/₂ pounds veal cubes
4 tablespoons olive oil
2 tablespoons butter
salt and pepper to taste
granulated garlic to taste
1 clove garlic, pressed
2 teaspoons parsley, chopped
$^1/_4$ teaspoon sage
$^3/_4$ cup Sebastiani Chardonnay,
   slightly heated
$^1/_2$ cup green olives, coarsely chopped

Brown veal in oil and butter, adding salt, pepper and granulated garlic to all sides. Turn frequently with spatula until brown.

Add garlic clove, parsley, sage and heated wine. Add olives and cover. Simmer for 20 minutes or until veal is tender. Add extra wine if moister veal is desired.

SUGGESTED WINE:
Sebastiani Chardonnay

Per serving: 408 Calories; 26g Fat (62% calories from fat); 35g Protein; 1g Carbohydrate; 158mg Cholesterol; 668mg Sodium
Food Exchanges: 5 Lean Meat; 4 1/2 Fat

NOTES:
GREAT OVER POLENTA, RISOTTO OR
CREAMY, MASHED POTATOES.

NOTES:

NOTES:

MISCELLANEOUS

■

CHARDONNAY-POACHED EGGS

FROM CHATEAU CHANTAL WINERY/BED & BREAKFAST, MICHIGAN

Serves 1

1 tablespoon butter
$1/4$ cup Chardonnay
2 large eggs
dash grated Parmesan cheese
1 English muffin, halved,
   or two pieces of toast
1 teaspoon all-purpose flour
2 tablespoons low-fat sour cream
salt and white pepper to taste

In small omelet or sauté pan, melt butter and add wine; slip in eggs. Sprinkle grated Parmesan over each egg. Cook over low heat until whites are firm (covering pan speeds up this process). Lift out eggs onto toasted, buttered English muffin halves or toast. Add flour, sour cream, white pepper and salt to liquid in pan. Cook until thickened, then pour over eggs.

SUGGESTED WINE:
Chateau Chantal Sparkling Wine

Per serving: 443 Calories; 23g Fat (52% calories from fat); 18g Protein; 30g Carbohydrate; 464mg Cholesterol; 551mg Sodium
Food Exchanges: 2 Starch/Bread; 2 Lean Meat; 3 1/2 Fat

NOTES:
HOW ABOUT EGGS CHANTAL?
A NOTCH ABOVE EGGS BENEDICT.

CHEDDAR SWISS FONDUE

FROM DEBONNE VINEYARDS, OHIO

Serves 4

1 $1/4$ cups Debonne Pinot Gris
1 clove garlic, chopped
8 ounces Swiss cheese, cubed
4 tablespoons flour
2 cans condensed cheddar cheese soup
   (10 $1/2$-ounce cans)

Heat wine and garlic in saucepan or fondue pot to simmering. Combine cheese and flour. Gradually blend into wine. Heat until cheese is melted, stirring occasionally. Blend in soup, stirring until smooth.

Dip bread cubes into fondue.

NOTES:
FUN FOR GUESTS AND FAMILY; DELICIOUS TOO!

SUGGESTED WINE:
Debonne Pinot Gris

Per serving: 389 Calories; 22g Fat (58% calories from fat); 20g Protein; 15g Carbohydrate; 70mg Cholesterol; 743mg Sodium
Food Exchanges: 1/2 Starch/Bread; 2 1/2 Lean Meat; 3 Fat

CHERRY CHEESE STRATA

FROM CHATEAU CHANTAL WINERY/BED & BREAKFAST, MICHIGAN
CHEF CHRISTINE CAMPBELL

Serves 6

4 ounces cream cheese, softened
16 slices French bread
$1/_2$ cup Chateau Chantal Cherry
   Merlot cherry preserves
1 cup frozen cherries
4 large eggs, slightly beaten
2 cups half and half
$2/_3$ cup sugar
1 $1/_2$ teaspoons orange zest, finely shredded
1 teaspoon vanilla
$1/_4$ cup turbinado raw sugar
$1/_4$ cup sliced almonds

NOTES:
IT'S WORTH GETTING OUT OF BED FOR
THIS BREAKFAST DISH.

Preheat oven to 350° F. Coat 2-quart square baking dish with cooking spray. Spread cream cheese on slices of bread and fit a few slices into baking dish in single layer. Spread cherry preserves over top. Scatter frozen cherries on top of preserves. Build another layer with bread slices. Tear remaining bread into bite-size pieces and fill in around slices.

In medium bowl, combine eggs, half and half, sugar, orange zest and vanilla. Pour over bread in baking dish. Sprinkle with turbinado sugar and sliced almonds. Bake uncovered about 45 minutes or until knife inserted in center comes out clean. Let stand 15 minutes before serving.

Serve with dollop of vanilla yogurt or ice cream for an added treat.

SUGGESTED WINE:
Chateau Chantal Sparkling Wine

Per serving: 662 Calories; 24g Fat (33% calories from fat); 16g Protein; 98g Carbohydrate; 194mg Cholesterol; 541mg Sodium
Food Exchanges: 2 1/2 Starch/Bread; 1 Lean Meat; 2 1/2 Fruit; 1/2 Non-Fat Milk; 4 1/2 Fat; 3 Other Carbohydrates

LAVASH CRACKER BREAD

FROM CHATEAU CHANTAL WINERY/BED & BREAKFAST, MICHIGAN
CHEF NADINE BEGIN

Serves 30

2 cups unbleached all-purpose flour
1 teaspoon salt
1 envelope active dry yeast
2 tablespoons soft corn oil margarine
$^1/_2$ teaspoon granulated sugar
  (fructose is better)
$^2/_3$ cup warm water
2 tablespoons sesame seeds, divided

Combine flour, salt and yeast in large bowl. Mix together margarine, sugar or fructose and warm water. Slowly add to dry ingredients, stirring constantly. Knead dough until smooth and elastic. Shape into ball and rub margarine over entire surface.

Place dough in bowl and cover with plastic wrap or foil. Place hot, damp towel over covered bowl and let dough rise until doubled in bulk, 1 to 2 hours.

Preheat oven to 400° F. Punch dough down and cut into 2 pieces. Place $^1/_2$ tablespoon sesame seeds on sheet of waxed paper cut to fit cookie sheet. Place $^1/_2$ of dough on paper and press out as thinly as possible. Sprinkle another $^1/_2$ tablespoon of sesame seeds on another cookie sheet, turn dough over onto seeds and roll dough out again as thinly as possible. Remove waxed paper.

Bake 10 to 12 minutes until light golden brown. While lavash is baking, repeat process with second ball of dough. To serve, break lavash into pieces.

SUGGESTED WINE:
Chateau Chantal Riesling

Per serving: 42 Calories; 1g Fat (25% calories from fat); 1g Protein; 7g Carbohydrate; 0mg Cholesterol; 82mg Sodium
Food Exchanges: 1/2 Starch/Bread

NOTES:
WONDERFUL WITH BRIE, ASSORTED CHEESE, GRAPES AND A GLASS OF WINE.

PAULA'S PANNAKUKU (FINNISH PANCAKE)

FROM CHATEAU CHANTAL WINERY/BED & BREAKFAST, MICHIGAN
CHEF PAULA WASEK

Serves 6

8 large eggs
$1/2$ cup sugar
1 $1/2$ cups all-purpose flour
$1/2$ teaspoon salt
4 cups milk
$3/4$ cup melted butter, divided
nutmeg to sprinkle

Preheat oven to 400° F. In large bowl mix eggs, sugar, flour, salt, milk and $1/2$ cup butter. Set aside. Heat remaining $1/4$ cup of butter in 9x13-inch pan. Pour in batter and sprinkle with sugar and nutmeg. Bake 30 minutes.

Remove from oven and cool for several minutes before cutting into big squares.

Serve with Chateau Chantal Strawberry Riesling jam.

NOTES:
THERE'S NO NEED TO SETTLE FOR THE SAME OLD BORING BREAKFAST.

SUGGESTED WINE:
Chateau Chantal Celebrate

Per serving: 578 Calories; 35g Fat (54% calories from fat); 17g Protein; 49g Carbohydrate; 371mg Cholesterol; 574mg Sodium
Food Exchanges: 1 1/2 Starch/Bread; 1 Lean Meat; 1 Fruit; 1/2 Non-Fat Milk; 6 Fat; 1 Other Carbohydrates

PEAR WALNUT MUFFINS

FROM CHATEAU CHANTAL WINERY/BED AND BREAKFAST, MICHIGAN
CHEF CHRISTINE CAMPBELL

Serves 9

$1/2$ cup unsalted butter, softened
1 cup firmly packed brown sugar
2 large eggs, beaten
$1/2$ cup sour cream
2 teaspoons vanilla extract
1 $2/3$ cups unbleached flour
2 teaspoons baking powder
$1/2$ teaspoon ground nutmeg
pinch salt
1 medium pear, peeled, cored and chopped
$1/2$ cup chopped walnuts

NOTES:
A BREAKFAST TREAT FOR YOUNG AND OLD.

Preheat oven to 375° F. Grease muffin tin or line with paper muffin cups.

Beat butter with sugar in large bowl until light and fluffy. Beat in eggs, sour cream and vanilla. In another bowl, stir together flour, baking powder, ground nutmeg and salt.

Add dry ingredients to wet ingredients and stir until just blended. Fold in pears and walnuts. Do not over mix or muffins will be tough. Spoon batter into prepared tin, filling cups about $2/3$ full. Bake about 20 minutes, until lightly browned and springy to touch. Let muffins cool in pan 5 minutes before transferring to cooling rack.

■

SUGGESTED WINE:
Chateau Chantal Sparkling Wine

Per serving: 373 Calories; 19g Fat (45% calories from fat); 6g Protein; 46g Carbohydrate; 83mg Cholesterol; 113mg Sodium
Food Exchanges: 1 Starch/Bread; 1/2 Lean Meat; 3 1/2 Fat; 1 1/2 Other Carbohydrates

NOTES:

PASTA
&
RICE

■

CLAM-GUINE WITH CHARDONNAY

FROM LYNFRED WINERY, ILLINOIS
CHEF CHRIS SMITH

Serves 4

1 pound linguine
4 tablespoons olive oil, divided
2 tablespoons pesto sauce, homemade
　or store-bought
4 cloves garlic, minced
2 cups clams, canned with liquid
　or fresh minced
$^1/_2$ cup Lynfred Chardonnay
1 cup fresh flat leaf parsley, chopped
1 teaspoon dried oregano
salt and pepper to taste
$^1/_3$ cup Parmesan cheese, freshly grated

NOTES:
SERVE WITH A CRUSTY LOAF OF FRENCH
BREAD, A GARDEN GREEN SALAD AND A
BIG GLASS OF CHILLED CHARDONNAY.
MAKES A COMPLETE MEAL.

In large pot cook linguine to al dente, according to package directions. Drain and return to pot. Stir in 2 tablespoons olive oil and pesto sauce to coat pasta. Cover to keep warm.

While pasta is cooking, heat 2 tablespoons olive oil in heavy skillet over medium heat. Add minced garlic and sauté until golden, about 1 minute. Do not burn. Add clams including juice, wine, chopped parsley and oregano. Simmer until clams are cooked, 10 minutes for fresh clams and 5 minutes for canned clams. Do not overcook. Season to taste with salt and freshly ground black pepper.

Place linguine on heated platter. Spoon clam sauce over pasta and sprinkle with Parmesan cheese.

SUGGESTED WINE:
Lynfred Chardonnay

Per serving: 642 Calories; 21g Fat (30% calories from fat); 20g Protein; 88g Carbohydrate; 11mg Cholesterol; 469mg Sodium
Food Exchanges: 5 1/2 Starch/Bread; 1/2 Lean Meat; 1/2 Vegetable; 3 1/2 Fat

GOLDEN SEAFOOD RISOTTO

FROM PETRONI VINEYARDS, CALIFORNIA
NORTH BEACH RESTAURANT

Serves 6

$3/4$ large onion, chopped and divided
$1/2$ cup extra virgin olive oil, divided
1 pound Arborio rice
$1/2$ teaspoon saffron
1 pound snapper filet, cut in chunks
1 $1/4$ cups dry white wine, divided
2 quarts fish stock, plus 1 cup
6 whole calamari, sliced in rings
1 pound bay scallops
12 medium shrimp, peeled and deveined
2 cloves garlic, chopped
12 small clams
12 mussels
$1/4$ cup Italian parsley, chopped
salt and pepper to taste

Sauté $1/2$ large onion in $1/4$ cup extra virgin olive oil until translucent. Add rice and saffron; cook until mixture reaches a golden color. Stir frequently and do not allow to brown. Add snapper and sauté for a few minutes. Add 1 cup wine and allow to evaporate halfway. Meanwhile, bring 2 quarts fish stock to a boil in separate pot. Add enough boiling stock to rice to cover by about 1 inch. Reduce heat by half. After about 7 minutes add calamari, scallops and prawns.

Continue cooking, adding stock as needed to keep rice covered. Stir occasionally. Stop adding stock toward end of cooking time, approximately 20 minutes. Allow rice to completely absorb stock.

While rice is cooking, heat $1/4$ cup extra virgin olive oil in pan, add $1/4$ large onion and garlic and sauté until golden. Add clams and mussels. Sauté for a few minutes on high heat, add $1/4$ cup wine and allow to evaporate. Add 1 cup fish stock, cover and cook about 5 to 7 minutes or until clams and mussels open. Add chopped parsley. Add salt and pepper to taste.

Put rice in dishes and decorate with shellfish sauce.

NOTES:
LOVELY TO LOOK AT, AND DELICIOUS TO EAT.

SUGGESTED WINE:
California Pinot Blanc

Per serving: 1150 Calories; 37g Fat (32% calories from fat); 93g Protein; 82g Carbohydrate; 409mg Cholesterol; 1498mg Sodium
Food Exchanges: 4 1/2 Starch/Bread; 11 Lean Meat; 1/2 Vegetable; 4 Fat; 1/2 Other Carbohydrates

GRILLED SHRIMP OVER LINGUINE AND ARUGULA

FROM LAMOREAUX LANDING WINE CELLARS, NEW YORK

Serves 4

MARINADE:
1 ounce fresh lemon juice
(about $1/2$ a lemon)
1 $1/2$ ounces fresh orange juice
(about $1/2$ an orange)
1 ounce fresh lime juice (about $1/2$ a lime)
1 $1/2$ teaspoons Tabasco sauce
1 teaspoon black pepper, freshly ground
$1/2$ teaspoon salt
3 cloves garlic, minced
1 tablespoon grated lemon rind, divided
1 $1/2$ pounds jumbo shrimp,
peeled and deveined

PASTA:
$2/3$ pound linguine
1 teaspoon black pepper, freshly ground
$1/2$ cup Parmesan cheese, grated
3 cups arugula, chopped

NOTES:
SERVE WITH A SIMPLE CUCUMBER, RED
PEPPER AND RADISH SALAD, SOME
FRENCH BREAD AND A BOTTLE OF WINE.

Mix marinade ingredients with 1 teaspoon lemon rind and pour over shrimp in medium bowl. Light charcoal grill or preheat gas grill. When grill is ready, remove shrimp from marinade and bring marinade to a boil in small pot. Thread shrimp onto skewers and grill quickly over high heat, 1 to 2 minutes per side. Remove shrimp to platter; cover loosely with foil.

Meanwhile, cook pasta in large pot of water until al dente. Drain in colander, saving $1/2$ cup cooking water. Toss pasta into cooking pot with marinade, remaining lemon rind, pepper and cooking water. Cook over low heat 1 to 2 minutes, then sprinkle with Parmesan cheese and arugula. Divide pasta into bowls and place shrimp on top.

SUGGESTED WINE:
Lamoreaux Landing Wine Cellars Reserve Chardonnay

Per serving: 538 Calories; 8g Fat (14% calories from fat); 50g Protein; 63g Carbohydrate; 269mg Cholesterol; 772mg Sodium
Food Exchanges: 4 Starch/Bread; 5 1/2 Lean Meat; 1/2 Vegetable; 1/2 Fat

HAM MOUSSE-STUFFED MANICOTTI WITH DILL MUSTARD SAUCE

FROM CEDAR MOUNTAIN WINERY, CALIFORNIA

Serves 8

1 pound pasta (8 manicotti tubes)

HAM MOUSSE:
2 $1/4$ pounds smoked ham, coarsely chopped
1 cup bread crumbs
1 large egg
3 tablespoons cream
$1/2$ teaspoon salt
$1/2$ teaspoon white pepper
$1/2$ tablespoon butter for baking sheet

SAUCE:
1 tablespoon butter
3 shallots, finely chopped
3 cups cream
$1/4$ cup Dijon mustard
2 tablespoons fresh dill, finely chopped
8 sprigs fresh dill for garnish

Cook manicotti tubes according to directions on package. Drain and set aside.

NOTES:
AN IMPRESSIVE AND DELICIOUS PASTA COURSE.

HAM MOUSSE:
Put smoked ham, bread crumbs, egg, cream, salt and pepper into food processor and process until smooth. Pipe mixture into pasta tubes and place on buttered baking sheet. Set aside.

SAUCE:
Melt butter in medium saucepan over medium heat. Add shallots and sauté for about 2 minutes. Add cream, bring to a boil, then reduce heat and cook until mixture has reduced by half. Add mustard and dill and stir for 1 minute. Sieve sauce and keep warm.

While sauce is reducing, preheat oven to 375º F. Cover stuffed manicotti with damp kitchen towel and bake until heated through, about 15 minutes.

Spoon sauce into center of each warmed serving plate. Top with stuffed manicotti and garnish with sprig of fresh dill.

SUGGESTED WINE:
Cedar Mountain Cabernet Sauvignon - Gold

Per serving: 771 Calories; 42g Fat (49% calories from fat); 35g Protein; 62g Carbohydrate; 188mg Cholesterol; 2095mg Sodium
Food Exchanges: 3 1/2 Starch/Bread; 3 1/2 Lean Meat; 1/2 Vegetable; 6 Fat

LASAGNA SUPREME

FROM GRAY GHOST VINEYARDS, VIRGINIA

Serves 8

8 ounces lasagna noodles
$1/2$ pound Italian sausage, hot style
$1/2$ pound ground beef or venison
1 medium onion, chopped
2 cloves garlic, minced
4 ounces Gray Ghost Cabernet Sauvignon
14 $1/2$ ounces canned tomatoes,
   chopped and undrained
6 ounces tomato paste
2 teaspoons dried basil
1 teaspoon dried marjoram
4 ounces canned mushrooms, drained
2 large eggs
1 pound creamed cottage cheese
   or ricotta cheese
$3/4$ cup Parmesan cheese, grated and divided
2 tablespoons dried parsley
salt to taste
freshly ground black pepper to taste
2 cups cheddar cheese, shredded
3 cups mozzarella cheese, shredded

Cook lasagna noodles according to package directions and drain.

NOTES:
HERE'S A RECIPE THE WHOLE FAMILY WILL LOVE. LEFTOVERS ALSO FREEZE WELL.

Remove any casings from sausage. Sauté meats, onion and garlic in large skillet over medium-high heat until meat is brown, stirring to separate meat. Drain excess fat. Add wine, tomatoes with juice, tomato paste, basil and marjoram. Reduce heat to low and cover. Simmer 15 minutes, stirring often. Stir in mushrooms and set aside.

Preheat oven to 375º F. Beat eggs in large bowl and add cottage or ricotta cheese, $1/2$ cup Parmesan cheese, parsley, salt and pepper. Mix well. Place a layer of noodles in bottom of 9x13x2-inch baking pan. Spread half cottage or ricotta cheese mixture over layer of noodles, then add a layer of meat mixture and a layer of cheddar and mozzarella cheeses. Repeat layers until everything is used and top with $1/4$ cup Parmesan cheese.

Bake lasagna 40 to 45 minutes or until bubbly. Let stand 10 minutes before cutting.

SUGGESTED WINE:
Gray Ghost Cabernet Sauvignon

Per serving: 713 Calories; 44g Fat (56% calories from fat); 43g Protein; 34g Carbohydrate; 183mg Cholesterol; 1291mg Sodium
Food Exchanges: 1 1/2 Starch/Bread; 5 1/2 Lean Meat; 1 1/2 Vegetable; 5 1/2 Fat

LOBSTER LINGUINE

FROM MARTINI & ROSSI, ITALY

Serves 4

1 pound linguine
2 tablespoons olive oil
4 cloves garlic, minced
1 cup onion, chopped
1 cup Martini & Rossi Extra Dry Vermouth
$1/2$ teaspoon saffron threads
1 pound raw lobster meat
salt and pepper to taste
2 tablespoons Italian parsley, chopped

Prepare linguine according to package directions.

While linguine is cooking, heat olive oil in large skillet over medium heat. Add garlic and onion and sauté until just soft. Add vermouth and saffron to skillet. Increase heat to high. Cook about 1 minute. Add lobster meat and cook, stirring constantly, until meat is just cooked. Remove from heat. Season with salt and pepper to taste. Add parsley and stir well.

When pasta is cooked, drain and return to pot. Add lobster sauce and mix well. Serve on plates.

SUGGESTED WINE:
Pinot Grigio

Per serving: 673 Calories; 10g Fat (14% calories from fat); 37g Protein; 93g Carbohydrate; 108mg Cholesterol; 357mg Sodium
Food Exchanges: 5 1/2 Starch/Bread; 3 Lean Meat; 1 Vegetable; 1 1/2 Fat

NOTES:
FOR PEOPLE LIVING ALONG THE MEDITERRANEAN, PAIRING FRESH SEAFOOD AND HEARTY PASTA IS QUITE OBVIOUS. FOR THE REST OF US, IT IS INSPIRED.

MUSHROOM RAVIOLI

FROM VALLEY OF THE MOON WINERY, CALIFORNIA
CHEF LAURIE SOUZA

Serves 6

RAVIOLI:
1 1/2 pounds assorted fresh mushrooms
3 tablespoons unsalted butter
1 small onion, finely chopped
1 clove garlic, minced
1/2 cup Valley of the Moon Pinot Noir
2 tablespoons Italian parsley, chopped
salt and pepper to taste
1 basic recipe for pasta dough or
   1 package wonton wrappers
water and flour as needed

BROTH:
3 tablespoons unsalted butter
1 large onion, coarsely chopped
1 pound fresh mushrooms,
   coarsely chopped
salt and pepper to taste
4 cups water

RAVIOLI:
Clean and finely chop any assortment of fresh mushrooms. Heat butter in wide, non-corrosive sauté pan and cook mushrooms and onion over high heat, stirring constantly. Cook until any liquid released evaporates and mushrooms and onions begin to brown. Add garlic and wine and cook until all liquid evaporates. Season with chopped parsley, salt and pepper to taste.

When mixture is cool, assemble ravioli: Lay out a thin sheet of pasta dough or wonton wrappers. Place about a teaspoon of mushroom mixture for each individual ravioli, leaving about a 3/4-inch border of dough around mixture. Continue until sheet is full of individual squares. Place another sheet of dough on top. Seal each ravioli square with a little water to moisten edges, eliminating air pockets as much as possible. Use a knife or pizza cutter to cut out each ravioli square. Lay out individual ravioli on wax paper-lined baking sheets dusted with a little flour. Cover and refrigerate or freeze until ravioli is to be cooked.

BROTH:

Melt butter in wide, heavy-bottomed pot. Add onion and mushrooms. Stir and cook over low heat until caramelized, about 1 hour. Season with salt and pepper to taste. Increase heat to high, add water and cook 15 minutes. Taste, correct seasoning and strain. For more intense broth, return stock to pot and reduce to 2 cups.

Cook ravioli in simmering salted water until tender, about 1 to 2 minutes. Transfer to hot mushroom broth and serve immediately, garnished with fresh mushroom slices.

SUGGESTED WINE:
Valley of the Moon Sangiovese

Per serving: 191 Calories; 13g Fat (61% calories from fat); 5g Protein; 14g Carbohydrate; 33mg Cholesterol; 36mg Sodium
Food Exchanges: 2 1/2 Vegetable; 2 1/2 Fat

NOTES:
FOR PASTA AND MUSHROOM LOVERS!

PASTA MARE CHIARO

FROM PETRONI VINEYARDS, CALIFORNIA
NORTH BEACH RESTAURANT

Serves 6

3 tablespoons unsalted butter
3 tablespoons olive oil
8 cloves garlic, thinly sliced
2 cups half and half
$1/2$ teaspoon crushed red pepper
1 cup bay shrimp
1 $1/2$ pounds linguine or spaghetti, cooked
1 cup Parmesan cheese
1 large tomato, peeled, seeded and chopped
salt and pepper to taste

Melt butter and oil in pan and sauté garlic. Do not allow garlic to change color.

Add half and half, crushed red pepper and bay shrimp.

Sauté until heated. Add pasta and Parmesan cheese. Sauté until well blended and add tomatoes. Season with salt and pepper and serve on hot dishes.

SUGGESTED WINE:
Petroni Cabernet Sauvignon

Per serving: 753 Calories; 29g Fat (35% calories from fat); 31g Protein; 91g Carbohydrate; 117mg Cholesterol; 351mg Sodium
Food Exchanges: 5 1/2 Starch/Bread; 1 1/2 Lean Meat; 1/2 Vegetable; 1/2 Non-Fat Milk; 5 Fat

NOTES:
SHRIMP LOVERS REJOICE!

PASTA WITH A FRESH TOMATO-SALMON SAUCE

FROM GRAY GHOST VINEYARDS, VIRGINIA

Serves 6

1 small onion, finely chopped
2 green onions, finely chopped
2 cloves garlic, minced
$1/4$ cup extra virgin olive oil
1 pound salmon filet, cut in 1-inch pieces
6 ounces Gray Ghost Chardonnay
1 teaspoon crushed red pepper flakes
9 plum tomatoes, cubed
salt and freshly ground black pepper to taste
1 pound pasta, any type
$1/4$ cup fresh basil, finely chopped

Sauté onions and garlic in oil until wilted. Add salmon, wine, crushed pepper, tomatoes, salt and freshly ground black pepper. Mix and simmer 8 minutes.

While preparing pasta according to package directions, have a few sips of Gray Ghost Chardonnay.

Drain pasta and transfer to large, deep dish. Add basil and stir throughly. Pour sauce over pasta and toss.

■

SUGGESTED WINE:
Gray Ghost Vineyards Chardonnay

Per serving: 534 Calories; 14g Fat (24% calories from fat); 28g Protein; 72g Carbohydrate; 39mg Cholesterol; 95mg Sodium
Food Exchanges: 4 Starch/Bread; 2 Lean Meat; 3 Vegetable; 2 Fat

NOTES:
USE ANY PASTA YOU LIKE, BUT WE FAVOR LINGUINE OR ANGEL HAIR WITH THIS SAUCE.

PORTOBELLO FLORENTINE PASTA

FROM STONE HILL WINERY & RESTAURANT, MISSOURI

Serves 4

1 pound linguine
4 medium Portobello mushrooms
4 tablespoons butter
16 ounces fresh spinach, rinsed and drained
1 tablespoon garlic, minced
$1/_2$ cup Stone Hill Steinberg White
1 pint heavy whipping cream
salt and white pepper to taste

Prepare linguine al dente according to package directions.

Peel, de-stem and scrape insides of Portobello mushrooms. Slice into thin strips. Heat butter in large sauté pan. Add mushrooms, spinach and garlic and sauté until tender. Add wine and deglaze. Add cream and reduce until slightly thickened. Add salt and white pepper to taste. Serve immediately over linguine.

NOTES:
A VEGETARIAN PASTA DISH THAT WILL STICK TO YOUR RIBS.

SUGGESTED WINE:
Stone Hill Winery Steinberg White

Per serving: 986 Calories; 58g Fat (53% calories from fat); 21g Protein; 94g Carbohydrate; 194mg Cholesterol; 261mg Sodium
Food Exchanges: 5 1/2 Starch/Bread; 1 Vegetable; 1/2 Non-Fat Milk; 11 Fat

PUMPKIN RISOTTO

FROM CITRA/PALM BAY IMPORTS, ITALY

Serves 8

4 tablespoons olive oil
$1/2$ cup onion, chopped
$1/2$ cup pancetta or bacon, shredded
2 cups pumpkin, cut in $1/2$-inch cubes
  or 15 ounces canned, unseasoned
2 cups dry red wine
salt and pepper to taste
2 cups Arborio rice
5 cups beef broth, divided
$1/4$ cup Parmesan cheese, grated

Put olive oil, onion and pancetta or bacon in large, sturdy pot over medium-high heat. Cook until onion turns translucent. Add diced pumpkin, wine and season with salt and pepper to taste. Reduce heat to medium and cook 10 minutes. Add rice to pot and stir thoroughly to coat grains. Add $1/2$ cup beef broth and stir until liquid is absorbed. Continue to add broth, $1/2$ cup at a time, stirring constantly until all liquid has been absorbed and rice is fully cooked.

Serve promptly with grated Parmesan.

SUGGESTED WINE:
Citra Montepulciano d'Abruzzo

Per serving: 360 Calories; 9g Fat (25% calories from fat); 16g Protein; 43g Carbohydrate; 12mg Cholesterol; 1300mg Sodium
Food Exchanges: 2 1/2 Starch/Bread; 1 1/2 Lean Meat; 1 1/2 Fat

NOTES:
A NORTHERN ITALY SPECIALTY!
ALTHOUGH A WHOLE PUMPKIN THAT IS
CUBED IS PREFERRED, YOU MAY USE
UNSEASONED PUMPKIN FROM A CAN.

RISOTTO WITH SNAP PEAS AND PRAWNS

FROM PEDRONCELLI WINERY, CALIFORNIA

Serves 4

5 cups low-sodium chicken broth
$1/2$ cup butter, divided
2 tablespoons olive oil, divided
1 medium onion, finely chopped
1 cup Arborio rice
2 cloves garlic, minced
1 tablespoon shallots, minced
$1/2$ cup Pedroncelli Chardonnay
1 teaspoon fresh lemon juice
$1/2$ pound shrimp, 32 to 50 count
$1/4$ pound pea snaps, strung and sliced
1 teaspoon lemon zest
1 cup Parmesan cheese, freshly grated

Bring chicken broth to a simmer in separate saucepan.

In heavy wide-bottomed pan on medium heat, add a little over $1/4$ cup butter and 1 tablespoon olive oil. Once melted, add onion and sauté until soft. Add rice and garlic and sauté until rice is well heated and covered with butter/oil liquid.

Add $1/2$ cup broth, stirring constantly until absorbed (heat should be adjusted to medium-low once stock has been added). Continue adding broth as above until rice is tender and creamy, approximately 25 minutes. (Broth may not be fully used, but most of added broth will be absorbed.)

In separate pan, melt remaining butter and 1 tablespoon olive oil over medium heat, add shallots and sauté until lightly browned. Add wine and lemon juice then reduce volume by half. Add shrimp, peas and lemon zest. Sauté until just done (careful not to overcook shrimp).

Once risotto is done, remove from heat and add shrimp mixture and Parmesan cheese. Serve immediately.

NOTES:
CALL THEM PRAWNS OR SHRIMP; THEY ADD TO A PERFECT RISOTTO.

SUGGESTED WINES:
Pedroncelli Chardonnay or
Sauvignon Blanc

Per serving: 692 Calories; 37g Fat (49% calories from fat); 39g Protein; 47g Carbohydrate; 163mg Cholesterol; 1365mg Sodium
Food Exchanges: 2 1/2 Starch/Bread; 4 Lean Meat; 1 Vegetable; 6 1/2 Fat

RISOTTO WITH SWISS CHARD (RISOTTO E BIETE)

FROM MARTINI & ROSSI, ITALY

Serves 6

4 tablespoons butter, divided
2 cloves garlic, finely chopped
1 shallot, finely chopped
1 1/2 cups Arborio rice
1/4 cup Martini & Rossi Rosso
    Sweet Vermouth
3 cups low-sodium chicken broth, divided
1 1/2 cups Swiss chard, steamed,
    drained and chopped
1 ounce dried porcini mushrooms
1 tablespoon Parmesan cheese, grated

Heat 3 tablespoons butter in medium sauté pan. Sauté garlic and shallot 1 to 2 minutes. Add rice and sauté 1 to 2 minutes. Add vermouth, 1 cup chicken broth, chopped Swiss chard and porcini mushrooms. Bring to a boil and then simmer, stirring frequently.

As liquid is absorbed, slowly add chicken broth and continue stirring until rice is soft and mixture thickens (about 15 to 20 minutes).

Stir in Parmesan cheese and 1 tablespoon butter. Serve immediately.

NOTES:
COOKING GREAT RISOTTO IS ABOUT ADDING LAYERS OF FLAVOR, EACH IN PROPER SUCCESSION.

SUGGESTED WINE:
Martini & Rossi Rosso Sweet Vermouth

Per serving: 289 Calories; 9g Fat (28% calories from fat); 10g Protein; 44g Carbohydrate; 21mg Cholesterol; 142mg Sodium
Food Exchanges: 2 1/2 Starch/Bread; 1/2 Lean Meat; 1 Vegetable; 1 1/2 Fat

SPAGHETTI CARBONARA

FROM BARTON & GUESTIER, FRANCE

Serves 4

2 tablespoons butter
$1/2$ pound pancetta or bacon, diced
1 pound spaghetti
3 extra-large eggs
$1/3$ cup heavy cream
$1/2$ cup Parmesan cheese,
   freshly grated and divided
salt and pepper to taste
1 tablespoon parsley, minced

NOTES:
A CLASSIC PASTA DISH THE WORLD OVER.

Heat butter (may substitute with 1 tablespoon butter and 1 tablespoon olive oil) in large nonstick skillet over medium heat and add pancetta or bacon, stirring to brown lightly. Set aside in pan.

Prepare spaghetti in lightly salted water. Beat eggs in bowl with heavy cream, $1/3$ cup Parmesan cheese, good pinch salt and few grinds pepper until well mixed. When pasta is al dente, drain and add immediately to pancetta in skillet over low heat. Quickly add egg mixture and mix until spaghetti is well coated with creamy sauce and heated through. Sprinkle with remaining Parmesan and parsley and serve immediately.

■

SUGGESTED WINE:
Barton & Guestier Vouvray

Per serving: 752 Calories; 26g Fat (32% calories from fat); 40g Protein; 86g Carbohydrate; 252mg Cholesterol; 1836mg Sodium
Food Exchanges: 5 1/2 Starch/Bread; 3 1/2 Lean Meat; 3 Fat

SPAGHETTI CON VODKA

FROM PETRONI VINEYARDS, CALIFORNIA
NORTH BEACH RESTAURANT

Serves 4

1 medium onion, thinly sliced
$1/4$ pound sweet butter, divided
3 cups half and half
1 pound spaghetti, cooked and drained
1 cup Parmesan cheese, grated
1 cup vodka
salt and white pepper to taste

NOTES:
TRULY A "SAN FRANCISCO TREAT" —
ITALIAN STYLE.

Sauté onion in $1/8$ pound butter until onion becomes transparent.

Add half and half and bring to a boil.

Add spaghetti, $1/8$ pound butter, Parmesan cheese and vodka.

Sauté, stirring constantly until well blended. Season with salt and pepper to taste.

Serve on warm plates.

SUGGESTED WINE:
Soave

Per serving: 1118 Calories; 53g Fat (48% calories from fat); 31g Protein; 97g Carbohydrate; 149mg Cholesterol; 787mg Sodium
Food Exchanges: 5 1/2 Starch/Bread; 1 1/2 Lean Meat; 1/2 Vegetable; 1/2 Non-Fat Milk; 9 1/2 Fat

SPAGHETTINI BASTA PASTA

FROM PETRONI VINEYARDS, CALIFORNIA
NORTH BEACH RESTAURANT

Serves 6

1 pound pasta, spaghettini (thin spaghetti)
1 medium onion, chopped
4 cloves garlic, chopped
1 stalk celery, chopped
1 small carrot, chopped
2 tablespoons olive oil
1 pound ground veal
$^1/_4$ cup dry white wine
2 cups mushrooms, sliced
$^1/_4$ pound prosciutto or pancetta
1 $^1/_2$ cups heavy cream or white sauce
4 medium tomatoes, chopped
2 tablespoons parsley, chopped
$^1/_2$ cup Parmesan cheese, grated

Prepare pasta al dente.

Sauté onion, garlic, celery and carrot in olive oil. Add veal. Cook until browned, then add wine. Add mushrooms, prosciutto or pancetta and sauté. Add cream or white sauce, tomatoes, parsley and Parmesan cheese. Heat thoroughly until sauce is well blended and pour over pasta.

SUGGESTED WINE:
Petroni Cabernet Sauvignon

Per serving: 763 Calories; 37g Fat (44% calories from fat); 36g Protein; 69g Carbohydrate; 163mg Cholesterol; 776mg Sodium
Food Exchanges: 4 Starch/Bread; 3 1/2 Lean Meat; 2 Vegetable; 5 1/2 Fat

NOTES:
OH, GO AHEAD AND INDULGE.
YOU'LL LOVE IT.

VENISON BOLOGNESE OVER PASTA

FROM LAKE SONOMA WINERY, CALIFORNIA
CHEF ROBIN LEHNHOFF

Serves 6

2 ounces pancetta or bacon, diced
4 tablespoons olive oil, divided
1 pound ground venison
2 tablespoons unsalted butter
4 cups yellow onion, diced
1 $1/2$ cups carrots, diced
1 cup celery, diced
1 cup green bell pepper, diced
4 cups tomatoes,
    chopped in food processor
1 cup Lake Sonoma Cabernet Sauvignon
1 cup veal stock
1 bay leaf
$1/4$ teaspoon nutmeg, freshly grated
$1/2$ teaspoon ground cinnamon
1 teaspoon kosher salt
freshly ground black pepper, to taste
1 tablespoon fresh rosemary, chopped
1 pound pasta of choice

NOTES:
A HUNTER'S PASTA DISH!

In heavy-bottomed saucepot, sauté pancetta or bacon in 2 tablespoons olive oil until browned. Add venison and sear until cooked.

In another pan, heat 2 tablespoons olive oil and butter. Sauté onion, carrot, celery and bell pepper until soft. Add tomatoes and wine and cook 10 minutes. Add to meat along with veal stock and bay leaf. Simmer 30 minutes. Add spices, salt, pepper and rosemary and let cook another 20 minutes.

Serve over freshly cooked pasta such as spaghetti, linguine, penne, etc.

SUGGESTED WINE:
Lake Sonoma Alexander Valley Cabernet Sauvignon

Per serving: 623 Calories; 18g Fat (27% calories from fat); 33g Protein; 77g Carbohydrate; 82mg Cholesterol; 872mg Sodium
Food Exchanges: 4 Starch/Bread; 3 Lean Meat; 3 1/2 Vegetable; 2 1/2 Fat

NOTES:

POULTRY
&
GAME

■

BRAISED MUSCOVY DUCK LEGS WITH LAVENDER & WILD MUSHROOMS

FROM WENTE FAMILY ESTATES, CALIFORNIA, CHEF KIMBALL JONES

Serves 4

4 duck legs with thigh, without skin
salt and pepper for seasoning plus to taste
$^1/_2$ bunch thyme
1 bunch lavender
2 medium carrots, peeled and diced
1 medium onion, peeled and diced
1 leek, cleaned and sliced
1 stalk celery, cleaned and sliced
2 bay leaves
12 black peppercorns
$^1/_2$ bottle Wente Pinot Noir
water to cover
$^1/_4$ pound porcini or other wild mushrooms
2 tablespoons olive oil
2 tablespoons butter

Season duck legs with salt and pepper. Chop thyme and lavender and rub all over duck legs. Place duck legs in container with another container that fits into the first one. Place second container on top of duck. Place in refrigerator with about 5 pounds of weight on top (a gallon of milk will work). Season 3 to 4 hours.

NOTES:
MUSCOVY IS THE DUCK OF CHOICE, BUT ANOTHER TYPE WILL DO.

Preheat oven to 350º F. Remove duck legs from container and place in roasting pan with carrots, onion, leek, celery, bay leaves, peppercorns, wine and water to cover. Bring to a boil on top of stove. Place in oven and braise until very tender, about 1$^1/_2$ hours. Remove duck legs from liquid and reserve. Strain liquid and place in saucepan. Reduce to about half.

Clean mushrooms, removing any dirt with damp towel. Heat olive oil in frying pan over high heat. When very hot, add mushrooms and season with salt and pepper. Cook until golden brown, stirring often.

Reheat duck legs in reduced sauce, then remove to heated plates. Add mushrooms to remaining sauce and swirl in butter. Serve over duck legs.

HINT: Lavender is available at most health food stores.

SUGGESTED WINES:
Wente Family Estates Pinot Noir or Syrah

Per serving (excluding unknown items): 527 Calories; 27g Fat (45% calories from fat); 46g Protein; 28g Carbohydrate; 190mg Cholesterol; 268mg Sodium Food Exchanges: 1 Starch/Bread; 5 1/2 Lean Meat; 2 1/2 Vegetable; 2 1/2 Fat

CANADIAN GOOSE STEW

FROM SIX MILE CREEK VINEYARD, NEW YORK

Serves 6

4 goose breasts, cut into $1/2$-inch cubes
2 tablespoons olive oil
salt and pepper to taste
$1/2$ cup onion, diced
$1/2$ cup carrots, diced
$1/2$ cup celery, diced
1 $1/2$ cups nonfat chicken broth
  or beef broth
1 bottle Six Mile Creek Quintessence
  Red Wine
2 bay leaves
1 tablespoon coriander

NOTES:
SIX MILE CREEK QUINTESSENCE IS A
CABERNET BLEND THAT ADDS A VELVETY
RICHNESS TO THE STEW.

In heavy-bottomed pot or Dutch oven sear goose meat in olive oil over medium-high heat. Season with salt and pepper while cooking.

When browned, remove goose from pot and toss in onion, carrots and celery. Sauté until onions are just translucent. Return goose to pot and add broth and wine while scraping any bits from bottom of pan. Add bay leaves, coriander and season with salt and pepper. Bring to a boil, then simmer on low heat 2 to 2 $1/2$ hours, or until meat is tender.

Garnish with parsley and serve with grilled bread.

SUGGESTED WINE:
Six Mile Creek Vineyard Quintessence

Per serving: 304 Calories; 15g Fat (46% calories from fat); 37g Protein; 3g Carbohydrate; 127mg Cholesterol; 272mg Sodium
Food Exchanges: 5 Lean Meat; 1/2 Vegetable; 1 Fat

CHERRY GLAZED CORNISH GAME HENS

FROM VALLEY OF THE MOON WINERY, CALIFORNIA
CHEF LAURIE SOUZA

Serves 4

4 Rock Cornish game hens
salt and pepper to taste
1 jar cherry preserves (any brand)
1 teaspoon cinnamon
1 teaspoon vanilla extract
snow peas and beets for garnish

Preheat oven to 350º F. Remove gizzards from hens. Season hens with salt and black pepper. Place hens in steamer basket inside of saucepan. Fill with water to bottom of hens. Steam 30 to 45 minutes, depending on size. Place cherry preserves in sauté pan and heat until melted. Add cinnamon and vanilla extract. Boil and remove from heat. Place hens on sheet pan and brush with cherry glaze. Place in oven approximately 30 minutes. Garnish with snow peas and beets.

NOTES:
IF THE GAME HEN CROSSES THE ROAD, SERVE HER UP WITH THIS SIMPLE RECIPE.

SUGGESTED WINE:
Valley of the Moon Sangiovese

Per serving: 1529 Calories; 106g Fat (64% calories from fat); 130g Protein; 4g Carbohydrate; 764mg Cholesterol; 462mg Sodium
Food Exchanges: 18 Lean Meat; 10 1/2 Fat

CHICKEN ALLA MATTONE

FROM PETRONI VINEYARDS, CALIFORNIA
NORTH BEACH RESTAURANT

Serves 2

3 pounds whole chicken, free range
4 tablespoons extra virgin olive oil, divided
2 rosemary sprigs, divided
pinch salt to taste
pinch black pepper, freshly ground

NOTES:
WITH THIS RECIPE YOU FINALLY FIND THE
REASON YOU ARE SAVING GRANDMA'S
OLD IRON SKILLET OR THAT ONE LONELY
BRICK THE KIDS BROUGHT HOME.

Cut chicken in half and disjoint, but not completely. Pound chicken until flat. Marinate overnight with 3 tablespoons olive oil, 1 rosemary sprig, salt and pepper.

Preheat oven to 350° F. Place pan on stove with 1 tablespoon olive oil and 1 sprig rosemary. Turn heat on high and when pan is hot, remove rosemary and place marinated chicken in pan, skin down. Wait 1 to 2 minutes, and then place weight on top of chicken and put pan in oven 12 minutes.

Remove pan from oven, remove weight, turn chicken over and return to oven an additional 12 minutes with no weight on it.

Serve with favorite vegetables and roasted potatoes.

SUGGESTED WINE:
Petroni Vineyards California Sauvignon Blanc

Per serving: 1180 Calories; 90g Fat (70% calories from fat); 86g Protein; 1g Carbohydrate; 423mg Cholesterol; 330mg Sodium
Food Exchanges: 11 1/2 Lean Meat; 10 1/2 Fat

CHICKEN CACCIATORE

FROM TRENTADUE WINERY, CALIFORNIA

Serves 6

4- to 5-pound whole roasting chicken
salt and pepper to taste
1 cup flour
6 tablespoons olive oil
1/2 pound fresh mushrooms
1 medium onion, diced
1/2 cup dry white wine
16 ounces canned tomatoes
1 tablespoon brandy
small bunch parsley, chopped
1 clove garlic, chopped
1 tablespoon butter

Cut chicken into pieces. Sprinkle with salt and pepper. Roll in flour and fry in olive oil until golden brown. Remove chicken from pan and add mushrooms and diced onions to remaining oil. Cook until slightly brown. Add wine and tomatoes. Cook 5 minutes. Put chicken back in pan and cook about 15 minutes or until chicken is fully cooked.

Add brandy, 3 to 4 tablespoons chopped parsley and garlic. Cover and cook slowly. When chicken is tender, add butter.

NOTES:
EASY TO PUT TOGETHER AND ALWAYS A HIT WITH "LA FAMILIA".

SUGGESTED WINE:
Trentadue La Storia Meritage

Per serving: 935 Calories; 65g Fat (65% calories from fat); 57g Protein; 23g Carbohydrate; 231mg Cholesterol; 395mg Sodium
Food Exchanges: 1 Starch/Bread; 7 1/2 Lean Meat; 1 1/2 Vegetable; 8 1/2 Fat

CHICKEN CACCIATORE A LA LOMBARDA

FROM SEBASTIANI VINEYARDS, CALIFORNIA

Serves 6

1 whole chicken, cut into pieces
2 tablespoons all-purpose flour
4 tablespoons olive oil
2 tablespoons butter
salt and pepper to taste
$^1/_2$ medium onion, chopped
1 stalk celery, chopped
1 clove garlic, pressed
1 tablespoon parsley, chopped
1 small can sliced mushrooms
1 $^1/_2$ cups Sebastiani Chardonnay
$^1/_2$ teaspoon thyme
$^1/_2$ teaspoon rosemary

Dust chicken lightly with flour. Brown well in oil and butter; sprinkle all sides with salt and pepper while cooking. Add chopped onion and celery, salt and pepper to taste. Stir frequently with pancake turner until celery and onion are limp, then add garlic and parsley, stirring constantly. Add mushrooms, wine, thyme and rosemary. Cover and simmer about 45 minutes. If there seems to be too much liquid, cook without cover the last 10 to 15 minutes.

SUGGESTED WINE:
Sebastiani Chardonnay

Per serving: 637 Calories; 47g Fat (69% calories from fat); 43g Protein; 5g Carbohydrate; 180mg Cholesterol; 319mg Sodium
Food Exchanges: 6 Lean Meat; 1 1/2 Vegetable; 5 1/2 Fat

NOTES:
A HEARTY FAMILY DISH SERVED OVER RICE OR POLENTA AND TOPPED WITH FRESHLY GRATED PARMESAN CHEESE.

CHICKEN IN WHITE WINE

FROM VON STIEHL WINERY, WISCONSIN

Serves 4

3/4 cup Italian bread crumbs
1/4 cup Parmesan cheese
1/8 teaspoon garlic powder
salt and pepper to taste
4 skinless, boneless chicken breasts
1 large egg, beaten
1 stick butter
1/4 cup Von Stiehl Chenin Blanc
1/4 cup white Worcestershire sauce

NOTES:
AN IMPRESSIVE DISH FOR THE MIDDLE
OF THE WEEK DINNER.

Mix seasoned bread crumbs, Parmesan cheese, garlic powder, salt and pepper.

Dip chicken breasts in beaten egg, then in bread crumb mixture. Place in 9x13-inch glass baking dish.

Melt butter, then add wine and Worcestershire sauce. Mix together and pour over chicken. Bake uncovered 40 to 45 minutes.

SUGGESTED WINE:
Von Stiehl Winery Chenin Blanc

Per serving: 354 Calories; 8g Fat (22% calories from fat); 45g Protein; 19g Carbohydrate; 161mg Cholesterol; 990mg Sodium
Food Exchanges: 1 Starch/Bread; 6 Lean Meat; 1 Fat

CHICKEN SATAY

FROM BEAULIEU VINEYARD, CALIFORNIA

Serves 4

1 pound skinless, boneless chicken breasts

MARINADE:
$^1/_2$ cup coconut milk
1 tablespoon fish sauce, "nam pla"
2 teaspoons red curry paste
1 teaspoon brown sugar or palm sugar
1 tablespoon cilantro, chopped
$^1/_2$ teaspoon ground turmeric
salt and pepper to taste

PEANUT SAUCE:
1 cup canned coconut milk, unsweetened
2 tablespoons red curry paste
$^1/_2$ cup chunky peanut butter
$^1/_2$ cup low-sodium chicken broth
$^1/_4$ cup brown sugar or palm sugar
2 tablespoons fresh lime juice
1 teaspoon salt

cilantro, whole leaves for garnish

NOTES:
LOOKING FOR SOMETHING DIFFERENT
AND ADVENTUROUS?

Soak bamboo skewers in cold water.

In bowl, combine all marinade ingredients. Slice chicken into long, thin strips and flatten by pounding gently between sheets of plastic wrap. Add chicken to marinade and turn to coat both sides. Cover and refrigerate at least 1 hour. Prepare medium-hot barbecue fire and thread each chicken strip onto skewer. Grill 3 to 4 minutes or until done, turning once. Serve with jasmine rice and peanut sauce. Garnish plates with cilantro leaves.

PEANUT SAUCE:
Heat coconut milk to a boil in small saucepan. Whisk in curry paste until dissolved. Whisk in peanut butter, broth and sugar. Reduce heat and simmer until smooth, stirring constantly, about 5 minutes. Remove from heat and add lime juice and salt. Cool to room temperature.

SUGGESTED WINES:
Beaulieu Vineyard Viognier or Sauvignon Blanc

Per serving: 625 Calories; 43g Fat (59% calories from fat); 38g Protein; 28g Carbohydrate; 68mg Cholesterol; 1144mg Sodium
Food Exchanges: 1/2 Starch/Bread; 4 1/2 Lean Meat; 7 1/2 Fat; 1 Other Carbohydrates

CHICKEN TOSCANA

FROM PETRONI VINEYARDS, CALIFORNIA
NORTH BEACH RESTAURANT

Serves 4

3 pounds whole chicken
1/2 cup flour
salt and pepper to taste
3 tablespoons olive oil
1 sprig rosemary, chopped
1 tablespoon unsalted butter
1/2 cup zucchini, diced
1/2 cup fresh mushrooms, sliced
1/2 cup artichoke hearts
12 black olives
1/2 cup dry white wine

NOTES:
BASIC TUSCAN COOKING, AND IT'S SO
DELICIOUS.

Preheat oven to 325° F. Cut chicken into 4 pieces. Dry chicken sections with paper towel and flour lightly on both sides. Season with salt and pepper to taste. Heat olive oil in ovenproof sauté pan and place chicken, skin down, in hot oil. Add rosemary. Cook 3 minutes on each side. Place pan in oven and bake about 15 to 20 minutes.

Remove pan from oven. Remove chicken to warm plate and cover. Drain fat from pan. Add butter, zucchini, mushrooms, artichokes and olives and sauté for a minute. Add wine and bring to a boil. Sauté for a while longer.

Place chicken on plate and pour sauce over each piece.

SUGGESTED WINE:
Petroni Sangiovese Grosso

Per serving: 727 Calories; 50g Fat (64% calories from fat); 46g Protein; 17g Carbohydrate; 220mg Cholesterol; 303mg Sodium
Food Exchanges: 1 Starch/Bread; 6 Lean Meat; 1/2 Vegetable; 6 Fat

FRISKI CHICKEN

FROM ROCKBRIDGE VINEYARD, VIRGINIA

Serves 8

1 jar dried beef
8 skinless, boneless chicken breasts
8 slices bacon
1 can mushroom soup
$1/2$ cup dry red wine
$1/2$ cup sour cream

Preheat oven to 325º F. Coat ovenproof casserole dish with vegetable spray. Line bottom of dish with dried beef. Wrap each piece of chicken with 1 slice bacon. Combine soup, wine and sour cream. Pour over top of chicken and bake for 1 $1/2$ hours.

This can be prepared ahead and stored uncooked (covered) in refrigerator for up to 12 hours.

■

SUGGESTED WINE:
Rockbridge Pinot Noir

NOTES:
NOT YOUR ORDINARY BAKED CHICKEN BREASTS.

Per serving: 283 Calories; 9g Fat (33% calories from fat); 42g Protein; 2g Carbohydrate; 110mg Cholesterol; 459mg Sodium
Food Exchanges: 5 1/2 Lean Meat; 1 1/2 Fat

GRILLED CHICKEN WITH DIJON MARINADE

FROM PEDRONCELLI WINERY, CALIFORNIA

Serves 6

1 cup Pedroncelli Chardonnay
2 tablespoons Dijon mustard
black pepper, freshly ground to taste
1 teaspoon kosher salt
1 teaspoon fresh sage, minced
1 teaspoon fresh rosemary, minced
1 teaspoon fresh thyme, minced
1/4 cup olive oil
6 skinless, boneless chicken breast halves

NOTES:
YOU'LL NEVER GRILL "NAKED" CHICKEN
BREASTS AGAIN.

Combine all ingredients but chicken in bowl and whisk until blended to make marinade. Place chicken breasts in self-sealing plastic bag and pour in marinade. Refrigerate at least 1 hour and up to 8 hours.

Heat grill to medium-high. Cook marinated chicken on grill about 3 to 4 minutes on each side for tender, moist chicken. Pour marinade in bowl and baste chicken once on each side while grilling.

Serve with favorite pasta or rice dish, salad and fresh bread.

SUGGESTED WINE:
Pedroncelli Chardonnay

Per serving: 207 Calories; 10g Fat (52% calories from fat); 21g Protein; 1g Carbohydrate; 51mg Cholesterol; 458mg Sodium
Food Exchanges: 3 Lean Meat; 2 Fat

LEMON CHICKEN WITH GEWÜRZTRAMINER SAUCE

FROM FIRELANDS WINERY, OHIO

Serves 6

$1/2$ cup fresh lemon juice
(about 1 large lemon)
6 skinless, boneless chicken breasts
1 large egg
$2/3$ cup flour
$2/3$ cup fresh bread crumbs,
preferably sourdough
3 teaspoons lemon zest
(about 1 large lemon)
$1/2$ teaspoon dried dill
1 teaspoon salt
pepper to taste
4 tablespoons olive oil, divided
2 tablespoons butter, divided

SAUCE:
2 cups low-sodium chicken broth
2 cups Firelands Gewürztraminer
$1/2$ pint cream
3 tablespoons cold butter

Pour lemon juice into glass baking dish. Add chicken breasts. Cover and refrigerate 45 minutes. Turn chicken and refrigerate an additional 45 minutes. Remove chicken from marinade and pat dry with paper towels. Reserve marinade. Beat egg

and $1/4$ cup lemon marinade in shallow bowl. Set aside.

Combine flour, bread crumbs, lemon zest, dill, salt and pepper in plastic bag.

Heat 2 tablespoons olive oil and 1 tablespoon butter in large, heavy skillet.

Dip each chicken breast in egg mixture, then shake in crumb mixture. Place in hot oil mixture. Cook until golden brown on 1 side (6 to 8 minutes). Add 2 tablespoons olive oil and 1 tablespoon butter, turn chicken and cook an additional 8 minutes.

SAUCE:
Blot up all oil in skillet with paper towels, leaving any browned bits. Add chicken broth and reduce to 1 cup. Add wine and continue to reduce to 2 cups total liquid. Add cream and bring to a boil. Reduce heat to low and whisk in butter a little at a time. Each addition should be well incorporated before more butter is added. Spoon over chicken and serve.

SUGGESTED WINE:
Firelands Gewürztraminer

Per serving: 595 Calories; 32g Fat (53% calories from fat); 46g Protein; 18g Carbohydrate; 192mg Cholesterol; 788mg Sodium
Food Exchanges: 1 Starch/Bread; 6 Lean Meat; 6 Fat

NOTES:
THE SPICINESS OF THE GEWÜRZTRAMINER AND THE ZESTINESS OF THE LEMON MAKE THIS A VERY TASTY DISH.

MUSTARD-GRILLED CHICKEN

FROM GRAY GHOST VINEYARDS, VIRGINIA

Serves 6

$2/3$ cup Dijon-style mustard, divided
2 tablespoons cayenne, divided
$1/4$ cup vegetable oil
$1/4$ cup Gray Ghost Victorian White
6 skinless, boneless chicken breasts

NOTES:
NO WIMPY OR DULL TASTING CHICKEN
BREASTS ON THIS GRILL!

Stir together $1/3$ cup mustard, 1 tablespoon cayenne, vegetable oil and wine. Place chicken in large self-sealing plastic bag and pour in mustard mixture. Press out air and seal tightly. Massage to distribute marinade. Set in large bowl and refrigerate at least 2 hours, or longer.

Combine rest of mustard and cayenne. Remove chicken from marinade, allowing as much marinade as possible to cling to surface of chicken. Grill, turning frequently, for about 20 to 30 minutes, brushing several times with mustard/cayenne mixture.

SUGGESTED WINE:
Gray Ghost Victorian White

Per serving: 295 Calories; 13g Fat (40% calories from fat); 40g Protein; 3g Carbohydrate; 96mg Cholesterol; 443mg Sodium
Food Exchanges: 5 1/2 Lean Meat; 2 Fat

PEACHY CHICKEN MARINADE

FROM LAKEWOOD VINEYARDS, NEW YORK

Serves 4

1/2 cup grapeseed oil
2 cups Lakewood Riesling wine
2 tablespoons capers
1/2 cup lemon juice
22 ounces diced peaches
1/2 teaspoon thyme
1/2 teaspoon cumin
1/2 teaspoon marjoram
1/4 teaspoon cayenne pepper
4 skinless, boneless chicken or duck breasts

Combine all ingredients, except chicken, in blender to make marinade. Blend until peaches are pureed. Cover chicken or duck breasts with marinade and refrigerate overnight. Cook over low heat on grill until done, but still moist. Keep warm.

Bring marinade to a boil and reduce until it is a pourable consistency. Drizzle reduced marinade over chicken or duck.

SUGGESTED WINE:
Lakewood Vineyards Riesling

Per serving: 565 Calories; 30g Fat (54% calories from fat); 39g Protein; 17g Carbohydrate; 96mg Cholesterol; 153mg Sodium
Food Exchanges: 5 1/2 Lean Meat; 1 Fruit; 5 1/2 Fat

NOTES:
FOR A PLEASANT SMOKY FLAVOR, PUT GRAPE CUTTINGS IN THE GRILL WHILE COOKING.

PORCINI-STUFFED CHICKEN BREAST

FROM ZD WINERY, CALIFORNIA

Serves 4

3 strips thick-sliced bacon
1 stalk celery, finely diced
1 small onion, finely diced
2 ounces dried porcini mushrooms
1/2 loaf baguette, crust removed, cubed
1/4 cup heavy cream
1 sprig thyme, chopped
4 chicken breasts, skin on
4 tablespoons olive oil
salt and pepper to taste

Slice bacon crosswise and render out fat in sauté pan. When fat starts releasing from bacon, add celery and onions and cook until translucent.

NOTES:
PLAIN OLD CHICKEN BREASTS WILL NEVER BE THE SAME.

In small saucepan re-hydrate mushrooms by covering with boiling water and let steep for about 15 minutes. Drain excess water and roughly chop.

Put bacon mixture, bread, mushrooms and cream into mixing bowl. Add thyme.

With boning knife, form pocket in chicken breast starting at fattest part of breast and moving knife around inside of breast without making opening too large. Stuff breasts generously with mixture.

Preheat oven to 350º F. Heat ovenproof skillet over high heat. Add olive oil. Generously season chicken breasts with salt and pepper and place in skillet. Reduce heat slightly and sauté until skin is golden brown. Leave skin side down and place in oven about 5 minutes. Turn chicken over and cook an additional 10 to 15 minutes, depending on size of chicken breasts.

■

SUGGESTED WINE:
ZD Pinot Noir

Per serving: 1064 Calories; 59g Fat (51% calories from fat); 85g Protein; 45g Carbohydrate; 260mg Cholesterol; 743mg Sodium
Food Exchanges: 2 Starch/Bread; 11 1/2 Lean Meat; 2 1/2 Vegetable; 5 Fat

SAUTÉED CHICKEN WITH PROSECCO-MUSHROOM CREAM SAUCE

FROM MARTINI & ROSSI, ITALY

Serves 6

6 skinless, boneless chicken breast halves
salt and pepper
2 tablespoons vegetable oil
2 tablespoons butter
6 ounces shiitake or crimini mushrooms, sliced
1/4 cup shallots, chopped
1/2 cup Martini & Rossi Prosecco
1/2 cup chicken broth
1 cup cream
1 teaspoon dried thyme

Lightly pound chicken filets until uniform in thickness. Season with salt and pepper. Heat oil in large skillet over medium-high heat. Add chicken and sauté 5 to 6 minutes on each side until browned and cooked through. Remove from skillet and keep warm in oven set at lowest temperature.

Melt butter in skillet, add mushrooms and shallots and sauté until mushrooms are limp. Add wine and chicken broth; increase heat to high and cook until liquid is boiled down to a syrupy stage. Add cream and thyme and continue boiling until sauce thickens lightly. Season to taste with salt and pepper.

Serve sauce over chicken.

NOTES:
NORTHERN ITALIAN-STYLE CHICKEN WITH EGG NOODLES, BUTTER AND PARMESAN CHEESE OR LEMON RISOTTO.

SUGGESTED WINE:
Martini & Rossi Prosecco

Per serving: 377 Calories; 20g Fat (48% calories from fat); 25g Protein; 24g Carbohydrate; 96mg Cholesterol; 247mg Sodium
Food Exchanges: 3 Lean Meat; 3 1/2 Vegetable; 3 1/2 Fat

SEARED QUAIL WITH LENTIL RAGOUT

FROM ZD WINERY, CALIFORNIA

Serves 4

2 slices thick-sliced bacon
1 carrot, diced
1 stalk celery, diced
1 small leek, white part diced
1 cup lentils
1 bay leaf
2 cups water
2 tablespoons sherry vinegar
1 tablespoon whole grain mustard
1 tablespoon honey
salt and pepper as needed
3 tablespoons olive oil
5 tablespoons grapeseed oil, divided
2 whole quail
2 teaspoons butter, divided
2 cloves garlic, smashed whole
1 head frisee lettuce, washed

In shallow pan with lid, render bacon over medium heat. Then add carrot, celery and white part of leek. Sauté until vegetables soften. Add 1 cup lentils, bay leaf and cover with water. Simmer 10 to 15 minutes. Taste lentils and if they have begun to soften, add salt to taste. If not, continue to simmer and when they soften, add salt. (If lentils are seasoned too soon, they will never soften.) Cool lentils on sheet pan and set aside.

To make vinaigrette for frisee lettuce, whisk sherry vinegar, mustard, honey and a little salt and pepper. Slowly drizzle in olive oil and 4 tablespoons grapeseed oil while whisking. Season to taste with salt and pepper.

Butcher quail into 4 pieces, 2 legs and 2 breasts each. Heat medium-size skillet over high heat. Pat quail dry with paper towel and generously season each side with salt and pepper. Put 1 tablespoon grapeseed oil in pan and when it begins to smoke, place quail pieces skin side down. When skin becomes golden brown and crispy (about 4 minutes), flip quail over, add 1 teaspoon butter and 2 smashed garlic cloves. Let butter foam and melt. Turn off heat and let quail continue to cook another 1 to 2 minutes in pan.

Meanwhile, heat lentils slowly over low heat. Add 1 tablespoon vinaigrette, 1 teaspoon butter and check seasoning.

To serve, place a spoon of warmed lentils in center of plate. Toss a little frisee lettuce with a little vinaigrette and put on top of lentils. Then put down a quail leg with a quail breast on top.

■

SUGGESTED WINE:
ZD Winery Pinot Noir

Per serving: 597 Calories; 37g Fat (55% calories from fat); 29g Protein; 40g Carbohydrate; 57mg Cholesterol; 228mg Sodium
Food Exchanges: 2 Starch/Bread; 3 Lean Meat; 1 1/2 Vegetable; 6 Fat; 1/2 Other Carbohydrates

NOTES:
THIS DISH IS A NICE COMPONENT IN A MULTI-COURSE MEAL OR JUST BY ITSELF AS A SNACK.

SPAGHETTI SQUASH WITH SMOKED MOZZARELLA AND CHICKEN

FROM GRAY GHOST VINEYARDS, VIRGINIA

Serves 4

2 1/2 pounds spaghetti squash
2 ounces smoked mozzarella or
  Gouda cheese, shredded
2 whole tomatoes, diced
1/2 teaspoon salt, divided
1/4 teaspoon coarsely ground pepper,
  divided
1 tablespoon olive oil
1 medium onion, diced
12 ounces skinless, boneless chicken breast,
  cut for stir-fry
1/2 cup Gray Ghost Seyval Blanc
1/4 cup fresh basil leaves, coarsely chopped

With tip of sharp knife, pierce squash in about 10 places. Microwave on high 6 or 7 minutes. Turn squash over and pierce in another 10 places and microwave 6 to 7 minutes longer or until squash is soft to the touch.

Shred cheese and mix with diced tomatoes, 1/4 teaspoon salt and 1/8 teaspoon pepper.

When squash is done, cut in half lengthwise and lift out pulp in strands. Place in large bowl. Discard squash skin. Mix cheese and tomatoes with hot squash. Keep warm.

In nonstick 12-inch skillet, heat olive oil over medium heat. Add onion and cook until tender and golden, about 8 minutes, stirring occasionally. Add chicken, wine, 1/4 teaspoon salt, 1/8 teaspoon black pepper and cook until chicken is done, about 6 to 8 minutes, stirring occasionally.

Spoon squash mixture into 4 bowls and top with chicken and onion mixture. Garnish with basil.

NOTES:
A TASTY DISH, COMPLETE WITH ALL THE FOOD GROUPS FOR AN INCLUSIVE ENTREE.

SUGGESTED WINE:
Gray Ghost Seyval Blanc

Per serving: 291 Calories; 10g Fat (32% calories from fat); 25g Protein; 22g Carbohydrate; 62mg Cholesterol; 431mg Sodium
Food Exchanges: 3 Lean Meat; 4 Vegetable; 1 Fat

NOTES:

NOTES:

SOUP
&
SALAD

■

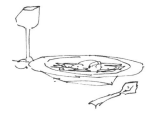

"IRS 1040" BEAN SOUP

FROM CEDAR MOUNTAIN WINERY, CALIFORNIA

Serves 8

48 ounces refried beans
29 ounces chicken stock
2 cloves garlic, mashed
2 drops liquid smoke flavoring
$1/4$ teaspoon Tabasco sauce
juice of $1/2$ lemon
salt and pepper to taste

Mix together all ingredients thoroughly and bring to a boil. Serve.

SUGGESTED WINE:
Cedar Mountain Duet - Gold

Per serving: 194 Calories; 2g Fat (9% calories from fat); 11g Protein; 33g Carbohydrate; 0mg Cholesterol; 1627mg Sodium
Food Exchanges: 2 Starch/Bread

NOTES:
LIKE DEATH AND TAXES, THIS SOUP IS A SURE THING.

ASPARAGUS & DUNGENESS CRAB SALAD

FROM WENTE FAMILY ESTATES, CALIFORNIA
CORPORATE CHEF KIMBALL JONES

Serves 4

2 bunches asparagus
  (approximately 40 spears)
2 ounces extra virgin olive oil
  plus 1 tablespoon olive oil plus to taste
3 shallots, finely chopped
1 tablespoon Dijon mustard
1 medium lemon, juice and zest
2 large eggs
salt and pepper to taste
1 pound freshly cooked Dungeness crab
1 tablespoon parsley, coarsely chopped

Trim ends of asparagus spears by snapping them. They should snap easily, leaving none of the white woody part. Peel asparagus from spear end down. Set aside.

Preheat oven to 350º F.

Heat 2 ounces olive oil in ovenproof pan over medium heat. Add shallots. Place in oven and roast approximately $1/2$ hour,

turning occasionally so that shallots brown evenly. Cool shallots and chop finely. Place in mixing bowl with mustard, lemon juice and zest. Slowly whisk in 1 tablespoon olive oil. Set aside.

Place eggs in saucepan and cover with water. Bring to a boil. Turn off heat and let stand for 8 minutes. Centers of yolks should be just cooked through. Cool, peel and chop.

Bring large quantity of salted water to a boil. Add asparagus and cook $1 \ 1/2$ minutes. Drain and immediately season to taste with olive oil, salt and pepper. Let cool for a few minutes.

To serve, toss asparagus with shallot vinaigrette and divide among 4 plates. Top with crabmeat. Sprinkle with chopped egg and parsley.

SUGGESTED WINE:
Wente Sauvignon Blanc

Per serving: 320 Calories; 21g Fat (59% calories from fat); 25g Protein; 9g Carbohydrate; 175mg Cholesterol; 419mg Sodium
Food Exchanges: 3 Lean Meat; 1 Vegetable; 4 Fat

NOTES:
A DELECTABLE SALAD TO COMPLEMENT YOUR WEEKEND DINNER MENU.

BLANCHE'S GRILLED CHICKEN SALAD

FROM CEDAR MOUNTAIN WINERY, CALIFORNIA

Serves 6

MARINADE:
2 cloves garlic, coarsely chopped
$1/_2$ medium onion, coarsely chopped
$1/_4$ cup olive oil
$1/_4$ cup Cedar Mountain Duet
$1/_4$ cup cider vinegar or red wine vinegar
$1/_2$ tablespoon tomato paste
$1/_2$ tablespoon liquid smoke flavoring
$1/_4$ teaspoon black pepper, freshly ground
1 jalapeno pepper, seeded and chopped
1 tablespoon Worcestershire sauce
4 boneless, skinless chicken breasts

SALAD:
$1/_4$ cup currants or white raisins
$1/_4$ cup dry white wine plus 2 tablespoons
1 medium apple, seeded and chopped
$1/_4$ cup walnuts, pecans or pine nuts
1 ounce crumbled blue cheese
1 stalk celery, sliced
lettuce leaves, assorted

DRESSING:
6 tablespoons olive oil
2 tablespoons balsamic vinegar
salt and pepper to taste

MARINADE:
Put all marinade ingredients in food processor or blender and process until smooth. Put chicken breasts in glass bowl or self-sealing container with marinade over them. Turn breasts at least once to make sure marinade coats them. Cover bowl with plastic wrap and let chicken marinate at least 3 hours, or up to 24 hours, in refrigerator.

SALAD:
Combine currants and $1/_4$ cup wine and let soak at least 3 hours, or up to 24 hours, in refrigerator.

While heating grill, toss chopped apple with 2 tablespoons wine and drain. Combine apple, walnuts, blue cheese and celery in salad bowl. Add torn assorted lettuce leaves and mix. Arrange whole leaves on serving plates or shred and place on plates.

Grill chicken breasts, being careful to not overcook. Slice or coarsely chop chicken and add to salad bowl.

DRESSING:
Whisk together olive oil, balsamic vinegar, salt and pepper. Pour over salad, toss lightly and serve immediately or chill.

SUGGESTED WINE:
Cedar Mountain Duet - Gold

Per serving: 432 Calories; 28g Fat (61% calories from fat); 29g Protein; 13g Carbohydrate; 68mg Cholesterol; 186mg Sodium
Food Exchanges: 4 Lean Meat; 1/2 Vegetable; 1/2 Fruit; 5 Fat

NOTES: A TASTY LUNCHEON SALAD ANY TIME OF THE YEAR.

CALAMARI SALAD

FROM PALMER VINEYARDS, NEW YORK

Serves 4

$^1/_2$ pound squid, cleaned and sliced
$^1/_8$ cup chamomile vinegar
$^1/_8$ cup pomegranate juice or syrup
$^1/_8$ cup olive oil
salt and pepper to taste
1 pint cherry tomatoes, cut in half
1 medium avocado, peeled and cut in cubes
1 medium cucumber,
    peeled and cut in cubes
$^1/_4$ pound lettuce, chopped
1 medium green pepper, sliced in strips
$^1/_8$ cup fresh herbs, minced
$^1/_8$ cup toasted almonds

Sauté squid in hot pan or grill.

Whisk chamomile vinegar, pomegranate syrup, olive oil and salt and pepper to taste. Toss with squid and vegetables.

Top with minced herbs of choice (basil, parsley, oregano, etc.) and toasted almonds.

SUGGESTED WINE:
Palmer Vineyards Reserve Chardonnay

Per serving: 270 Calories; 18g Fat (57% calories from fat); 13g Protein; 18g Carbohydrate; 132mg Cholesterol; 46mg Sodium
Food Exchanges: 1 1/2 Lean Meat; 2 Vegetable; 1/2 Fruit; 3 Fat

NOTES:
A TASTY ADVENTURE INTO THE SEAWORLD OF SALADS.

CECI BEAN SOUP WITH PANCETTA AND ROSEMARY

FROM LAKE SONOMA WINERY, CALIFORNIA
CHEF ROBIN LEHNHOFF

Serves 6

3 cups dry garbanzo beans
6 cups no-salt-added chicken broth
2 cups yellow onions, chopped
2 tablespoons chopped garlic
4 cups canned tomatoes, pureed
$1/2$ pound pancetta or bacon,
   diced and cooked crisp
2 tablespoons fresh rosemary, chopped
1 tablespoon kosher salt
2 teaspoons black pepper

Cover garbanzo beans with water and soak overnight.

Drain and add chicken broth, onion, garlic and pureed tomatoes. Bring to a boil and then add pancetta or bacon. Simmer until beans are tender. Add rosemary, salt and pepper.

Remove half of soup and process in blender until smooth. Return to remaining soup, stir and check seasonings.

NOTES:
NOW HERE'S A FULL-FLAVORED SOUP!

SUGGESTED WINE:
**Lake Sonoma Winery Saini
Old Vine Zinfandel**

*Per serving: 532 Calories; 12g Fat (19% calories from fat); 43g Protein; 77g Carbohydrate; 26mg Cholesterol; 2368mg Sodium
Food Exchanges: 4 Starch/Bread; 3 Lean Meat; 2 1/2 Vegetable; 1 Fat*

CITRUS SALAD

FROM ZD WINERY, CALIFORNIA

Serves 4

1 medium red bell pepper
1 bunch pea shoots
3 oranges, peeled and segmented
6 large basil leaves
2 tablespoons olive oil
1 tablespoon fresh lime juice
salt and pepper to taste
1 tablespoon honey

Roast red bell pepper over open flame until skin is black on all sides. Put in small bowl and cover with plastic wrap. Let pepper sit 10 minutes then peel, seed and dice.

Meanwhile, tear pea shoots into bite-size pieces.

Mix together oranges, basil, roasted red bell pepper, olive oil, lime juice, salt, pepper and honey. Let marinate for at least 20 minutes before serving.

SUGGESTED WINE:
ZD California Chardonnay

Per serving: 161 Calories; 7g Fat (36% calories from fat); 4g Protein; 25g Carbohydrate; 0mg Cholesterol; 9mg Sodium
Food Exchanges: 2 Vegetable; 1/2 Fruit; 1 1/2 Fat; 1/2 Other Carbohydrates

NOTES:
A REFRESHING SALAD MIXTURE WITH AN ENTREE OF FISH OR CHICKEN.

CRAB CIOPPINO

FROM SIERRA VISTA VINEYARDS & WINERY, CALIFORNIA

Serves 6

2 tablespoons olive oil
1 large onion, minced
2 cloves garlic, minced
2 teaspoons fresh marjoram, minced
2 teaspoons dried basil
1 teaspoon dried oregano
2 teaspoons dried thyme
$^1/_4$ teaspoon white pepper
$^1/_4$ teaspoon red pepper flakes
$^1/_4$ teaspoon cayenne
3 cups chicken stock
1 cup Chardonnay, without barrel oak
$^1/_2$ can tomato paste
2 whole Dungeness crab,
   cooked and cracked
1 teaspoon parsley to garnish

Heat olive oil in 6-quart pan over medium-high heat. Sauté onion and garlic until translucent, then add spices. Stir 1 minute until fragrant. Add broth, wine and tomato paste. Bring to a boil, stirring often. Reduce heat and simmer 25 to 30 minutes to blend flavors. Adjust seasonings. This mixture may be made a day or two ahead.

Break crabs apart and clean. Cut body in fourths and crack legs. Add to hot soup and simmer until hot, about 7 to 10 minutes. Garnish with parsley.

SUGGESTED WINE:
Sierra Vista Syrah

Per serving: 149 Calories; 5g Fat (41% calories from fat); 11g Protein; 7g Carbohydrate; 32mg Cholesterol; 1347mg Sodium
Food Exchanges: 1 1/2 Lean Meat; 1 Vegetable; 1 Fat

NOTES:
A SPICY AND FULL-FLAVORED MEAL WITH A GREEN SALAD AND CRUSTY BREAD.

CRISP CUCUMBER-RED ONION SALAD

FROM SAKONNET VINEYARDS, RHODE ISLAND

Serves 4

3 medium cucumbers
1 tablespoon kosher salt
$1/2$ medium red onion, peeled
and thinly sliced
2 $1/2$ tablespoons sugar
$1/2$ cup Vidal Blanc
$1/4$ cup fresh dill, coarsely chopped

NOTES:
A CRISP, REFRESHING SALAD FOR A PICNIC OF GRILLED CHICKEN OR SALMON.

Peel cucumbers, trim ends and cut in half, lengthwise. Remove seeds by scooping out centers of cucumbers with teaspoon. Slice cucumbers crosswise into $1/4$-inch pieces. Place cucumbers in colander, set in bowl and toss with kosher salt. Weigh cucumbers down lightly with another bowl placed inside colander. Put in refrigerator to drain 1 to 2 hours. Lightly rinse and pat dry.

Transfer cucumbers to mixing bowl and toss with onion slices. In separate small bowl, dissolve sugar in wine. Pour wine over top of cucumbers and toss in dill. Let salad stand, marinating in refrigerator, at least 1 hour before serving.

SUGGESTED WINE:
Sakonnet Vineyards Vidal Blanc

Per serving: 117 Calories; 1g Fat (5% calories from fat); 3g Protein; 22g Carbohydrate; 0mg Cholesterol; 12mg Sodium
Food Exchanges: 3 Vegetable; 1/2 Fruit; 1/2 Other Carbohydrates

CURRIED SQUASH SOUP

FROM FENN VALLEY VINEYARDS, MICHIGAN

Serves 12

1 large butternut squash, halved and cleaned
1 large Bosc pear, peeled and cored
1 tablespoon olive oil
1 large onion, chopped
3 cloves garlic, minced
$1/2$ cup carrots, chopped
$1/2$ cup celery, chopped
3 large apples, peeled, cored and chopped
2 $1/4$ teaspoons curry powder
$1/2$ teaspoon salt
$1/4$ teaspoon black pepper
1 tablespoon honey
$3/4$ teaspoon fresh ginger, chopped
6 cups chicken broth
$1/8$ teaspoon cayenne pepper
$3/4$ teaspoon cumin
2 tablespoons fresh chives,
    chopped for garnish

Preheat oven to 350º F. Place squash in roasting pan. Put Bosc pear in squash cavity. Cover with foil. Bake 1 $1/2$ hours. Cool and scoop into soup bowl. Set aside.

In stockpot with olive oil, sauté onion and garlic until transparent. Add carrots, celery, apples and curry powder. Simmer approximately 3 minutes. Add squash and pear plus rest of ingredients, except chives. Simmer 1 hour. Puree and garnish with chopped chives.

SUGGESTED WINE:
Fenn Valley White Riesling

Per serving: 118 Calories; 3g Fat (20% calories from fat); 7g Protein; 18g Carbohydrate; 1mg Cholesterol; 881mg Sodium
Food Exchanges: 1/2 Starch/Bread; 1/2 Lean Meat; 1/2 Vegetable; 1/2 Fruit

NOTES:
THIS SOUP GETS RAVE REVIEWS AT THE WINERY. WHY NOT GET THEM FROM YOUR KITCHEN?

DUNGENESS CRAB AND CORN SOUP

FROM BRASSFIELD ESTATE VINEYARD, CALIFORNIA

Serves 4

2 tablespoons butter
$^3/_4$ cup red bell pepper, diced
$^1/_2$ cup green onions, diced
2 tablespoons flour
4 cups low-sodium chicken broth
2 cups fresh or frozen corn kernels
$^1/_4$ cup milk
$^1/_4$ cup heavy cream
1 teaspoon cumin
1 teaspoon salt
1 teaspoon white pepper
$^1/_2$ pound precooked crab meat

Melt butter in 2-quart stock pan. Add red bell pepper and sauté 2 minutes. Add green onions. Cook another minute, then add flour and cook 2 more minutes. Add chicken broth and corn. Bring to a boil, then turn down to a simmer for 5 minutes. Add milk, cream and seasonings; return to a simmer.

Divide crab among 4 bowls and pour soup over crab. Soup will heat crab.

SUGGESTED WINE:
Brassfield Estate Sauvignon Blanc

NOTES:
WHETHER FOR LUNCH OR FOR THE EVENING'S SOUP COURSE, THEY'LL BE ASKING FOR MORE.

Per serving: 296 Calories; 15g Fat (39% calories from fat); 27g Protein; 26g Carbohydrate; 88mg Cholesterol; 837mg Sodium
Food Exchanges: 1 1/2 Starch/Bread; 3 Lean Meat; 1/2 Vegetable; 2 1/2 Fat

FRUIT AND NUT SALAD

FROM CEDAR MOUNTAIN WINERY, CALIFORNIA

Serves 8

SALAD DRESSING:
4 tablespoons salad oil (olive, canola, etc.)
1 tablespoon cider vinegar
1 tablespoon dry sherry
$1/8$ teaspoon cinnamon

SALAD:
4 medium apples
1 teaspoon lemon juice
1 can mandarin oranges, sliced and drained
$1/4$ cup walnuts, chopped
1 tablespoon toasted pine nuts
8 cups lettuce, assorted

NOTES:
"SOMETIMES YOU FEEL LIKE A NUT,
SOMETIMES YOU DON'T."
THIS ONE IS FOR WHEN YOU DO.

SALAD DRESSING:
Mix ingredients in pint jar with screw top. Shake for about 30 seconds to make sure ingredients are well mixed.

SALAD:
Peel and core apples. Cut into thin slices and toss with lemon juice. Add drained mandarin orange slices, chopped walnuts and pine nuts. Lightly toss with salad dressing.

Arrange assorted lettuces on salad plates. Top with fruit and nut mixture.

◼

SUGGESTED WINE:
Cedar Mountain Winery Estate Chardonnay

Per serving: 148 Calories; 10g Fat (58% calories from fat); 2g Protein; 14g Carbohydrate; 0mg Cholesterol; 5mg Sodium
Food Exchanges: 1/2 Vegetable; 1 Fruit; 2 Fat

JAMBALAYA

FROM JANKRIS WINERY, CALIFORNIA

Serves 6

SEASON MIX:
$1/_3$ teaspoon salt
$1/_8$ teaspoon red pepper
$1/_4$ teaspoon black pepper

SOUP:
6 $3/_4$ ounces small shrimp,
   shelled and cleaned
4 ounces bay scallops
2 tablespoons unsalted butter
10 ounces canned tomato sauce
1 cup onions, finely chopped
$1/_2$ cup green onions, finely chopped
$1/_2$ medium green pepper, chopped
2 ounces parsley, chopped
1 tablespoon garlic, chopped
1 bay leaf
2 ounces thyme
16 ounces seafood stock or clam juice
$1/_2$ cup uncooked rice
$1/_2$ teaspoon salt
$1/_4$ teaspoon black pepper
$1/_2$ teaspoon chili pepper oil
2 $3/_4$ ounces andouille sausage, chopped

Make seasoning mix and add to shrimp and scallops. Mix and refrigerate.

Mix together butter and tomato sauce. Add remaining ingredients. Cook until rice is tender, stirring frequently.

SUGGESTED WINE:
 JanKris Zinfandel

Per serving: 298 Calories; 12g Fat (34% calories from fat); 15g Protein; 36g Carbohydrate; 74mg Cholesterol; 1062mg Sodium
Food Exchanges: 1 Starch/Bread; 1 1/2 Lean Meat; 1 1/2 Vegetable; 2 Fat; 1/2 Other Carbohydrates

NOTES:
SPICE UP THAT BARBECUE WITH A CUP OF THIS FLAVORFUL SOUP.

LOBSTER AND MOREL PASTA SALAD

FROM CEDAR MOUNTAIN WINERY, CALIFORNIA

Serves 4

$^1/_2$ cup elbow macaroni, uncooked
2 tablespoons extra virgin olive oil
8 medium morels, dried or fresh
1 medium lobster tail
2 tablespoons butter
$^1/_8$ teaspoon ground nutmeg
salt and pepper to taste
4 cups assorted lettuce leaves, torn

NOTES:
LOBSTER, MORELS AND CEDAR
MOUNTAIN WINERY CHARDONNAY
COMBINE FOR A DECADENT WAY TO
END A WEEK.

Cook macaroni according to directions on package. Drain and combine with olive oil. Set aside.

If morel mushrooms are dried, reconstitute in water for $^1/_2$ hour. Cut mushrooms into 4 pieces each. Cut lobster tail into $^1/_2$-inch cubes. Sauté lobster and mushrooms in butter; add nutmeg. When lobster and morels are just barely cooked, remove from heat and add macaroni. Toss lightly and add salt and pepper to taste. Let cool slightly.

Arrange assorted lettuces on serving plates. Put $^1/_4$ of lobster, morels and pasta mixture on each plate. Serve immediately.

SUGGESTED WINE:
Cedar Mountain Winery Chardonnay

Per serving: 246 Calories; 14g Fat (50% calories from fat); 18g Protein; 14g Carbohydrate; 83mg Cholesterol; 293mg Sodium
Food Exchanges: 1/2 Starch/Bread; 2 Lean Meat; 1 1/2 Vegetable; 2 1/2 Fat

MERITAGE PASTA FAGIOLA

FROM DR. KONSTANTIN FRANK VINIFERA WINE CELLARS,
NEW YORK

Serves 8

1 pound beans (northern beans, navy
    pea, etc.)
1 large onion, diced
2 tablespoons olive oil
8 cups water
$1/2$ cup stewed tomatoes
    or 1 cup meatless spaghetti sauce
$1/2$ cup Salmon Run Meritage
salt and pepper to taste
1 pound soup pasta (ditalini)

Cover dry beans with water and soak at
least 4 to 5 hours, then drain.

In large stockpot, sauté diced onions in
olive oil. Add water and bring to a boil.
Add beans and simmer 2 hours.

Add stewed tomatoes or meatless spaghetti
sauce. Add wine and salt and pepper to
taste. Let simmer and cook soup pasta per
package directions. Add cooked pasta to
soup and let simmer 5 to 10 minutes.

Serve with grated Parmesan cheese.

SUGGESTED WINE:
Salmon Run Meritage

NOTES:
HEARTY AND DELICIOUS.

*Per serving: 452 Calories; 5g Fat (10% calories from
fat); 20g Protein; 79g Carbohydrate; 0mg
Cholesterol; 70mg Sodium
Food Exchanges: 5 Starch/Bread; 1 Lean Meat; 1/2
Vegetable; 1/2 Fat*

MIXED GREENS SALAD WITH VERMOUTH VINAIGRETTE

FROM MARTINI & ROSSI, ITALY

Serves 4

1 bag prepackaged mixed salad greens
1 cucumber, sliced
2 tablespoons Martini & Rossi Rosso
   Sweet Vermouth
2 tablespoons balsamic vinegar
1 tablespoon fresh basil, chopped,
   plus sprig for garnish
1 tablespoon Dijon-style mustard
$1/2$ teaspoon sea salt
$1/4$ teaspoon black pepper, freshly ground
$1/3$ cup extra virgin olive oil
   or more if needed
$1/8$ cup Parmesan cheese, shaved

In large bowl, toss mixed salad greens with cucumber slices.

In small bowl, mix next 6 ingredients. Add oil gradually, whisking until well blended.

Toss mixed salad greens and cucumber with just enough vinaigrette to coat lightly. Add shaved Parmesan cheese and garnish with sprig of fresh basil.

SUGGESTED WINE:
Martini & Rossi Prosecco

Per serving: 207 Calories; 19g Fat (84% calories from fat); 2g Protein; 6g Carbohydrate; 2mg Cholesterol; 334mg Sodium
Food Exchanges: 1 Vegetable; 3 1/2 Fat

NOTES:
SOON TO BE YOUR "SIGNATURE" SALAD!

SUN-DRIED TOMATO AND ROASTED RED PEPPER SOUP

FROM VALLEY OF THE MOON WINERY, CALIFORNIA
CHEF LAURIE SOUZA

Serves 4

5 slices bacon, julienned
1 tablespoon olive oil
1 large onion, chopped
2 cloves garlic, minced
2 Roma tomatoes, seeded and chopped
1 cup sun-dried tomatoes, julienned
3 medium roasted red bell peppers,
    peeled and seeded
4 cups no-salt-added chicken broth
salt and pepper to taste
fresh basil for garnish

Sauté bacon in large stockpot with olive oil until crispy and brown. Remove with slotted spoon and reserve.

Sauté onion in fat until soft and translucent. Add garlic and chopped tomatoes. Cook 2 to 3 minutes. Add sun-dried tomatoes, red bell peppers and chicken broth. Simmer 30 minutes.

Puree soup in blender. Season with salt and freshly ground black pepper. Garnish with bacon and fresh basil.

SUGGESTED WINE:
Valley of the Moon Zinfandel

Per serving: 180 Calories; 11g Fat (40% calories from fat); 17g Protein; 18g Carbohydrate; 7mg Cholesterol; 457mg Sodium
Food Exchanges: 1/2 Starch/Bread; 1 1/2 Lean Meat; 1 1/2 Vegetable; 1 Fat

NOTES:
AN INTRIGUING BLEND OF FLAVORS
THAT ONLY GET BETTER THE NEXT DAY.

YUM WOON SEN - ASIAN NOODLE SALAD

FROM SIERRA VISTA VINEYARDS & WINERY, CALIFORNIA

Serves 6

DRESSING:
2 jalapeno chili peppers, minced
3 tablespoons lime juice
2 tablespoons Thai fish sauce (nam pla)
1 teaspoon sugar
3 shallots, peeled and chopped
1/2 cup fresh cilantro, coarsely chopped

SALAD:
1 1/2 tablespoons vegetable oil
1/2 boneless, skinless chicken breast halves,
    coarsely chopped
salt and pepper to taste
2 ounces Asian-style noodles
1/2 carrot, julienned and blanched
1/2 zucchini, julienned
2 tablespoons shallots,
    fried crisp for garnish

DRESSING:
Mix together jalapeno, lime juice, fish sauce, sugar, shallots and cilantro.

SALAD:
Pour oil into hot wok or skillet. Add chopped chicken and sauté until it loses pink color. Season with salt and pepper to taste. Cool. Toss with small amount of dressing. Chill.

Add noodles to large pot of boiling water. Cook until just done and drain. Mix with dressing, carrot, zucchini and chicken. Garnish with fried shallots.

SUGGESTED WINE:
Sierra Vista Viognier

NOTES:
WITH OR WITHOUT CHICKEN, THIS IS A HEALTHY ASIAN DISH.

Per serving: 113 Calories; 5g Fat (37% calories from fat); 4g Protein; 14g Carbohydrate; 14mg Cholesterol; 13mg Sodium
Food Exchanges: 1/2 Starch/Bread; 1 Vegetable; 1 Fat

NOTES:

NOTES:

VEGETABLES

■

BAKED SQUASH MEDLEY

FROM OLIVER WINERY, INDIANA

Serves 6

3 tablespoons olive oil, divided
1 medium yellow squash,
  sliced in $1/2$-inch rounds
1 medium zucchini,
  sliced in $1/2$-inch rounds
1 small eggplant, sliced in $1/4$-inch rounds
1 medium onion, diced
3 cloves garlic, minced
1 teaspoon black pepper, divided
15 ounces canned tomatoes, crushed
$1/2$ teaspoon rosemary
$1/2$ teaspoon garlic powder
$1 1/2$ teaspoons oregano, divided
$2/3$ cup Parmesan cheese, shredded
  and divided

NOTES:
A VEGETABLE CASSEROLE THAT IS NOT
ONLY HEALTHY BUT WONDERFULLY
DELICIOUS.

Preheat oven to 350º F. Add 2 tablespoons olive oil to large frying pan. Stir-fry yellow squash, zucchini, eggplant, onion, garlic and $1/2$ teaspoon black pepper. Cook until mixture begins to soften.

Pour crushed tomatoes into medium saucepan, and stir in $1/2$ teaspoon of black pepper, rosemary, garlic powder and 1 teaspoon oregano. Simmer 10 minutes, stirring mixture occasionally.

Grease 2-quart rectangular casserole dish with 1 tablespoon olive oil. Layer bottom of greased casserole dish with $1/2$ of squash mixture. Sprinkle $1/2$ teaspoon oregano and $1/3$ cup Parmesan cheese over mixture. Top this mixture with another layer of same ingredients, finishing off with $1/3$ cup Parmesan cheese. Bake about 25 minutes.

SUGGESTED WINE:
Oliver Zinfandel

Per serving: 157 Calories; 10g Fat (54% calories from fat); 6g Protein; 13g Carbohydrate; 7mg Cholesterol; 286mg Sodium
Food Exchanges: 1/2 Lean Meat; 2 Vegetable; 1 1/2 Fat

CHUNKY GAZPACHO

FROM MARTINI & ROSSI, ITALY

Serves 4

$^1/_2$ cup red onion, diced
$^1/_2$ cup yellow peppers, diced
$^1/_2$ cup red peppers, diced
1 $^1/_2$ cups tomatoes, diced
$^1/_3$ cup Martini & Rossi
   Extra Dry Vermouth
1 cup tomato or V8 juice
$^1/_4$ cup cilantro, chopped
$^1/_2$ tablespoon Worcestershire sauce
$^1/_2$ tablespoon diced jalapeno pepper
$^1/_2$ cup diced avocado

Combine all ingredients and chill at least 2 hours.

Serve chilled.

SUGGESTED WINE:
Martini & Rossi Prosecco

Per serving: 117 Calories; 5g Fat (42% calories from fat); 2g Protein; 13g Carbohydrate; 0mg Cholesterol; 255mg Sodium
Food Exchanges: 1 1/2 Vegetable; 1 Fat

NOTES:
THE JALAPENO PEPPER GIVES THIS SOUP AN EXTRA KICK.

EGGPLANT CAPONATA MIX

FROM TABOR HILL WINERY, MICHIGAN

Serves 8

2 teaspoons garlic, minced
$1/3$ cup fresh mushrooms, sliced
$1/3$ cup yellow squash, diced
$1/3$ cup zucchini, diced
1 tablespoon olive oil
$3/4$ cup fresh tomatoes, diced
$3/4$ cup artichoke hearts, coarsely chopped
$1/8$ cup roasted red peppers, diced
$1/4$ cup kalamata black olives, chopped
1 teaspoon fresh parsley, chopped
1 teaspoon fresh basil, chopped
1 teaspoon crushed capers
$1/8$ teaspoon red pepper flakes
fresh ground black pepper to taste
$1/2$ teaspoon kosher salt
1 tablespoon balsamic vinegar
$1/4$ cup Tabor Hill Cabernet Franc
1 medium eggplant, roasted and
   coarsely chopped

Sauté garlic, mushrooms, squash and zucchini in olive oil. When just translucent, add rest of ingredients except eggplant. Simmer until thickened. Add eggplant and mix well.

Place on serving platter and drizzle with extra virgin olive oil.

Makes approximately 1 quart.

■

SUGGESTED WINE:
Tabor Hill Cabernet Franc

Per serving: 57 Calories; 2g Fat (37% calories from fat); 2g Protein; 8g Carbohydrate; 0mg Cholesterol; 181mg Sodium
Food Exchanges: 1 1/2 Vegetable; 1/2 Fat

NOTES:
A FLAVORFUL VEGETABLE WHEN SERVED WARM ON A PLATTER WITH A GOOD GOAT CHEESE AND TOASTED OR GRILLED BREAD.

GRILLED MARINATED VEGETABLE KABOBS

FROM MARTINI & ROSSI, ITALY

Serves 4

$1/_2$ cup Martini & Rossi Rosso
  Sweet Vermouth
$1/_4$ cup extra virgin olive oil,
  or more if needed
2 tablespoons garlic, chopped
1 tablespoon fresh basil, chopped
1 tablespoon fresh oregano, chopped
1 teaspoon salt
$1/_2$ teaspoon cracked black pepper
1 medium zucchini,
  cut into $1/_2$-inch thick slices
1 medium yellow squash,
  cut into $1/_2$-inch thick slices
$1/_2$ medium eggplant, cut in 1-inch cubes
1 large red bell pepper, cut in 1-inch cubes
1 large yellow pepper, cut in 1-inch cubes

In large bowl, combine vermouth, olive oil, garlic, basil, oregano, salt and pepper. Add vegetables and toss to coat. Cover and refrigerate at least 4 hours.

Prepare grill. Thread vegetables onto skewers. Grill until tender, about 10 minutes.

Serve with a side of vine-ripe tomato salsa.

■

SUGGESTED WINE:
Martini & Rossi Prosecco

Per serving: 235 Calories; 14g Fat (59% calories from fat); 3g Protein; 19g Carbohydrate; 0mg Cholesterol; 543mg Sodium
Food Exchanges: 3 Vegetable; 2 1/2 Fat

NOTES:
A PERFECT COMPANION FOR YOUR
GRILLED STEAK AND A BOTTLE OF WINE.

HEIRLOOM TOMATO GAZPACHO

FROM JUSTIN VINEYARDS, CALIFORNIA
EXECUTIVE CHEF RYAN SWARTHOUT

Serves 8

1 slice bread, crust removed
1 clove garlic, peeled
1 whole shallot, peeled
2 teaspoons salt
1 teaspoon sugar
2 tablespoons balsamic vinegar
$^1/_2$ teaspoon ground cumin
2 pounds tomatoes, cored, quartered
  and divided
2 cups extra virgin olive oil
1 cup Chardonnay, reduced to $^1/_4$ cup

Cut crustless bread into large cubes. Soak bread in about $^1/_2$ cup water 1 minute, then squeeze dry and discard soaking water.

NOTES:
THIS IS A PERFECT WARM WEATHER VEGETARIAN SOUP WITH EXQUISITE FLAVOR AND DEPTH. BE SURE TO CHOOSE TOP QUALITY, RIPE HEIRLOOM TOMATOES FOR FULL FLAVOR.

In food processor, combine bread, garlic, shallot, salt, sugar, vinegar, cumin and 1 pound tomatoes. Puree.

While food processor is running, add remaining 1 pound tomatoes and continue pureeing. Slowly drizzle in olive oil in steady stream and blend until smooth, about 1 minute. Strain soup through fine sieve into bowl. Push solids through strainer firmly and discard any leftovers. Taste for seasoning and adjust with salt and pepper if necessary. Add wine reduction after it has cooled. Serve immediately or refrigerate for later.

CHIVE OIL — OPTIONAL GARNISH:
2 cups olive oil
1 bunch of chives

Place both ingredients in blender and puree 2 minutes. Strain pureed oil and drizzle over top of finished soup just before serving.

■

SUGGESTED WINE:
Justin Chardonnay

Per serving: 523 Calories; 54g Fat (92% calories from fat); 1g Protein; 10g Carbohydrate; 0mg Cholesterol; 568mg Sodium
Food Exchanges: 1 Vegetable; 11 Fat

MOREL MUSHROOM & ASPARAGUS TART WITH BLACK PEPPERCORN CREAM

FROM PINE RIDGE WINERY, CALIFORNIA, CHEF ERIC MACZKO

Serves 4

2 pieces puff pastry sheet
1 bunch asparagus
1 pint heavy cream
2 tablespoons whole black peppercorns
6 ounces morels or 2 ounces dried
2 tablespoons unsalted butter
kosher salt as needed
cracked black pepper as needed
1 tablespoon thyme, chopped and divided
1 teaspoon tarragon, chopped
1 large egg yolk, mix with 1 tablespoon water
4 ounces Gruyère cheese, grated
1 tablespoon parsley, whole leaves

NOTES:
MOREL MUSHROOMS ARE A FORAGER'S DELICACY IN SPRING AND FANTASTIC IN THIS CHEF'S RECIPE.

Preheat oven to 375º F. Allow puff pastry dough to come up to room temperature for 20 minutes prior to rolling out. On lightly floured work surface, roll dough lightly to form approximately 8-x10-inch sheets. Cut into four 5-inch circles, reserving remaining dough for another use. Puncture each tart 3 or 4 times with fork. Double over outside edge to form raised $1/2$-inch crust. Chill on parchment-lined sheet pan.

Blanch asparagus in 4-quart saucepot of boiling salted water until tender (3 minutes). Shock asparagus immediately in ice water. Dry on paper towels. Cut off tips and reserve. Dice remaining stems and reserve separately.

Steep heavy cream and whole black peppercorns 10 minutes. Do not boil.

Lightly brush away any dirt from morels. (If using dried mushrooms soak in hot water or hot mushroom stock 15 to 30 minutes. Remove and reserve soaking liquid.) Sauté mushrooms lightly in butter until tender. Season with salt and pepper, half of thyme and tarragon. Strain heavy cream through fine mesh strainer over mushrooms. Simmer and reduce by $1/4$.

Brush puff pastry rounds with egg wash.

Continued on next page

Bake 15 to 20 minutes, until lightly browned and gently raised. If under-cooked bake an additional 5 minutes.

To assemble: Spoon mushrooms and cream into center of tarts. Arrange asparagus tips upright in a circle around mushrooms. Place diced stems in middle and sprinkle with Gruyère. Bake an additional 8 minutes until cheese is melted and golden. Remove from oven and garnish with remaining herbs. Plate and serve immediately.

SUGGESTED WINE:
Pine Ridge Crimson Creek Merlot

Per serving (excluding unknown items): 1101 Calories; 85g Fat (68% calories from fat); 14g Protein; 77g Carbohydrate; 233mg Cholesterol; 457mg Sodium
Food Exchanges: 4 1/2 Starch/Bread; 1/2 Vegetable; 1/2 Non-Fat Milk; 17 Fat

RED WINE-GLAZED PEARL ONIONS

FROM DUCK POND CELLARS, OREGON

Serves 4

30 pearl onions, red or white
3 tablespoons butter
$1/3$ cup Duck Pond Merlot
$1/8$ teaspoon dried thyme
salt and pepper to taste

Preheat oven to 450º F.

Blanch onions in boiling water 2 to 3 minutes. Drain and peel, removing tough stem ends.

Melt butter in large ovenproof skillet over medium heat. Add onions and sauté until golden, about 12 minutes. Stir in wine and thyme.

Transfer skillet to oven and cook until onions are tender and glazed, stirring occasionally, about 10 to 15 minutes. Season to taste with salt and pepper. Transfer to bowl and serve.

SUGGESTED WINE:
Duck Pond Merlot

Per serving: 264 Calories; 9g Fat (32% calories from fat); 6g Protein; 40g Carbohydrate; 23mg Cholesterol; 1599mg Sodium
Food Exchanges: 7 1/2 Vegetable; 1 1/2 Fat

NOTES:
A SUPER SIMPLE RECIPE THAT IS SURPRISINGLY DELICIOUS AND A FAVORITE AT FAMILY GATHERINGS.

ROASTED ROOT VEGETABLES

FROM PINE RIDGE WINERY, CALIFORNIA
CHEF ERIC MACZKO

Serves 6

5 parsnips, peeled and diced
2 turnips, peeled and diced
3 carrots, peeled and diced
salt and pepper to taste
2 tablespoons vegetable oil as needed
2 tablespoons sage

Toss diced root vegetables with salt and pepper and oil.

Roast root vegetables in roasting pan or sheet tray 45 minutes to an hour, stirring periodically, until all vegetables are soft and sweetly roasted. Toss sage into vegetables. Cover with aluminum foil and keep warm in oven until ready to serve.

NOTES:
THESE VEGGIES ARE GREAT WITH BRAISED PORK OR BEEF.

SUGGESTED WINE:
Pine Ridge Rutherford Cabernet Sauvignon

Per serving: 154 Calories; 5g Fat (28% calories from fat); 2g Protein; 27g Carbohydrate; 0mg Cholesterol; 55mg Sodium
Food Exchanges: 4 1/2 Vegetable; 1 Fat

TRUFFLED MUSHROOM AND ARUGULA RAGU

FROM BYINGTON VINEYARD & WINERY, CALIFORNIA

Serves 4

1 tablespoon butter
1 tablespoon garlic, minced
4 medium shallots, sliced
4 cups fresh mushrooms,
   assorted 1-inch pieces
salt and pepper to taste
1 cup Santa Cruz Mountains
   Cabernet Sauvignon
2 cups beef stock
1 tablespoon fresh thyme leaves
15 ounces canned tomatoes, peeled
   and chopped
2 cups arugula, chiffonade
dash white truffle oil

In medium saucepan, melt butter and sauté garlic and shallots. Add mushrooms and sauté; season with salt and pepper.

Deglaze with red wine and reduce liquid by 80 percent.

Add stock and thyme, then simmer 15 to 20 minutes.

Add tomatoes and adjust seasoning. Right before serving, add arugula and white truffle oil.

SUGGESTED WINE:
Byington Santa Cruz Mountains Cabernet Sauvignon

Per serving: 142 Calories; 4g Fat (30% calories from fat); 4g Protein; 15g Carbohydrate; 8mg Cholesterol; 1364mg Sodium
Food Exchanges: 2 1/2 Vegetable; 1/2 Fat

NOTES:
SERVE ALONGSIDE YOUR FAVORITE GRILLED STEAK OR ON A BED OF SHORT NOODLES SUCH AS PENNE OR FARFALLE.

VEGETARIAN PASTA TERRINE

FROM CEDAR MOUNTAIN WINERY, CALIFORNIA

Serves 12

CARROT MIXTURE:
1 pound carrots
1 tablespoon butter
salt and pepper to taste
$1/2$ teaspoon fresh tarragon, minced

BROCCOLI MIXTURE:
1 bunch fresh broccoli
4 quarts water, rapidly boiling
2 tablespoons butter, melted

RED BELL PEPPER MIXTURE:
4 medium red bell peppers
1 tablespoon butter

CUSTARD MIXTURE:
1 cup cream cheese
6 large eggs
1 cup milk
salt and pepper to taste
dash nutmeg

2 cups Swiss cheese, shredded and divided
1 pound lasagna noodles

CARROT MIXTURE:
Trim and peel carrots; cut into julienne sticks the size of toothpicks. Sauté carrots in 1 tablespoon butter until just tender. Do not overcook. Season with salt, pepper and tarragon.

BROCCOLI MIXTURE:
Trim and wash broccoli. Cut off flowerets. Peel tough part of stems until white flesh shows. Cut stems in 2-inch lengths. Drop peeled broccoli stems and flowerets into 4 quarts of rapidly boiling water and boil uncovered about 3 minutes, or until just barely tender. Drain immediately. Chop into $1/4$-inch pieces. Toss in 2 tablespoons melted butter and set aside.

RED BELL PEPPER MIXTURE:
Seed red bell peppers and chop into $1/4$-inch pieces. Sauté in 1 tablespoon butter until peppers are just barely tender.

CUSTARD MIXTURE:
In food processor or blender, combine cream cheese, eggs, milk, salt, pepper and nutmeg. Process until smooth.

Cook lasagna noodles according to directions on package.

Continued on next page

Lightly butter bottom and sides of 9x5x3-inch loaf pan. Arrange layer of lasagna noodles so they cover bottom of pan and overhang sides by 3 inches all around pan. Spread $1/3$ of grated Swiss cheese in bottom of pan, cover with carrot mixture and press into place. Add just enough of custard mixture to come to the level of carrots. Arrange layer of lasagna noodles on top of carrots. Spread $1/3$ of Swiss cheese on noodles, cover with broccoli mixture and press into place. Add just enough custard mixture to come to level of broccoli. Arrange layer of lasagna noodles on top of broccoli. Spread remaining Swiss cheese on noodles, cover with red bell pepper mixture and press into

place. Add just enough custard mixture to come to level of peppers. Fold noodles that were hanging over edges of pan to cover pepper layer. Lightly butter noodles. Place layer of aluminum foil lightly over terrine.

Preheat oven to 350° F. Bake on lower middle rack with drip pan below in case terrine overflows during baking. After about 1 hour, increase temperature to 400° F. Insert meat thermometer into middle of terrine and continue baking until thermometer reads 165° F.

Remove from oven and let rest at room temperature about 15 minutes. Run thin-bladed knife around inside of pan and unmold onto platter. Serve warm or cold. Serves 8 as a vegetable course or 12 as an appetizer.

NOTES:
COLORFUL AND DELICIOUS AS A VEGETABLE COURSE OR APPETIZER.

SUGGESTED WINE:
Cedar Mountain Estate Chardonnay

Per serving: 400 Calories; 21g Fat (48% calories from fat); 16g Protein; 36g Carbohydrate; 164mg Cholesterol; 221mg Sodium
Food Exchanges: 2 Starch/Bread; 1 1/2 Lean Meat; 1 Vegetable; 3 1/2 Fat

VIDAL ASPARAGUS WITH LEMON HERB SAUCE

FROM CEDAR CREEK WINERY, WISCONSIN

Serves 6

1 cup Cedar Creek Vidal Blanc
2 cups low-sodium chicken broth
1 1/2 pounds thin asparagus spears, trimmed
2 tablespoons extra virgin olive oil, divided
1 1/4 cups green onions, chopped, divided
1/3 cup shallots, minced
1 teaspoon sugar
1 tablespoon garlic, minced
1 1/2 tablespoons Dijon mustard
1 tablespoon fresh lemon juice
1 teaspoon fresh thyme, minced
1/2 teaspoon lemon rind, grated (zest)
1/2 cup red bell pepper, seeded and diced

NOTES:
VEGGIES NEVER TASTED SO GOOD. IT'S DELICIOUS AND HEALTHY EATING.

Bring wine and broth to a boil in large pot. Add asparagus; cook until crisp-tender, about 4 minutes. Using tongs, transfer asparagus to large bowl of ice water. Reserve 1 cup broth/wine in small bowl. Drain asparagus; pat dry.

Heat 1 tablespoon oil in medium nonstick skillet over medium heat. Add 1 cup green onions, shallots and sugar. Sauté until onions and shallots are tender, about 5 minutes. Add garlic and sauté 2 minutes. Stir in reserved broth/wine, 1 tablespoon oil, mustard, lemon juice, thyme and lemon zest. Simmer until slightly thickened and liquid is reduced to 1 1/4 cups, about 5 minutes.

Season with salt and pepper. Cool to room temperature.

Arrange asparagus on platter. Spoon sauce over asparagus. Sprinkle with red bell peppers and remaining 1/4 cup green onions.

■

SUGGESTED WINE:
Cedar Creek Vidal Blanc

Per serving: 122 Calories; 5g Fat (42% calories from fat); 6g Protein; 9g Carbohydrate; 0mg Cholesterol; 226mg Sodium
Food Exchanges: 1/2 Lean Meat; 1 1/2 Vegetable; 1 Fat

NOTES:

NOTES:

GOLD MEDAL CONTRIBUTING WINERIES

ALBA VINEYARD
269 ROUTE 627
MILFORD, NJ 08848
WWW.ALBAVINEYARD.COM

BARGETTO WINERY
3535 NORTH MAIN ST.
SOQUEL, CA 95073
WWW.BARGETTO.COM

BARTON & GUSTIER
1200 JEFFERSON ST.
NAPA, CA 94559

BEAULIEU VINEYARD
1200 JEFFERSON ST.
NAPA, CA 94559

BRASSFIELD ESTATE VINEYARD
PO BOX 1661
10915 HIGH VALLEY RD.
CLEARLAKE OAKS, CA 95423
WWW.BRASSFIELDESTATE.COM

BYINGTON VINEYARD & WINERY
21850 BEAR CREEK RD.
LOS GATOS, CA 95033
WWW.BYINGTON.COM

CAMARADERIE CELLARS
334 BENSON RD.
PORT ANGELES, WA 98363
WWW.CAMARADERIECELLARS.COM

CEDAR CREEK WINERY
N 70 W 6340 BRIDGE RD.
CEDARBURG, WI 53012
WWW.CEDARCREEKWINERY.COM

CEDAR MOUNTAIN WINERY
7000 TESLA RD.
LIVERMORE, CA 94550
WWW.WINES.COM/CEDARMOUNTAIN

CHATEAU CHANTAL
15900 RUE DE VIN
TRAVERSE CITY, MI 49686
WWW.CHATEAUCHANTAL.COM

CITRA/PALM BAY IMPORTS
313 UNDERHILL BLVD.
SYOSSET, NY 11791
WWW.PALMBAYIMPORTS.COM

CONCANNON VINEYARD
4590 TESLA RD.
LIVERMORE, CA 94550
WWW.CONCANNONVINEYARD.COM

CROWN VALLEY WINERY
23589 ST. RT WW
STE GENEVIEVE, MO 63670
WWW.CROWNVALLEYWINERY.COM

DEBONNE VINEYARDS
7743 DOTY RD.
MADISON, OH 44057
WWW.DEBONNE.COM

**DR. KONSTANTIN FRANK
VINIFERA WINE CELLARS**
9749 MIDDLE RD.
HAMMONDSPORT, NY 14840
WWW.DRFRANKWINES.COM

DUCK POND CELLARS
PO BOX 429
23145 HWY 99 WEST
DUNDEE, OR 97115
WWW.DUCKPONDCELLARS.COM

EAST VALLEY VINEYARDS
4960 BASELINE AVE.
SANTA YNEZ, CA 93460

EOS ESTATE WINERY
5625 HWY 46 EAST
PASO ROBLES, CA 93446
WWW.EOSVINTAGE.COM

FENN VALLEY VINEYARDS, INC.
6130 122ND AVE.
FENNVILLE, MI 49408
WWW.FENNVALLEY.COM

FIRELANDS WINE CO.
917 BARDSHAR RD.
SANDUSKY, OH 44870
WWW.FIRELANDSWINERY.COM

GRAY GHOST VINEYARDS
14706 LEE HIGHWAY
AMISSVILLE, VA 20106
WWW.GRAYGHOSTVINEYARDS.COM

HARMONY CELLARS
3255 HARMONY VALLEY RD.
HARMONY, CA 93435
WWW.HARMONYCELLARS.COM

HOSMER WINERY
6999 ROUTE 89
OVID, NY 14521
WWW.HOSMERWINERY.COM

JANKRIS WINERY
1266 BETHEL RD.
TEMPLETON, CA 93465
WWW.JANKRISWINERY.COM

JUSTIN VINEYARDS & WINERY
11680 CHIMNEY ROCK RD.
PASO ROBLES, CA   93446
WWW.JUSTINWINE.COM

KENWOOD VINEYARDS
9592 SONOMA HIGHWAY
KENWOOD, CA   95452
WWW.KENWOODVINEYARDS.COM

KING ESTATE WINERY, INC,
80854 TERRITORIAL RD.
EUGENE, OR   97405
WWW.KINGESTATE.COM

KOVES-NEWLAN VINEYARDS & WINERY
5225 SOLANO AVE.
NAPA, CA   94558
WWW.KOVESNEWLANWINE.COM

LAKE SONOMA WINERY
9990 DRY CREEK RD.
GEYSERVILLE, CA   95441
WWW.LAKESONOMAWINERY.COM

LAKEWOOD VINEYARDS, INC.
4024 STATE RTE 14
WATKINS GLEN, NY   14891
WWW.LAKEWOODVINEYARDS.COM

LAMOREAUX LANDING WINE CELLARS
9224 RTE 414
LODI, NY   14860
WWW.LAMOREAUXWINE.COM

LYNFRED WINERY
15 S ROSELLE RD.
ROSELLE, IL   60172
WWW.LYNFREDWINERY.COM

MAGNOTTA WINERY CORP.
271 CHRISLEA RD.
VAUGHAN ONTARIO, CANADA   L4L8N6
WWW.MAGNOTTA.COM

MARTINI & ROSSI/BACARDI USA
2100 BISCAYNE BOULEVARD
MIAMI, FL   33186
WWW.BACARDI.COM

NAVARRO VINEYARDS
PO BOX 47
5601 HWY 128
PHILO, CA   95466
WWW.NAVARROWINE.COM

OLIVER WINE CO., INC.
8024 N STATE RD 37
BLOOMINGTON, IN   47404
WWW.OLIVERWINERY.COM

PALMER VINEYARDS
108 SOUND AVE.
PO BOX 2125
AQUEBOGUE, NY   11931
WWW.PALMERVINEYARDS.COM

PEDRONCELLI WINERY
1220 CANYON RD.
GEYSERVILLE, CA   95441
WWW.PEDRONCELLI.COM

PETRONI VINEYARDS
1512 STOCKTON
SAN FRANCISCO, CA   94133
WWW.PETRONIVINEYARDS.COM

PINE RIDGE WINERY
5901 SILVERADO TRAIL
NAPA, CA   94558
WWW.PINERIDGEWINERY.COM

QUADY WINERY
13181 ROAD 24
MADERA, CA   93639
WWW.QUADYWINERY.COM

ROCKBRIDGE VINEYARD, INC.
35 HILL VIEW LANE
RAPHINE, VA   24472
WWW.ROCKBRIDGEVINEYARD.COM

RODNEY STRONG VINEYARDS
11455 OLD REDWOOD HIGHWAY
HEALDSBURG, CA   95448
WWW.RODNEYSTRONG.COM

SAKONNET VINEYARDS
BOX 197
162 W MAIN RD.
LITTLE COMPTON, RI   02837
WWW.SAKONNETWINE.COM

SEBASTIANI VINEYARDS
389 FOURTH ST EAST
SONOMA, CA   95476
WWW.SEBASTIANI.COM

SHARPE HILL VINEYARD
108 WADE RD.
PO BOX 1
POMFRET, CT   06258
WWW.SHARPEHILL.COM

SIERRA VISTA VINEYARDS & WINERY
4560 CABERNET WAY
PLACERVILLE, CA   95667
WWW.SIERRAVISTAWINERY.COM

SIX MILE CREEK VINEYARD
1551 SLATERVILLE RD.
ITHACA, NY   14850
WWW.SIXMILECREEK.COM

ST. JAMES WINERY
540 SIDNEY ST.
ST JAMES, MO   65559
WWW.STJAMESWINERY.COM

ST. JULIAN WINE COMPANY
716 S KALAMAZOO ST.
PAW PAW, MI   49079
WWW.STJULIAN.COM

STERLING VINEYARDS
1200 JEFFERSON ST.
NAPA, CA   94559
WWW.STERLINGVINEYARDS.COM

STONE HILL WINERY
1110 STONE HILL HWY
HERMANN, MO   65041
WWW.STONEHILLWINERY.COM

TABOR HILL WINERY
185 MT TABOR RD.
BUCHANAN, MI   49107
WWW.TABORHILL.COM

TOMASELLO WINERY
225 WHITE HORSE PIKE
HAMMONTON, NJ   08037
WWW.TOMASELLOWINERY.COM

TRENTADUE WINERY
19170 GEYSERVILLE AVE.
GEYSERVILLE, CA   95441
WWW.TRENTADUE.COM

UNIONVILLE VINEYARDS
9 ROCKTOWN RD.
RINGOES, NJ   08551
WWW.UNIONVILLEVINEYARDS.COM

VALLEY OF THE MOON WINERY
13250 RIVER RD.
GUERNEVILLE, CA   95446
WWW.VALLEYOFTHEMOONWINERY.COM

VON STIEHL WINERY
115 NAVARINO ST.
ALGOMA, WI   54201
WWW.VONSTIEHL.COM

WENTE FAMILY ESTATES
5565 TESLA RD.
LIVERMORE, CA 94550
WWW.WENTEVINEYARDS.COM

WINDSOR VINEYARDS
9600 BELL RD.
WINDSOR, CA 95492
WWW.WINDSORVINEYARDS.COM

ZD WINERY
8383 SILVERADO TRAIL
NAPA, CA 94558
WWW.ZDWINES.COM

NOTES:

FOOD AND WINE PAIRINGS

Experiment on your own with different foods and sauces. You'll be amazed at the different taste sensations that can be created by changing the wine companion. To get started, here are some suggested match-ups from Tasters Guild.

FOOD	SUGGESTED WINES TO TRY
Appetizers	
Dips & Canapés	Riesling, Sauvignon Blanc, Dry Chenin Blanc, Prosecco
Paté	Chilled Dry Sherry, Alsatian Pinot Gris, Fumé Blanc
Shellfish	Chablis, Chardonnay, Champagne, Pinot Blanc
Caviar	Brut Champagne (the classic pairing is iced Vodka)
Fish	
Freshwater Fish	Unwooded Chardonnay, Pinot Gris/Grigio, Sauvignon Blanc, Seyval Blanc, Proprietary Dry White Wines
Seafood (salmon, tuna, etc.)	Chardonnay, Viognier, French White or Red Burgundies
Grilled or Highly Seasoned	Reserve Chardonnay, Pinot Noir, Côtes du Rhone
Shellfish course	Riesling, Sauvignon Blanc, Muscadet, Semillon
Poultry	
Barbecue Chicken	Dry Rosé, Pinot Noir, Gamay, Beaujolais Villages, Dolcetto
Roasted Chicken or Turkey	Riesling, Chenin Blanc, Blush/Rosé, Beaujolais, Prosecco
Fried Chicken	Riesling, Semillon, Sauvignon Blanc, Pinot Blanc
For Basting Chicken or Ham	Gewürztraminer, Cherry Wine, other fruit wines
For Marinating Chicken	Sauvignon Blanc, Pinot Grigio/Gris, Dry Riesling
Roasted Game Birds	Syrah/Shiraz, Pinot Noir, Zinfandel
Duck or Goose	Mature Cabernet Sauvignon, Chateauneuf du Pape

Meats

Game Meat	Petite Sirah, Shiraz/Syrah, Barolo, Barbaresco
Grilled Beef Steak	Shiraz/Syrah, Malbec, Cabernet Sauvignon, Petite Sirah, Sangiovese
For Marinating Beef	An inexpensive dry, red wine
Roast Beef	Merlot, Cabernet Franc, Pinot Noir, Malbec
Stew or Casserole	Zinfandel, Shiraz/Syrah, Barbera, Burgundy-style wines
Broiled Veal	Valpolicella, Beaujolais, Pinot Noir, Merlot, Chianti Classico
Sautéed Veal	Vouvray, Pinot Gris/Grigio, Soave, Dry Riesling, Prosecco
Sausage and Cold Cuts	Riesling, Proprietary Dry White Wines, Dry Rosé, Malbec
Pork Roast or Chops	Chilean Merlot, French Beaujolais, Pinot Noir
Barbecue Ribs	Dry Rosé, Pinot Noir, Gamay, Beaujolais Villages
Ham	Gewürztraminer, Vouvray, Riesling, Blush wines
Lamb	Cabernet Sauvignon, Chambourcin, Spanish Rioja

Desserts

Cheesecake	Fruit (other than grape) wines, German Auslese, Late Harvest Riesling or Vidal, Sauternes, Cream Sherry
Chocolate	Port and Port-style wines, Zinfandel, Orange Muscat
Fresh Fruits	Riesling, Gewürztraminer, sparkling wines, Sauternes
Pastries	Canadian Ice Wine, Sauternes, German Auslese, Asti Spumante
Soufflé	Champagne, Vouvray, Late Harvest wines

Miscellaneous

Asian Dishes	Riesling, Gewürztraminer, Sparkling wines, Pinot Blanc, Pinot Noir
Blue Cheese	Sauternes and most fortified wines like port
Grilled or Sautéed Vegetables	Valpolicella, Merlot, Shiraz/Syrah, Tempranillo
Pasta with White Sauce	Pinot Gris/Grigio, Soave, Frascatti, Gavi
Pasta with Tomato Base	Zinfandel or any Italian red wine
Pizza	Chilled Beaujolais, Vin de Pays Rouge or Blush/Rosé
Sushi	Sauvignon Blanc, Pinot Blanc, Champagne

WINE BOTTLE SIZES

Miniature	100 ml	3.4 oz.
Split	187 ml	6.3 oz.
Half-bottle	375 ml	12.7 oz.
500 milliliter	500 ml	16.9 oz.
Standard Wine Bottle	750 ml	25.4 oz.
One liter	1 liter	33.8 oz.
Magnum	1.5 liter	50.7 oz.
Double Magnum of Table Wine	3.0 liter	101.5 oz.
Jeroboam of Champagne	3.0 liter	101.5 oz.
Rehoboam of Champagne	4.5 liters	152.2 oz.
Jeroboam of Table Wine	4.5 liters	152.2 oz.
Methuselah of Champagne	6.0 liters	202.9 oz.
Imperial of Table Wine	6.0 liters	202.9 oz.
Salmanazar	9.0 liters	304.4 oz.
Balthazar	12.0 liters	405.8 oz.
Nebuchadnezzar	15.0 liters	507.3 oz.

U.S. MEASUREMENT EQUIVALENTS

Pinch/dash	=	$1/16$ teaspoon
$1/2$ teaspoon	=	30 drops
1 teaspoon	=	$1/3$ tablespoon
3 teaspoons	=	1 tablespoon
$1/2$ tablespoon	=	$1 \, 1/2$ teaspoons
1 tablespoon	=	$1/2$ fluid ounce
2 tablespoons	=	1 fluid ounce; $1/8$ cup
3 tablespoons	=	$1 \, 1/2$ fluid ounces
4 tablespoons	=	$1/4$ cup; 2 fluid ounces
8 tablespoons	=	$1/2$ cup; 4 fluid ounces
$1/4$ cup	=	4 tablespoons; 2 fluid ounces
$1/3$ cup	=	5 tablespoons + 1 teaspoon
$1/2$ cup	=	8 tablespoons; 4 fluid ounces
$2/3$ cup	=	10 tablespoons + 2 teaspoons
$3/4$ cup	=	12 tablespoons; 6 fluid ounces
1 cup	=	16 tablespoons; $1/2$ pint; 8 fluid ounces
2 cups	=	1 pint; 16 fluid ounces
4 cups	=	1 quart; 32 fluid ounces
1 quart	=	2 pints; 4 cups; 32 fluid ounces
4 quarts	=	1 gallon; 8 pints
1 gallon	=	4 quarts; 8 pints; 16 cups; 128 ounces
8 quarts	=	1 peck
4 pecks	=	1 bushel

INGREDIENT YIELDS AND EQUIVALENTS

Anchovies	2 oz. can	= 10 to 12 anchovies
	1 filet	= $1/2$ teaspoon anchovy paste
Anchovy Paste	2 oz. tube	= 4 tablespoons
Apples	3 medium or 1 lb.	= 3 cups pared and sliced
Avocado	1 medium	= 1 cup cubed
Bay Leaf	1 whole leaf	= $1/4$ teaspoon crushed
Bananas	4 medium or 1 lb.	= $1\ 3/4$ cups mashed
	1 medium	= $3/4$ cup sliced
Bacon	1 pound, cooked	= $1\ 1/2$ cups crumbled
	1 slice, cooked	= 1 tablespoon crumbled
Bell Peppers	1 large or 6 oz.	= 1 cup diced
Blueberries, fresh	1 pint basket	= 2 cups
Blue Cheese	4 ounces	= 1 cup crumbled
Bread Crumbs, dry	1 slice of dried bread	= $1/3$ cup dry bread crumbs
Bread Crumbs, soft	1 slice of fresh bread	= $1/2$ cup soft bread crumbs
Brown Rice	2 cups uncooked	= $6\ 1/4$ cups cooked
Brown Sugar, packed	1 pound	= $2\ 1/4$ cups
Butter	$1/8$ stick or $1/2$ oz.	= 1 tablespoon
	$1/4$ stick or 1 oz.	= 2 tablespoons
	1 stick or $1/4$ lb.	= 8 tablespoons or $1/2$ cup
	4 sticks or 1 lb.	= 2 cups
Butter, whipped	1 lb. or 6 sticks	= 3 cups
Carrots	1 lb.	= 3 cups shredded
		= $2\ 1/2$ cups diced
Caviar	1 ounce	= 1 heaping tablespoon
Celery	1 stalk	= $3/4$ cup diced
	1 lb. bunch	= $2\ 3/4$ cups diced
Cheddar Cheese	4 oz. or $1/4$ lb.	= 1 cup shredded
Cheese, dry (Parmesan)	3 oz. chunk	= 1 cup grated

Cheese, soft (Mozzarella)	4 oz. or $1/4$ lb.	= 1 cup shredded
Chicken	3 $1/2$ pounds	= 2 cups cooked and diced
Chocolate Chips	6 oz.	= 1 cup
Confectioners' Sugar	1 lb.	= 3 $1/2$ cups unsifted
		= 4 $1/2$ cups sifted
Corn	6 ears	= 3 cups kernels
	10 oz. frozen kernels	= 2 cups cooked
Cornmeal	1 cup uncooked	= 4 cups cooked
Cottage Cheese	$1/2$ pound	= 1 cup
Crackers	22 crackers	= 1 cup crumbs
Cream Cheese	1 oz.	= 2 tablespoons
Eggs	Extra Large	= 4 eggs = 1 cup
	Large	= 5 eggs = 1 cup
	Medium	= 6 eggs = 1 cup
Egg Yolks	Extra Large	= 10 yolks = 1 cup
	Large	= 12 yolks = 1 cup
	Medium	= 14 yolks = 1 cup
Eggplant	1 pound	= 3 cups chopped
Flour, all-purpose	1 pound	= 4 cups sifted
		= 3 $1/2$ cups unsifted
Frozen Vegetables	10 oz. package	= 2 cups
	16 oz. package	= 3 cups
Fruit, processed	15 oz. can	= 1 $1/3$ cups, drained
	16 oz. frozen	= 1 $1/4$ cups
Garlic	1 large clove	= 1 teaspoon minced
	1 medium clove	= $3/4$ teaspoon minced
		= $1/8$ teaspoon garlic powder
Grapes	1 pound	= 2 $1/2$ cups
Ham	$1/2$ lb. boneless	= 1 $1/3$ cups

Herbs	$1/2$ teaspoon dried	= 1 tablespoon fresh minced
Honey	1 lb.	= 1 $1/3$ cups
Ketchup	16 oz. bottle	= 1 $2/3$ cups
Lard	1 pound	= 2 cups
Lemon	1 whole	= 3 tablespoons juice
		= 2 teaspoons grated rind
Lime	1 whole	= 2 tablespoons juice
		= 1 teaspoon grated rind
Milk, dry	$1/4$ cup dry	= 1 cup reconstituted
Mustard	1 teaspoon dry	= 1 tablespoon prepared
Mushrooms	1 pound fresh	= 4 cups chopped
	6 oz. canned, drained	= 1 cup or $1/2$ lb. fresh
	3 oz. dried	= 1 lb. fresh
Onions	1 pound	= 3 large
	1 large	= 1 cup chopped
Onions, green	5 white bulbs only	= $1/2$ cup chopped
	5 with green stalks	= 1 $3/4$ cups chopped
Orange	1 medium	= 6 tablespoon juice
		= 3/4 cup sections
		= 2 tablespoons grated rind
Pasta	1 cup uncooked	= 1 $3/4$ cup cooked
Peaches	1 medium or $1/4$ lb.	= $1/2$ cup sliced
Popcorn	3 tablespoons	= 6 cups popped
Potatoes	1 lb. sliced or diced	= 3 $1/2$ to 4 cups raw
	3 medium or 1 lb.	= 2 $1/2$ cups cooked, sliced
		= 1 $3/4$ cups mashed
Pumpkin	1 lb. fresh	= 1 cup cooked and mashed
	15 oz. can	= 1 $3/4$ cups mashed
Raisins	15 oz. package	= 2 $1/2$ cups

Rice	1 cup or $^1/_2$ lb. dry	= 3 cups cooked
	2 cups precooked	= 2 $^2/_3$ cups cooked
Ricotta Cheese	$^1/_2$ pound	= 1 cup
Spices	$^1/_3$ teaspoon dried	= 1 tablespoon fresh
	$^1/_2$ teaspoon granules	= 1 tablespoon fresh
Spinach	1 pound fresh	= 1 $^3/_4$ cups cooked
	10 oz. frozen	= 1 $^1/_2$ cups cooked
Squash	1 lb. summer	= 3 cups sliced
	1 lb. winter	= 1 cup cooked and mashed
Sugar, granulated	1 pound	= 2 cups
Sugar, brown	1 pound	= 2 $^1/_2$ cups packed
Tofu	1 pound	= 2 $^3/_4$ cups cubes
		= 2 cups crumbled
		= 1 $^2/_3$ cups puréed
Tomato Paste	6 oz.	= $^3/_4$ cup
Tomato Sauce	8 oz.	= 1 cup
Tomatoes	1 lb. fresh	= 2 large or 4 small
		= 2 cups chopped
	16 oz. can, drained	= 1 $^1/_4$ cups
	28 oz. can, drained	= 2 cups
Vegetable Shortening	8 oz.	= 1 $^1/_8$ cups
Walnuts	1 lb. unshelled	= 1 $^3/_4$ shelled
	1 lb. shelled	= 3 $^3/_4$ cups
Wild Rice	1 cup raw	= 4 cups cooked
Yeast, active dry	1 package	= 1 tablespoon
Zucchini	1 pound	= 3 cups sliced
		= 2 $^1/_2$ cups chopped
		= 1 $^1/_2$ cups cooked

BLANCHE'S CALIFORNIA WINE DIET

(CEDAR MOUNTAIN WINERY AT BLANCHE'S VINEYARD)

This diet is designed for quick weight loss while living in our fast-paced environment. There are no substitutions and all portions must be eaten on the schedule provided. You only use this diet for four days then you can eat normally for two days. Gradually your fat thermostat will reset to a lower calorie intake making maintenance easier. If you cannot have wine at lunchtime, unflavored yogurt or a glass of low-fat milk may be substituted. Coffee and tea are optional, but caffeine will stimulate your appetite and should be used sparingly. Of course, only artificial sweetener should be used.

First Day

Breakfast: Four ounces of Cedar Mountain Sauvignon Blanc. One slice of dry wheat toast, half of grapefruit.

Lunch: Four ounces of Cedar Mountain Estate Chardonnay. One-half of a large tomato stuffed with tuna, pepper, salt, lemon juice, one tablespoon of olive oil (no mayonnaise or dressing), two celery sticks, two rye crisp crackers.

Dinner: Four ounces of Cedar Mountain Estate Chardonnay. One-half of a chicken breast sautéed in two tablespoons of olive oil and seasoned with fresh rosemary. A small salad made from butter lettuce and the other half of the tomato from lunch. More celery and carrot sticks, if desired. One, and only one, small chocolate chip cookie.

Second Day

■

Breakfast: Four ounces of Cedar Mountain Sauvignon Blanc. One slice of dry wheat toast, half a papaya with lime juice, one poached egg with Tabasco and salt.

Lunch: Four ounces of Cedar Mountain Merlot. Half an avocado filled with fresh crabmeat and seasoned with one tablespoon of olive oil and chopped parsley, salt and white pepper. For starch, add either raw zucchini, one-half cup of pesole or one-half cup couscous.

Dinner: Four ounces of Cedar Mountain Estate Cabernet Sauvignon. Roast a small, sliced new potato on a cookie tray oiled with one tablespoon of olive oil, season with pressed garlic and salt. Carefully trim the fat from one filet mignon and grill over an open flame. Remove the seeds and septum from one medium sized Anaheim chili pepper. Rub the pepper with olive oil and grill along with the filet. By this time you will need another glass of wine, but then there is no dessert. Serve the above with a butter lettuce, sliced celery and tomato salad. Use one teaspoon of Balsamic vinegar as dressing. Dessert, if you did not have the extra wine, is another cookie.

Third Day

■

Breakfast: Four ounces of Cedar Mountain Sauvignon Blanc — the bottle is almost empty by now. Sauté a fresh de-boned trout in one tablespoon of olive oil; season with lemon zest and white pepper. Serve with half of a grapefruit and dry wheat toast.

Lunch: Four ounces of Cedar Mountain Estate Chardonnay — you'll need to open a new bottle since you drank the first one. Eat the remaining half of chicken breast, cold. Make a small salad of one tomato filled with couscous seasoned with lemon zest and one tablespoon of olive oil. Serve on butter lettuce leaf.

Dinner: Four ounces of Cedar Mountain Merlot. Stuff remaining papaya half with one-half cup of chopped cooked duck breast (cook duck by roasting dry on an oven rack with skin intact). Serve on a bed of lettuce and season with a vinaigrette made of balsamic vinegar and one tablespoon of olive oil. Starch is one small croissant.

Fourth Day

■

Breakfast: Four ounces of Cedar Mountain Estate Chardonnay. Fry one egg in spray food release (e.g. PAM dry fry). Arrange fried egg on a sliced croissant spread with one tablespoon of fat-free mayonnaise. Salt and pepper to taste.

Lunch: Four ounces of Cedar Mountain Duet. Slice one leg of roasted duck. Arrange on a plate with couscous and sliced zucchini. Garnish with kalamata olives and lettuce leaf. Season with lemon zest and black pepper.

Dinner: Four ounces of Cedar Mountain Estate Chardonnay. Sauté cubes of white chicken meat in a mixture of diced celery and diced onion. Season with lime juice, curry powder, one-fourth cup coconut milk and white pepper. Construct a salad of shredded lettuce, six kalamata olives and tomato. Use vinegar and one tablespoon of olive oil for dressing. Dessert is half of papaya.

Congratulations, you have made it for four days. You should have lost many pounds and feel great. If this is not the case, then just finish off all those opened bottles of wine and try someone else's diet.

NOTES:

INDEX

WINERY RECIPE INDEX

Improve Billing and Collections

Get the Money You Deserve Now

*hc*Pro | 2O YEARS
Since 1986
THE HEALTHCARE COMPLIANCE COMPANY

Improve Billing and Collections: Get the Money You Deserve Now is published by HCPro, Inc.

Copyright 2006 HCPro, Inc.

ISBN 1-57839-778-2

HCPro provides information resources for the healthcare industry.

HCPro is not affiliated in any way with the Joint Commission on Accreditation of Healthcare Organizations, which owns the JCAHO trademark.

Natalie Goodale, Associate editor
Debra Beaulieu, Managing editor
Michele L. Wilson, Executive editor
Lauren McLeod, Group publisher
Jean St. Pierre, Director of operations
Lauren Rubenzahl, Copy editor
Michael Michaud, Bookbuilder
Patrick Campagnone, Cover designer

Advice given is general. Readers should consult professional counsel for specific legal, ethical, or clinical questions.

Arrangements can be made for quantity discounts.

For more information, contact:
HCPro
P.O. Box 1168
Marblehead, MA 01945
Telephone: 800/650-6787 or 781/639-1872
Fax: 781/639-2982
E-mail: *customerservice@hcpro.com*

Visit HCPro at its World Wide Web site: *www.hcpro.com*

04/2006
20819

Contents

Contents

Contents

Introduction

Providing patients with quality care may be your first priority, but you still need to be knowledgeable about and aware of the financial side of practicing medicine—an element that, if overlooked, could be detrimental to your practice.

But the fiscal complications and challenges of practicing medicine today likely make it difficult for you to collect the money you deserve, whether you operate in a solo practice or as a member of a group, large or small.

Why is it so difficult to get paid for your work?

Many of these difficulties are simply out of your control. For example, code changes, trends in healthcare, and alterations in legislation regarding the amount of money the government reimburses you all affect your payment. Unfortunately, you have little say about these changes.

However, you do have more control over your staff, who also can act as speed bumps in the collections process. For example, if your receptionist doesn't schedule the maximum number of appointments, and the problem goes unidentified, you could lose all-important revenue dollars.

How can you ensure you get the payment you deserve?

Owning a private practice and letting the payments for your services disappear into the black hole of the medical world doesn't make sense. You deserve to get the money you've earned. This book can help you do just that with

- organizational ideas

- tips about training staff

- charts and forms

- guidance in dealing with managed-care contracts, patients' delinquent payments, and other obstacles on the road to getting paid

Here's a look at what the book covers:

Section One: Fine-tuning the financial-management processes

To receive all appropriate reimbursement, you need an efficient, organized collections process. This section describes how to get your billing system in order, establish goals, delegate responsibilities to staff, and establish coding criteria and an auditing process.

Section Two: Collecting from patients in-office

The best way to ensure payments from patients is to collect money before patients leave the office. In this section, you'll find tips about collecting money up front, as well as arranging advance and automatic payments with credit cards. You'll also learn how to manage patient referrals and deal with the trend toward consumer-directed healthcare. Lastly, this section details how adding ancillary services may increase your practice's revenue.

Section Three: Improving collections from third-party payers

Where would you be without the money from third-party payers? Like it or not, you must monitor these payers and make sure they act appropriately in regards to your patients and their claims. This section details how to work with payers, including building relationships, appealing denied claims, and negotiating and terminating contracts.

Section Four: Collecting from patients after they leave the office

When your patients walk out the door after their appointments, you may not see them again for months or even years. You don't want it to be that long until you see a payment. If you've attempted to collect payment from patients but still haven't received any money, you may need to employ extensive collections processes such as letters and calls or use collections agencies and bankruptcy courts.

Fine-tuning the financial-management process

Chapter 1

A revenue cycle overview

Many physicians still consider reimbursement a self-contained activity for getting paid for the services they perform. But that's a shortsighted view, because reimbursement doesn't start and end when the physician finishes treating the patient, warns consultant Max Reiboldt, CPA. You'll be better served—and better paid—to think of reimbursement as part of a larger revenue cycle.

Reiboldt, managing partner and CEO of the Alpharetta, GA–based physician-services firm The Coker Group, suggests treating the revenue cycle as an assembly-line process: Starting with appointment scheduling and working through to collection, if any part breaks down, you stand to lose revenue. The revenue cycle includes the following four major components:

1. Appointment scheduling. The more patients you see, the more revenue you will earn. But this positive effect cannot happen without a well-trained front-desk staff filling your schedule appropriately.

Reiboldt tells the story of a solo practitioner who couldn't figure out why he wasn't productive—until his scheduler went on vacation. It turns out the scheduler didn't fill appointment gaps or offer available slots to incoming callers. The temporary fill-in did exactly that, and the doctor started seeing more patients.

There are three types of appointment scheduling:

- **Wave scheduling.** Using this model, you schedule two, three, or more patients on the hour, half-hour, or both. You then see the patients scheduled for each block of time in the order of their arrival.

- **Modified wave scheduling.** With this technique, you schedule a cluster of patients at the beginning of each hour, and schedule individual appointments every 10, 15, or 20 minutes during the rest of the hour.

Wave or modified wave methods work well for primary care practices in which physicians see many patients for short visits. You will always have patients to see. For example, if one of two or three patients scheduled for 9:00 a.m. is late, you likely will have another patient waiting. Also, with these scheduling techniques, your staff can prep and take vitals of one patient while you treat another. This adjustment can greatly improve the flow of your practice.

- **Stream scheduling.** With this type of scheduling, each patient has a definite appointment time, which allows you to plan your day. However, late patients or no-shows can disrupt the flow of work with this scheduling pattern. Therefore, confirm appointments ahead of time, especially those that you expect to be lengthy.

2. Registration. Maximizing revenue and reimbursement speed requires collecting the right information from every patient. Make sure your front desk rigorously collects and verifies insurance data and obtains required preauthorizations from health plans.

3. Clean claims. Properly handling the so-called "traditional" reimbursement steps goes a long way toward prompt, maximum payment. A breakdown in any of the following will affect whether and when you get paid:

- Coding

- Capturing charges

- Collecting from self-pay patients up front

- Posting payments

- Filing claims

Many different people at your practice work on these tasks (e.g., the physicians and coders do the coding, the front-desk staff collect patient pays, etc.), so it's essential that you audit the process required to produce a clean claim. Everyone on the "assembly line" must do his or her job correctly. Stress physician coding and provide training if those skills aren't up to par. Top-notch coding not only avoids payment delays, but it often enhances revenue.

4. Account followup. If only it were as simple as filing a claim and getting paid for it, no practice would face financial trouble. Carriers reject claims for many reasons. Make sure that your manager and staff investigate claim denials and appeal or refile them as necessary.

Create your internal process

In the face of managed care, dwindling reimbursement levels, and skyrocketing malpractice premiums, remaining profitable while still practicing top-notch medicine depends largely on your commitment to taking firm control of all billing and collection activities. But problems in any one area of the revenue cycle—which inevitably influence the other areas—start with your practice's internal collections process.

To manage this complicated area effectively and efficiently, you must establish procedures, create a team, educate your patients, review the payments you receive, and track your performance regularly.

Establish procedures
The first step begins with understanding what every piece of the billing and collections process entails and why the process involves the entire staff. Every member of this team—whether one or two staffers or an entire department—must perform well to ensure satisfactory cash flow. Bottlenecks or miscommunication in one area can clog the entire process.

For example, procedures should include how to effectively

- ask for and receive collections from patients before they leave the practice

- call patients with outstanding balances

- check and file clean claims

• review reimbursement that comes in

• follow up with patients, insurers, etc., about late payments or denied claims

Build a team-oriented approach to billing and collections

Effective collecting takes teamwork. If all staff do their part and support each other, you'll soon see improved collections and financial performance; fewer billing errors, denials, and procedures for which you cannot collect reimbursement; streamlined administration; elevated staff satisfaction; and better patient communications and relations.

Educate your patients

An improved billing and collections process doesn't end with your staff. Clearly communicating your practice's financial policies to patients on their initial visits to your practice can boost collection rates substantially. Too often patients believe the responsibility of paying for medical care belongs to someone else (e.g., the insurer, your office, etc.). Making sure that your patients understand their responsibilities up front saves untold hassles later.

Review payments received

When payments arrive, your staff must properly check the claims as filed, examine denied charges, and determine the legitimacy of the denials. Insurers do make mistakes, so your staff must firmly protect your interest by holding the payer accountable to perform according to the contract you established. Staff should take appropriate action regarding the denials as soon as they arrive. Their doing so will greatly increase your collections.

Track performance regularly

With effective procedures established and well-communicated to staff and patients, you will have the opportunity to produce meaningful financial data you can analyze and use to improve your collection rates. For example, review your insurers' explanations of benefits, closely examining payments, denials, and contractual write-offs. Is payment predictable, or do you experience a sudden delay in reimbursement?

The monthly reports you generate with your practice-management software will help you watch for trends in the following key areas:

- Reasons for denials

- Collection rate by individual carrier

- Days in collection by payer class

- Contractual allowances

- Bad debt write-offs

- Accounts/receivable aging by third-party payer and patient

- Billing errors

Identify responsible parties

Trending may provide insight into whether a problem you notice is internal (i.e., at your practice) or external (i.e., the payer's). Internal problems range from not obtaining adequate billing information up front to not using effective collection controls. Perhaps a new staffer simply makes mistakes. Externally, perhaps the payer experiences a financial crunch that leads to inappropriate denials and adjustments, a slowdown in payments, or both. Either way, you must establish a response mechanism and know your recourse should you spot any such red flags.

Tracking key factors over time lets you develop a quality assurance program. Examine trends and know how they affect the practice, so you can make better-educated decisions. Moreover, set and monitor standards for your staff's handling of billing and collection functions, whether that means creating a new department to handle certain aspects of the process or reorganizing and training an existing team.

But it isn't enough to reorganize your department, establish new procedures, and put the process on autopilot. You must continually monitor ongoing billing operations to detect problems or glitches in the system. For example, does it take longer to submit initial claims than to follow up with outstanding claims? Are the majority of claims denied due to your internal errors? Has the payer's response time slowed?

Continued rising receivables or delays in payment call for increased attention to both your staff's work and the payer's situation. Explore the reason for the problem, determine the solution, and act quickly to make sure that every staffer does his or her job (for more about staff responsibilities, see Chapter 2). By doing so, staff know you mean business. Ultimately, this will produce better billing operations and higher staff morale.

Chapter 2

Staff
responsibilities

Putting together an effective billing team begins with the hiring process. Some applicants for medical office work just aren't cut out for billing and collecting. Individuals who have the five following personal characteristics—above and beyond the usual hiring criteria—are likely to be successful at billing and collection.

Look for a candidate whom you could describe in the following ways:

1. **Has a positive attitude.** You want someone who thinks, "I can do this," whatever the task.

2. **Is a self-starter.** A person who sets priorities—and then gets right to them—performs especially well in collection follow-up.

3. **Recognizes the importance of his or her job function.** A good business staffer avoids a "that's not my job" attitude, doing instead whatever the job requires.

4. **Believes in your practice.** An applicant who has faith in the mission/quality of your practice is more likely to be a loyal, enthusiastic worker.

5. **Has "street sense."** It's helpful to have someone who knows your community inside and out and has the savvy to address patients' potential ability to pay.

Conduct your employee searches—and especially your applicant interviews—with these traits in mind. Although you can't directly measure the characteristics, understanding their importance helps lead you to your best billing/collection employee choice.

Set up the chain for handling payment

Once you know what traits to look for, you can begin assembling your cracker-jack staff. But even with a top-notch staff, ensuring full, correct reimbursement is no easy matter. It involves everyone in your office working as a team so that all staff members can fulfill their interrelated responsibilities. Be sure your staff understand each other's individual roles by outlining the chain of responsibility for payment.

For the chain concept to work, you must make clear that the reimbursement challenge involves all staff, including physicians. It begins when the patient first contacts your office and doesn't end until long after the patient's visit. Following are the duties of each "link" in the chain:

The scheduler

The scheduler is also the screener—the first financial tool in the process. Before scheduling the patient, the scheduler must answer questions such as the following to determine and document whether the patient meets your requirements for treatment:

- Do you have a contract with the patient's insurer?

- Is every doctor in your group contracted with the plan?

- Is the patient eligible?

- What specific limitations/restrictions does the plan include?

- Is preauthorization required and, if so, what are the parameters?

- Is the patient responsible for noncovered services?

- What is the patient's shared responsibility (i.e., copay)?

- If your contract pays on a capitated basis, are you the provider of record who receives the patient's monthly payment?

For easy reference, the documentation goes either on the schedule or in the patient's record. If this all-important step—the first link in the chain—is not handled properly, you may not get paid for the visit.

The receptionist

Reception is far more than a "hello" job. The receptionist is the first person your patients see and has responsibilities in the billing and collection process. For that reason, consider a seasoned employee for the position. The person at your front desk must be smart and pay attention to detail.

Your receptionist must audit the patient's registration form for thoroughness and accuracy and cross-reference the data on the form with what was reported during the scheduling process. This includes obtaining a copy of the patient's insurance card, verifying coverage, and gathering the referral or authorization required by the plan.

To do so, your receptionist needs specific knowledge of each plan with which you contract. In addition, it's typically his or her task to keep individual patient information up-to-date so you don't render "free" services. Chapter 5 goes into more detail about validating patients' insurance and coverage information.

Provide your receptionist with a "cheat sheet" of questions to ask on a patient's first visit. This ensures that he or she consistently asks all of the essential questions about copays, deductibles, carve-outs, and preauthorizations. Print the sheet on the back of your regular patient information form, so the receptionist can fill it out immediately after taking care of the other intake information. Figure 2.1 on p. 15 provides a sample cheat sheet.

Clinical staff and physicians

Once the receptionist confirms the patient's coverage information, the patient enters your clinical area (presumably an exam room). It's important that your nurses, medical assistants, and physicians understand how the patient's plan limits authorized care. These limits delineate the clinical responsibilities you assumed—and identify which ones you didn't take on—under the contract you signed.

For example, you may be authorized for office visits and consultations but not for diagnostic procedures or testing. Or your payment may only cover consultation and office visits. Be sure that you also know where to send the patient for diagnostic studies and how to obtain authorization for therapeutic services and procedures. Mishandling these issues may result in losing the fees involved.

Figure 2.1: Sample insurance information form

Patient's name: _____   Employer: _____

Insured's name: _____   Policy or group #: _____

Insured's SS#: _____   Plan effective date: _____

Type of plan: _____

Major medical: _____   Basic: _____

Deductible: _____   Coinsurance: _____

Stop loss: _____   Copay: _____

Authorization requirements: _____

Cashier

When the patient arrives or is ready to leave the office, your cashier (in a smaller practice, this might be your receptionist or another regular staffer to whom you give this added responsibility) must clearly understand the patient's financial responsibilities. Right before the patient leaves is the time to collect the copay, deductible, or other direct patient pay element that is difficult to collect by mail. Your cashier needs an easy-to-access method—preferably within the computer system—to identify all of your plans' contract provisions.

Insurance biller

Once the patient leaves the office, the biller takes over. This employee must ensure accurate, complete data entries and charges and must submit claims according to plan requirements (e.g., within 60 days after service). Make your insurance biller responsible for training and updating your entire staff on procedural requirements as well. With this range of duties, your insurance biller becomes an integral link in the chain.

Collector

The collector has an easy job if everyone earlier in the chain does his or her part. But the collector must audit any balance remaining after the patient and insurer make their payments, in order to determine whether the patient has any further responsibility or whether the contract requires a write-off. Identify who is responsible—the biller or the collector—for writing off these adjustments.

The collector should be detail-oriented and understand the contract terms well enough to identify and appeal inappropriate payments. Don't let him or her assume that insurance payments are correct. Because you and your practice bear the financial burden for what isn't paid, make sure this last staffer is a real bird dog in evaluating claims and pursuing payment.

Patient advocate

Because patients often have a range of insurance complications, your staff are likely to encounter frustrating problems such as improper enrollment, lack of preauthorization, etc. At the same time, your patients don't want hassles and expect your staff to minimize them. Patients you cannot serve without such annoyances may go to another practice that can.

Consider shifting staffers' job titles and descriptions and naming a "patient advocate." It's a friendly sounding, service-oriented moniker for a person who handles a range of duties aimed at ensuring that patients sail smoothly through their visits and that you get fully paid for your work. You might prefer calling this staffer your "patient care coordinator" (or just "patient coordinator"). This person will do the following:

- Learn the rules for all of your managed-care plans: HMOs, hospitals, referral physician practices, pharmacies, etc.

- Develop relationships with the plans and other plan providers, staying current with changes and knowing who to call.

- Help patients with their billing and insurance hassles, focusing on patient satisfaction as well as proper reimbursement.

- Know who to use as referral physicians for various plans, how their practices run, and who to call at each practice. Conversely, this person will also know your referrers and the appropriate manner to smoothly handle their incoming referrals.

- Act as the patient liaison, communicating with each patient and on his or her behalf.

Consider appointing someone who is currently on your billing staff to this job. Because technology simplifies the mechanics of reimbursement, many good billing clerks can take on more responsibilities. It's a natural progression for an experienced biller.

Delegating the described duties to your patient advocate helps consolidate insurance responsibilities to one person (or in a larger practice, one section). Because billing and insurance problems are major causes of patient dissatisfaction, it's especially important for the advocate to keep a personal, working relationship with each company's representatives.

Patient financial counselor
A staffer who acts specifically as a patient financial counselor can help your patients prepare in advance for surgery or other expensive procedures, a step that

also can help improve your high-dollar collections. After discussing with the patient the need for a procedure, simply send him or her to the counselor to work out insurance precertification and scheduling, and make arrangements regarding how the patient will pay the balance.

More specifically, the financial counselor will do the following:

- Call the patient prior to the procedure to counsel him or her regarding facility fees and coverage

- Communicate all financial aspects of care to the patient

- Review with the patient/family estimated fees and coverage available explaining the fees and reimbursement process and documenting the review in the patient's record

- Suggest options to the patient regarding planning a payment schedule, filing insurance claims, and handling any problems that arise during the reimbursement process

- Interview the patient on the day of the procedure to confirm all demographic and insurance information for accuracy, making changes when applicable

- Reiterate financial obligations with the patient or family members, explaining the fees and reimbursement process

- Provide to the patient a written explanation of the estimated fee schedules by current procedural terminology code prior to treatment, and put a copy in the patient's record

- Review forms for the patient's signature, and obtain forms and signatures as needed

- Collect any copayment or deductible prior to the procedure

- Provide the patient with a promissory note, if necessary, and a payment schedule according to facility policy

Chapter 3

Coding and auditing processes

As a physician, you are ultimately responsible for both current procedural terminology (CPT) and ICD-9-CM coding accuracy. After all, you treat or oversee each patient, so only you know exactly what you do. Document those actions precisely, and be especially careful in selecting the level of evaluation and management (E/M) services. If it isn't documented, it wasn't done.

As a practice owner, you benefit most by capturing all of your charges. However, you pay the price for inaccurate coding, whether upcoding or downcoding. With the government placing a strong emphasis on coding accuracy, terrible problems—and potentially large paybacks and penalties—loom large for a doctor whose staff miscode, however unintentional the discrepancies.

Overcome your coding objections

Perhaps you have delegated all coding responsibilities for what you consider good reasons. But think about the following responses to common objections to coding by physicians:

"It's too complicated. Only my coding specialist understands."

Some of the rules are admittedly arcane and can require multistep analysis. But it is essential that you understand them. Work closely with your coding or billing specialist and take advantage of texts and seminars to educate yourself and keep up-to-date.

This advice is easier said than done and doesn't change the fact that you are pressed for time. But because third-party payers reimburse you for the lion's share of your work, you have no choice but to master the language of their realm. A cursory knowledge of CPT and ICD-9 coding simply won't suffice these days, and staying abreast of annual coding updates poses an even greater challenge.

"It takes too long."

Your time is valuable, but so is accurate coding because it gets you the reimbursement you deserve. Plus, it doesn't have to take long. You will occasionally come across a difficult coding problem, but you typically should be able simply to check off a superbill preprinted with your most common CPT and ICD-9 codes updated yearly to reflect new or deleted codes. You can also load software coding programs on a personal computer for use in your office, saving you time if you face a situation for which you don't know how to code.

"It's the same amount of money no matter who does it."

Although unbundling—using separate codes for procedures already accounted for in one code—is generally illegal, the fee-for-service world still offers legitimate opportunities for revenue enhancement when the patient's situation requires extraordinary application of your skills and judgment. Even with thorough charting and clear notes, experience shows that when physicians code, they more reliably appreciate and capture unusual circumstances that increase reimbursement—increases that add to your bottom line.

And keep this in mind: Some health systems make coding an explicit job requirement for their employed doctors and impose penalties for noncompliance. Correct coding helps your practice realize extra revenue and steers you clear of legal trouble.

Establish coding criteria

How well your practice codes depends first and foremost on how well you

- identify the CPT codes that most aptly describe the services you provided

- understand the ICD-9 codes and use them correctly to explain why you provided the service

Even if you delegate much of that to competent staffers, it's up to you to establish the criteria for selecting codes and ensure that their entries are correct. To fulfill your responsibility, follow this four-step process, which requires effort on your part but also gives you the tools you need to code well:

1. Read the books. If you don't already have them, get copies of the annual CPT-4, ICD-9-CM, and Healthcare Common Procedure Coding System Level II manuals and carefully read all of the sections that relate to your practice. Pay close attention to the instructions and explanatory sections that give you the lay of the land. For example, the CPT manual's introduction reveals which codes changed and how codes are formatted.

2. Consult explanatory materials. Because you may find the manuals as clear as mud, take advantage of readily available supplementary resources. For example, the American Medical Association publishes specialty-specific guidebooks for CPT coding. Don't limit yourself to print resources. Electronic tutorials are generally available. Ask your billing company for a licensed copy.

3. Attend seminars. Sign up for a coding seminar in your area. Widely offered by medical and specialty societies, carriers, and private consulting companies, such seminars generally combine an explanatory lecture with coding exercises and a question-and-answer session. Choose carefully which seminars you attend, particularly if you are on a budget (e.g., limit yourself to specialty workshops conducted at your state and national specialty society meetings).

4. Critique your coding. Review carrier denials and error notices with your billing staff. Make sure you have a regular procedure in place for staff to bring all potential mistakes to your attention. If your staff ignore or work around billing problems that start with your selection of an incorrect CPT or ICD-9 code, you lose an opportunity to learn from your mistakes. For better or worse, coding incorrectly the first time is often one of the best ways to learn how to do it right. Also learn to effectively critique your coding and billing processes. The best way to do that? Perform an internal coding/billing audit.

Conduct a worthwhile internal coding/billing audit

You can't afford to lose revenue, especially when you have done the work to earn it. So how can you ensure that your office both protects itself from legal trouble and collects what it should? To manage this task in a cost-effective manner, consider performing annual miniaudits of your reporting, coding, and billing activities. If you come across significant problems, schedule the audits more frequently (e.g., quarterly) until you have control over the process. Then return to performing them annually.

The audits serve the following four valuable purposes:

1. Identify discrepancies. By examining the information related to a specific service and comparing the documentation on various office records, your staff will see where and why services end up understated, overstated, or even lost.

2. Increase reimbursement IQ. As your reception and nursing staff examine explanations of benefits (EOB) and see 30%–40% adjustments, they should begin to understand why they must properly capture every charge. Tracking the steps that lead up to the EOBs shows how to improve the results, which is a direct educational approach.

3. Improve awareness of coding's revenue-enhancing importance. By examining charts and billing information, your staff can better grasp the importance of accounting for every service rendered. For example, a four-physician practice that misses charging for just one hospital consult per month per member takes an annual hit of $6,000. Failing to charge for just one electrocardiogram and one urinalysis each day may cost you as much as $12,000 per year in lost revenue.

4. Teach teamwork. Again, stress to staff the importance of their individual actions as they fit together with those of their coworkers. A miniaudit involves all staff who have a role in coding and billing, as they team up to examine the process.

To conduct an audit, pull 10 random patient charts from a specific date of service three to six months ago. This allows adequate time for insurance processing and receipt of third-party payment. Break the staff into teams of two—preferably one business/administrative staffer and one nurse or other clinical assistant—and have each team review at least five of the charts.

Ask both teams to document any discrepancies as they track the service and its codes through the chart, charge slip, computer record (i.e., patient ledger), insurance form, and EOB finally received. After the teams finish their reviews, have them analyze the results for any patterns. Are the same errors reoccurring? Are there specific job positions at which they occur? Are mistakes common for specific services?

Ask the teams to calculate the potential cost of the errors for a 12-month period. Also ask them to identify errors they fear represent possible overcoding or overbilling, and the reasons why the claims may be wrong. EOBs that show consistent downcoding, such as those with bundled services, also may signify a serious problem. Discontinue any such coding situations at once, conducting an in-service training session and monitoring for compliance. Finally, have the teams make specific recommendations on how to correct the deficiencies for the practice's long-term benefit.

Miniaudits nearly always turn up a variety of discrepancies. For surgical and other procedural services, the discrepancies can be dramatic because of the payers' coding requirements. A lot of revenue and legal risk is involved, which makes the audit a highly valuable staff undertaking. Audits typically uncover the following discrepancies:

- Wrong diagnoses

- Missing dictation

- Incomplete charge slips

- Missed office charges (e.g., procedures, labs, x-rays, etc.)

- Missed hospital charges (e.g., ER visits, consults, etc.)

- Unjustified insurance write-offs

- Patient balances written off (e.g., Medicare/HMO copays and deductibles)

- Service overcoding

- Improper unbundling

Problem areas revealed by an audit may seem disheartening, but once you know which billing areas cause you the most trouble, you can narrow your focus for improvements, for example, to in-office collections or problems with payers (topics discussed in Sections three and four of this book).

Collecting from patients in-office

Chapter 4

Importance of in-office collections

With the emphasis on managed care—including capitation—doctors and managers too often think almost solely in terms of payments that come from third parties (e.g., the government or insurers). Copays and deductibles become almost an annoyance rather than an important source of income.

To increase in-office collections, inform patients of their up-front payment obligations and actually ask for payment. It's that simple. Unfortunately, most practices and physicians don't think that way.

Why bother to collect the $10–$15 copay from each patient when the HMO will pay you thousands of dollars each month? Besides, patients grumble when you press them about paying for visits, and your office probably isn't set up to handle these little payments (e.g., no one can collect the money, you have no where to store it, and you cannot make change). You may believe that copays and deductibles are more trouble than they're worth.

A negative attitude about copayments not only comes across to patients, but costs you money and negatively affects your bottom line and relationships with third-party payers.

For one, patient payments are part of your contract with most of your payers; your practice signed an agreement stating that you would collect those payments. In addition, if you don't insist on a consistent pattern of collecting, your staff and patients will lose a sense of the importance of direct patient payment.

Although each fee may seem small, you miss out on a significant amount of revenue if you don't collect direct payments. For example, a $10 copay could amount to at least $10,000 per year for a specialist and $12,000 yearly for a primary care doctor—all of which goes directly to your bottom line. Deductibles and payment for noncovered services add dramatically to that figure.

And many copays aren't as small as you may believe. Increasing carrier and employer costs are pushing average copays into the $20–$25 range. Specific deductibles and fees for noncovered services may be even larger. In addition, consumer-directed healthcare (CDH), particularly when attached to a high-deductible health plan, requires patients to pay more of their own money, which may further complicate collecting up front. (See Chapter 7 for more information about CDH.) That's why you should try various approaches to make sure that each patient pays the copay fee portion of his or her bill before leaving your office.

Over-the-counter payments

Collecting copays from patients adds up to large sums that all fall right to your bottom line. Getting patients to pay while still at the office for their visits—often referred to as "over-the-counter" (OTC) collection—is one of the best means to ensure that you actually receive payment from patients.

Besides producing the revenue you deserve, OTC collection helps reduce your overhead. It costs money to send out statements to request payment. And although you immediately collect each dollar that you receive in-house, someone who is able to pay OTC today may become unable or unwilling to pay later, especially if he or she owes large balances, according to Wisconsin practice-management consultant James Tripp. In other words, get it today while the patient can pay.

One more reason to enforce in-office collection: Many managed-care plans routinely check whether practices ask for copayments at the time of service and sometimes drop those practices that do not. Likewise, the plans sometimes drop practices whose patients routinely refuse to pay.

Techniques for collecting OTC payments from patients include the following:

Credit cards

Back when patient balances accounted for a larger portion of your receivables (a trend that may return), many doctors wrestled with the question of accepting credit card payments. But the times are long past when medical offices or their patients considered taking credit card payments unprofessional; indeed, patients generally view it as a convenience.

There's no minimum amount for credit card usage, and the "bother" of handling plastic is much less of an annoyance than catching up with a patient who leaves your office without paying a copay. Most patients carry credit cards with them and will happily charge their visit copays.

In addition, some credit card companies offer preauthorized healthcare forms with which patients can charge copays, deductibles, etc., for all of their visits during a year. Asking your patient to sign the form on the first visit of the year takes care of the collection hassle for the rest of the year. Present this as a benefit to your patient, as well as to your office.

When considering accepting credit cards, avoid the "minimum charge" philosophy (i.e., refusing to take credit cards for amounts below a stated minimum). There's simply no legal basis for doing so, and although you may not like to bear the 3%–5% service charge on small amounts, those charges are less expensive than the cost of billing for your fees.

If you put in place a system to accept credit cards, don't assume that your staff already know how to do this. Review with them the following basic steps to improve credit card payments at your office:

- **Support it from the top.** Unless you strongly back credit card payments for patients, don't expect staff to emphasize it. Explain that it's far less expensive to accept a plastic payment today than to pursue a patient balance later.

- **Educate the staff.** Make sure your check-out staff, patient financial counselor, and in-house collector know how to promote credit card payments from patients. To help staff avoid feeling like they're hounding patients for money, teach them to present the option as a positive one that eases the burden for people who owe money.

- **Invest in the equipment.** Use electronic credit card terminals, and make sure that every practice site has at least one. Purchasing terminals and phone lines makes it easier on your staff and demonstrates your commitment. You'll earn back every cent with improved OTC collections.

- **Put up signs everywhere.** Once considered questionable taste for doctors' offices, most have found that clear signs announcing that you accept credit cards will increase payments.

- **Use promotional tools.** Some credit card companies offer "take one" brochures tailored for doctors' offices. They describe credit card payment opportunities and advantages for your patients.

- **Provide for payment by mail.** By all means, make sure that your patient-balance statements include a credit card payment form. Use your billing comments as encouragement for patients to exercise this option.

- **Encourage payment by phone.** Teach your collectors to offer credit card payment as an option when calling patients about outstanding balances.

- **Offer preauthorized payment.** If you secure a patient's signature on a preauthorization form prior to surgery, you can enter a credit card payment for the patient balance after insurance reimbursement. You also can apply this payment method for recurring treatments and budget payment plans.

Bank financing

Far too many providers accept almost any patient excuse to allow spreading payment over as many months as the patient finds convenient. It's not unusual to see a patient paying a $1,500 account at $35 per month, taking 43 months—more than three and a half years—to pay it off. That makes the net value to the provider less than $1,100, with interest, monthly billing costs, and inflation eating up the original figure.

Perhaps that's acceptable if your fee fell through the cracks of insurance/HMO deductibles, copays, and exclusions, and your patient cannot afford to pay faster. Doctors tend to accept such extensions. However, it puts your office into the finance business and leaves you managing the account for longer than you should.

You don't have to become a bank for patients who need time to pay off a large balance. Instead of arranging payment in installments—usually without interest and often over several months (or years)—set up a program for bank financing. This works best for surgery or other practices that bill for large amounts, but only you must know the payment amounts and patient responsibilities. Arrange with a bank for a simple application and approval process to be handled in your office, much the same as an auto dealer handles a car loan. Many national and local banks offer such programs.

Once the system is set up, tell your patients that your office can no longer make payment arrangements but that you have arranged for bank financing. There are several advantages for the patient as well as for you (e.g., lower interest than on credit card payments), so arm yourself with these points. Invite patients to complete a simple, one-page credit application supplied by your participating bank; the bank should process the form for approval in three or fewer working days.

This takes the billing, collection, and follow-up process completely out of your office, giving you your fee up front while the patient pays the bank. One caveat: These deals generally permit the bank to return an unpaid loan to you (albeit only after extensive collection effort), so you ultimately bear the risk of payment.

Your OTC collections success

Track over-the-counter success by regularly setting a goal based on the in-office collection ratio. Obtain this number by taking each day's in-office (i.e., not mail) collections and dividing that total by the day's office charges.

You get the best in-office collection performance if you set goals. Two fairly easy-to-track time-of-service collection standards are collecting

- 100% of all copays

- at least 80% of all patient responsibility balances

Ask your practice manager to monitor these numbers once per week, using daily reports to compare the number of copayments and balance bills collected against the number of patients who should have paid. Adjust the goals as you go, considering what is both realistic and challenging to the staffers involved.

Tripp, the Wisconsin practice-management consultant, likens that approach to another per-patient count method: Adding up the number of patients who made OTC payments and dividing that figure by the total number of patients seen in the office during the same period. Once again, after obtaining an initial count, establish a challenging goal for successive weeks or months, and report how staff actually perform each time. As they meet one goal, raise it for the next period.

Surgeons and specialty internists generally have the lowest in-office collection ratios. That's not surprising, because these doctors generate most of their revenue in the hospital, rather than from office visits. Some consider collecting OTC payments relatively unimportant. But just as for primary care providers, collecting in person from office-visit patients can dramatically reduce the costs of billing and collection. So the fewer bills you must send, the more money you save.

For example, an orthopedic surgeon or gastroenterologist may indeed generate most of his or her dollars in the hospital, but a surprisingly high percentage of his or her monthly bills almost surely represent office visits before and after patients' hospital procedures not included in the global period.

Do you know where your practice falls on the OTC-collections continuum? Larger practices actually compute specific OTC ratios, but smaller ones often don't take the time. All practices should add up the total collected in the office each day and compare that total to what it could have received. It's quick and easy, and it gives immediate feedback. Thus, if 50 patients came into the practice under a managed-care plan with a $10 copay, you should have collected $500 cash from them. Did you?

In a larger group, if you take the money you lost on those 50 patients' nonpayment and multiply it by the total number of such patients in the entire practice, you may come up with a rather large number. That number should convince you to improve your systems and further press staff to focus on OTC collections.

However you do it, be sure that you have procedures in place to ensure staff pay attention to OTC collections. It's your money—ask for it. Chapter 5 provides some other examples of means to improve your in-office collections.

Chapter 5

Methods to improve in-office collections

Now that you know the importance of collecting payments from patients before they leave your office, consider putting in place measures to improve your in-office collections (e.g., training staff, knowing which patients are self-pay and enforcing that method of payment, validating coverage, understanding preauthorizations, keeping a change fund, etc.).

Train your staff

Every employee must understand the importance of obtaining the OTC payment before each patient leaves your office. Most importantly, staff must know that collecting small amounts by mail costs your practice money and proves annoying to the patients.

Reception staff are essential to making these transactions happen, so focus on training them first. You can also provide tools such as a front-desk reference, so staff don't have to remember every detail of every plan in which you participate. The tool might include a separate page for each plan that contains the 10–20 most common office visits and procedures, each procedure's regular charge, plan allowances, deductibles, and copays. Provide access to health plans' Web sites for staff to verify coverage and check other details.

Your plan representatives can tell you the various dollar amounts involved. Ask for them in writing. Also, track your explanations of benefits to make sure that the reference tool is updated and as accurate as possible.

Armed with the training and tools, your front desk staff can see at a glance what an exiting patient owes over the counter before that patient leaves the office. Be absolutely sure staff know to politely and appropriately ask for payment. Of course you will come across patients who will not have the money on them or claim not to be able to pay. Invite them to use a credit card or to speak to your patient financial counselor (whose role was detailed in Chapter 2).

Good collections often depend on replacing an adversarial stance with a posture of helpfulness. Convince your patients that you're all in it together and that you're going to help them come up with a means to pay their bills.

Every little step you take—or don't take—affects the impression you create. Your staff can even make a difference by simply addressing patients by name more than once during each conversation. Whether speaking over the telephone, greeting someone at the front desk, or processing a patient after an office visit, regularly using the patient's name emphasizes interest and direct concern. Here are a few examples:

- "Mr. Jones, we look forward to seeing you at nine o'clock on Thursday."

- "Mr. Jones, will you be paying by cash, check, or credit card?"

- "Thank you, Mr. Jones. We'll look forward to receiving your payment by next Wednesday."

Whatever the format, repeating the patient's name is an important part of the process. Every time you do so, you reinforce your personal interest in the patient and in his or her responsibility to pay the bill.

Know which patients are self-pay

If your cashier or exit receptionist doesn't know whether a patient's contract calls for a copay, you may never receive that money. Set up your computer system so it flags the self-pay patients. This will remind the receptionist to ask for a copay, deductible, or noncovered fee. Some systems automatically create a bill for the charge as soon as someone from the practice logs in the patient. Select the method that works best for your practice and is most compatible with your computer system.

Furnish patients who refuse to pay with a special warning reminding them that they are required to pay the copay, deductible, etc., and that you will notify their insurers if the balances don't get paid or if the patients refuse to pay at their next office visit. Include such notices with patient bills or statements.

Validate patient coverage

Validating patient coverage before you begin treatment is increasingly important. You run a risk of financial loss if you mistakenly accept or treat patients whom you believe are current members of a plan that your practice accepts or whose treatments you mistakenly believe are covered services. On the other hand, not treating the patient comes across as poor customer service and could also put you at financial risk if the patient leaves for another practice.

You need an effective process and clearly assigned job duties to ensure validation of each patient's coverage before you begin treatment. Although no system is foolproof, taking the following four steps minimizes your risk of losses:

1. Print out schedules one or two days early. Also obtain schedules from each branch office.

2. Assign one employee to verify coverage for each patient on each day's schedule. Have this staffer keep a running list, organized by plan, of all of the questions to ask each patient about indicated service eligibility. One call to each insurer then verifies all of the patient questions for that plan.

Assign the validation task to a staffer who does not work at the front desk. Having the person handle the work in advance and in the back avoids slowing down the check-in process. Ushering patients with coverage problems to a separate, private space to discuss their situations also ensures that you do not breach their privacy.

3. Flag the charts of any patients whose coverage the staffer could not validate. Perhaps those patients dropped the plan without informing you, lost their coverage upon the termination of their employment, changed physicians, or became not covered in another way. Or perhaps the insurer has inaccurate or old records. Whatever the reason, flagged charts alert your staff to discuss the situation with those patients when they arrive at your practice.

If you have sufficient volume with a certain insurer or under a specific plan, consider linking to the insurer's online patient database. In an increasing number of practices, online links reduce the number of verification calls and confirmation mistakes that plague even the most conscientious staffers.

4. Photocopy both sides of patient insurance cards. You may already ask to photocopy new patients' insurance cards, but do you have a consistent procedure in place to capture this information? Your staff may ask new patients to write their insurance numbers on the new patient registration forms and then enter the information into your computers, but do they ask about insurance information after the first office visit?

Replace a hit-or-miss system with a new routine centered at the reception desk, during which the receptionist asks every new and existing patient for his or her insurance or plan card. For a new patient, the receptionist photocopies both sides of the cards. The copy then becomes the basis for computer entry of the billing information.

Then, at each visit after the patient's first, the receptionist asks to see the insurance or plan card. If the card has the same data that is on file, the receptionist simply returns it with a "thank you." If it is different, he or she photocopies it (front and back), writes the date on the copy, and returns the card. The new copy becomes the basis for revising the data on file.

If that system is not enough to maintain accurate information, remove the lines on the new-patient registration form that ask for insurance/plan numbers. Many patients struggle to record the proper data anyway, and dropping this question ensures that they won't provide incorrect information.

Why photocopy the back of each card? The reverse side often gives useful information such as deductibles/copays/preapproval provisions, claims department addresses, and insurance company phone numbers. Your staff may believe that they know this information for your most common plans, but they often have to search for it for others. Copying the back of every card greatly reduces the chance for errors. Your staff may argue that this routine applied to every patient is too much work for your office. But sticking to it without deviation can significantly reduce the number of returned claims.

Understand and secure preauthorizations

Paying attention to preauthorizations can also reduce the number of returned or denied claims. Increasingly, practices write off thousands of dollars for medical services because plans haven't preauthorized the services you performed and your practice didn't check ahead of time. In the past, plans had no problem authorizing services already performed, but now they hesitate to approve services retroactively.

So if you have no assurance of preauthorization for the service you are about to provide, payment for that service might be denied. If it's denied, you'll have to write off the fees involved or bill the patient, who may argue about paying because you accepted his or her insurance at the time of the visit, implying that you were willing to abide by the insurer's decision (even if that meant receiving no payment).

Although it's extremely important, securing authorizations can be a time-consuming process. It's not unusual for one staff member to spend most of the day verifying eligibility and garnering authorizations for care. Because this process takes so much time, avoid the temptation to delegate the task to your receptionist or scheduler. However, depending on the size of your practice, that may not be possible.

Whoever handles it—and at least several of your staff should be able to do so—should understand the following basic parameters of preauthorizations as they apply to each of your contracts:

What services in your practice require preauthorization?

One plan may require that you authorize all services before performing them, whereas another may call for preauthorization only of surgical procedures. Nearly all plans require precertification of hospitalizations.

How many services can you get authorized at once?

A plan may approve a consultation and two follow-up visits, or perhaps a consultation and surgery within a given range of current procedural terminology codes (e.g., a biopsy or removal of a skin lesion). Obtain as many authorizations as possible with your first request.

Where do you get the preauthorization?

Do you go directly to the insurance plan, or to the Independent Practice Association (IPA)? The answer will depend on who holds the contract with the plan and what that contract provides. Authorizations usually come from insurance plans. Some IPAs are set up to handle all insurance processes and will contact the insurance plan to obtain authorizations for you.

How must you secure preauthorization?

Must it be in writing, or can you get it by telephone? If it must be written, ask for the preauthorization by phone and a written confirmation by fax.

How long does it take to obtain the preauthorization?

It may take an hour, a day, or even a week. You must know this to decide how far ahead to schedule the patient's appointment.

How long is a preauthorization valid?

If you don't complete the authorized services within that time period, you'll have to apply for another approval.

What preauthorization information must you submit with your billings?

Once you perform the service, you must to tell the payer that you had the authority to provide it. Do this by providing an authorization number with your billing. Know each plan's numbering system (e.g., a nine-digit number or seven-figure alphanumeric code) so you can verify the validity of the number.

Who gave the authorization?

Always obtain the name of the person who provides approval, so you can identify the person who gave you the okay if your bill gets rejected for any reason.

Once you have the authorization in hand, where do you file it? Use a form such as the one shown in Figure 5.1 to make sure you have all the required information. The problem then becomes making it easy to find the form when your patient's appointment comes around. For established patients, put this information directly into their charts. You might also keep a folder of upcoming patients'

Figure 5.1 Sample telephone preauthorization form

Patient: *Silver, Shirley*   **Account:** *12345*

Insurance: *QualMed*   **Date received:** *4/4/06*

From: *QualMed*   **Contact:** *Ginger Green*

Phone: *888/555-1000*   **For:** *Consultation*

Good for: *90 days*   **Authorization:** *V786450*

Received by: *Betty Blue*

authorizations, especially for new patients who don't have established charts. The more authorizations you deal with, the more important it is to have a system in place to track them.

Keep a change fund

If a patient is willing to pay at the desk, don't lose that money because you lack change for a $5 or $10 bill. Keep a small fund, perhaps $50 in ones and fives, at the exit position to accommodate your patients. Maintain a simple system to reconcile and replenish the fund at the end of each day.

Assign this job to someone you trust. After all, even the smallest amount of money can add up to a large sum over the long term, so whomever you put in charge of this task should be someone who will not take advantage of this money. You or the practice administrator should check the change fund weekly (if not daily) to make sure it contains the appropriate amount of money and to replenish the funds when necessary.

Ensure payments for noncovered services

With reimbursement levels shrinking, you may begin looking toward elective procedures (e.g., ancillary services) for added income. But how can you be sure you'll get paid for these noncovered services? The best solution is to open communication with insurance companies and managed-care plans and have the patient sign a form that states he or she understands that the procedure may not be covered.

Some plans never cover certain services (e.g., cosmetic procedures) or cover certain procedures (e.g., preventive care) under specific plans. In either case, know what is and isn't covered by each insurance company and plan with which you participate. Further, know what services require authorization before being performed.

If you believe a service may not be covered, first verify its coverage status with the insurance company or plan. Then ask the patient to sign an agreement (also known as an advanced beneficiary notice) to make payment in full before you provide the service. Figure 5.2 on p. 49 provides a sample authorization and payment agreement.

This simple step removes all uncertainty regarding who is responsible for payment. If the payer denies coverage, explain to the patient that the plan—not your practice—said no. Don't assume that the patient will not want the service if the insurance company denies coverage. Many patients still want uncovered procedures and will pay out of pocket. Just make sure they sign the form and pay first.

You may run into trouble when patients don't realize how much they will have to pay, even after coverage by insurance. Few patients plan for big medical bills and are surprised when they owe a significant amount of money for the procedure. Use a patient counselor (or the equivalent) to help patients plan ahead. Educating them up front about what to expect—not just medically, but also financially—makes it more likely the patient will pay for the services rendered.

Create in-house (or even bank-financed) time-payment plans. Offer patients the option of signing up for these plans before the procedure is performed, and use forms such as those in Figures 5.3 on p. 50 and 5.4 on p. 51 to make such agreements.

Figure 5.2: Noncovered services authorization and payment agreement

I understand that the service listed below is deemed to be a "noncovered service" by my insurance plan. I am requesting that the service be performed. I will accept responsibility for the fee for the service, and understand that I must pay in full before the service is performed.

Patient name: _____ Account #: _____

Service requested: _____

Patient signature: _____ Date: _____

Service verified noncovered: _____ Date: _____

Insurance company and representative: _____

Fee: _____ Date paid: _____ Date of procedure: _____

Even with access to payment reference tables, your front desk cannot always know the exact amount the patient must pay immediately. And, some contracts prohibit collecting deductibles/coinsurance until the plan has paid. In those cases, it's best to ask for advance credit card authorization—just as hotels and car rental agencies do.

Some credit card companies (e.g., Visa, American Express, etc.) provide forms for patients to sign in advance. One form authorizes card charges upon the receipt of the partial insurance payments. Patients can indicate a charge limit to ensure that they won't run an inordinate risk of card misuse.

Although you should not thereafter require any patient action on that charge, send a zero-balance statement to the patient when you charge his or her card that shows the amount due after the insurance payment and a

Figure 5.3: Customized financial agreement for insurance patients

Patient name: _____

Patient address: _____

Responsible party: _____

Address: _____

City: _____ State: _____ ZIP: _____

Phone: _____ Fax: _____

E-mail: _____

Description of services to be rendered:

1. Fee for services $_____

2. Estimate of insurance benefits $_____

3. Estimate of patient portion $_____

☐   I prefer paying 100% ($_____) of the patient portion of what the insurance
     does not cover on the first appointment.

☐   I prefer paying 50% ($_____) of the patient portion of the first appointment.
     The remainder will be paid within 15 days after the insurance has paid its portion.

In the event that I fail to pay for a period of 30 days, I hereby acknowledge that I
will be responsible for all of the balance, interest, court costs, and attorney fees.

I hereby certify that I have read and received a copy of the foregoing disclosure
statement this _____ day of _____.

Signature_____

Figure 5.4: Customized financial agreement for noninsurance patients

Patient name: _____

Patient address: _____

Responsible party: _____

Address:_____

City: _____ State: _____ ZIP: _____

Phone: _____ Fax: _____

E-mail: _____

Description of services to be rendered:

1. Fee for services $_____

2. Estimate of insurance benefits $_____

3. Estimate of patient portion $_____

☐   I prefer paying the full amount ($_____) and receiving a 5% bookkeeping
     allowance.

☐   I prefer paying 50% ($_____) of the patient portion at the first appointment
     and the balance in two equal, consecutive monthly payments ($_____ per
     month).

☐   I prefer to pay 1/3 ($_____) at the first appointment, and the balance in
     two equal, consecutive monthly payments ($_____ per month).

In the event that I fail to pay for a period of 30 days, I hereby acknowledge that I
will be responsible for all of the balance, interest, court costs, and attorney fees.

I hereby certify that I have read and received a copy of the foregoing disclosure
statement this _____ day of _____.

Signature_____

notation that it was paid by credit card. That helps you avoid a patient calling to ask why a charge from your office showed up on his or her card.

Safeguard cash that enters the practice

Because the aim is to increase the amount of money you collect directly from patients at the time of service, you cannot ignore the importance of tracking that increased cash flow. Experts estimate that three out of every four physicians will suffer a significant loss due to employee dishonesty at least once during their careers. Serious—and expensive—trouble awaits the physician who grows lax in basic cash controls.

If your office lacks proper controls, even the most-trusted staffer may be tempted to embezzle. Unfortunately, in many practices, it's easy to borrow from the office kitty or forget to record patient payments. As already noted, those small amounts add up—especially if one of your employees pockets money that rightly belongs to you.

Your practice size dictates how complex you make your cash-control policies, but there are common-sense rules that almost any office can implement.

Generally accepted accounting principles call for a division of duties that ensures that no individual employee has control over a transaction from beginning to end. For example, assign balancing each day's office receipts to your check-out clerk, but require a supervisor or office manager to prepare the deposit.

Smaller practices with fewer staff have a difficult time following the division-of-duties principle, but you can still gain internal control by working closely with your accountant and being involved in certain transactions yourself. In fact, having your CPA audit and revise your internal controls as necessary may be money well spent. It demonstrates your awareness of what's going on in your office, without you having to hover over employees day in and day out.

To ensure that you actually receive all of the money that your staff collect in patient fees, take the time to establish and monitor the following controls in these three key areas:

1. Personnel

- Adequately screen applicants, including getting in touch with references and conducting background checks.

- Require that your employees take vacations. This is prime time to uncover possible thefts because they will not be in the office to stop you.

2. Cash handling

- Make the person who takes payments responsible for balancing the books, but have a second person verify all transactions. You or the practice administrator should sign off on daily journals and deposits.

- Require receipts for every payment received over the counter.

- Make deposits daily or set up a lock-box system with your bank.

- Establish separate petty cash and patient change funds and randomly verify balances.

- Reconcile bank statements monthly and consider having the statements sent directly to your accountant (or to a physician at home).

3. Accounts receivable

- Use and account for serially numbered encounter forms for every service.

- Track a random sample of cash receipts through your entire system, from the appointment register all the way to the computer ledger, to confirm that no payments are missing.

- Set up a clear policy for write-offs that involves either physician approval or review.

- Prohibit financial records or insurance claims from leaving the office.

Chapter 6

Patient referrals

Coping with today's medical environment requires setting up systems to ensure that referrals—both from you to other physicians and vice versa—work smoothly for all of those concerned: the practice, the doctor and staff, and especially the patient. Most HMOs and PPOs require some form of authorization for a patient to be referred to a specialist, so it's an important, valid concern.

The patient referral/preauthorization process is a two-way street; someone has to give and someone has to receive. Your practice may deal more often with one process or the other, or you may occasionally be on both the giving and receiving sides. For example, an orthopedist who ordinarily receives referrals may have to refer out a procedure that he or she doesn't perform. If a physician refers an HMO/PPO patient to another specialist, the referral must go back to the primary care physician (PCP) for authorization.

Sending out referrals

Before you authorize specialist services, make sure you know what your contract dictates. It may clearly state that as the PCP, you must first see the patient for each illness referred to the specialist. If the contract does not state that you must see each patient before granting a referral, establish a policy on how you will give authorizations without a visit.

Perhaps you will decide that all patients must see you before you refer; maybe you'll allow nonvisit referrals according to the patient's described symptoms. Consider, for example, a patient who phones and describes an itchy rash that showed up after a camping trip. Because the symptoms are those of a classic case of poison ivy, you grant the patient's request to see a dermatologist without first coming in to your office. If the plan allows, set your policy to allow direct referral of patients in defined situations.

Set a clear policy that holds the patient responsible for securing the needed written authorization form from your office in such cases. Post a sign at the front desk, and have check-out staff remind patients when necessary. This removes the burden from your staff of transmitting the form to the other office in time for the patient's appointment.

Referral information to capture

Your plan may provide a preprinted authorization form; if so, be sure that staff use it consistently. If there's no prescribed form, draft one that contains at least the following information:

- Patient's name

- Patient's ID

- Date

- Consultant/specialist/MD provider

- Referring diagnosis (can include symptoms)

- Authorized visits/procedures

- Effective date of authorization (either an actual date by which to provide the referred service or a time frame such as 30 days)

Make sure you copy the referral before you give it to the patient. Not having this
piece of paper may lead to more work for your office and can be construed as
poor customer service.

Form storage
In an electronic medical record system, design the form so that it saves automatically within the system when you print it. This will ensure that you have a copy
of the referral. If you do not have an electronic system, file copies of the forms
collectively or in individual patients' charts. Filing them collectively usually
helps in finding one without having to pull the patient's chart, but filing them in
patients' charts ensures all information about each patient is in one place.

Receiving referrals

When you end up on the receiving end of referrals, you must know for each
referral whether it should have come from the patient's PCP or plan. To save
staff time, ask patients to secure the authorization from their PCPs or plans.
However, understand that your staff may have to assist patients who can't obtain
the appropriate authorization. Otherwise, you will not get paid.

Establish a policy for seeing patients who arrive at your practice without the required authorization form. Consider

- whether you will see them at the risk of not being reimbursed for the visit

- whether you will first require the form

- whether your contract with the insurer offers a way to obtain retroactive authorization

- how you will handle patients who don't have authorizations but whom you must treat (i.e., those who are very sick when they come to your practice) without authorization forms

- whether you will accept authorizations by fax or e-mail if your contracted plans allow these methods

Have a phone available in your office so patients who arrive without authorizations can call for them. Make a note in your appointment schedule about each patient's authorization. Has it been requested? Has it arrived? How it is getting there (e.g., is the patient bringing it)?

Many offices appoint one staffer to review the next day's appointments and verify the availability of all authorizations. Assign the same person to review the forms as they arrive to ensure they include all the necessary information. Set up a filing system for referral forms that arrive by mail. Keep them in a separate file for daily review until the patient comes in or you send the authorization to the insurance company.

Finally, determine what you will do with the referral forms after patient visits.

Make sure the authorization number appears on the claim and then file the referral form in the patient's chart in case you need it for the appeals process.

Performing consultations at the hospital

It's difficult enough to gather necessary information and communicate clearly with patients in your office, but it's even tougher to get paid for performing hospital consultations on patients whom you do not know.

These patients often don't know that you are a separately practicing, fee-for-service doctor specifically called into the case by their regular doctors. Worse yet, previous consulting physicians—not even the patients' regular doctors—may have called on you for consultations, leaving the patients (and their families) still more puzzled about you.

If you handle such consults, educate the patient about your role—and your fee. Simply reciting the facts to weakened, worried patients often fails. Even when they're perfectly healthy, people tend to hear what they want to and not what might cost them money. Having third-party insurance doesn't change the problem because patients who have insurance still face deductibles, copays, and non-covered service obligations for consults they don't remember.

If you're a referral-oriented specialist plagued by this problem, draft an attractive "consultation card" such as the sample in Figure 6.1 on p. 60 to leave with each consult patient. The card confirms that you had a special role, that you in fact performed specific services, and that someone will eventually have to pay you for your work. The card remains with the patient so he or she knows about and remembers your involvement even after the actual encounter.

Fig 6.1: Sample referral consultation card

Your doctor, Dr. Smith, asked that I see you in consultation to advise her about your care. I am a heart specialist concerned with that aspect of your care.

This card confirms that I have reviewed your medical chart carefully and examined you in person. I will provide a report of my findings and suggestions to your doctor.

As a separately practicing doctor, I will charge my usual fee for the consultation. My office will gladly work with you to help you obtain any insurance reimbursement to which you are entitled.

John J. Jones, MD

Chapter 7

Consumer-directed healthcare

As we enter an era of consumer-directed healthcare (CDH), every year more insurers offer high-deductible health plans (HDHP), and employers—desperate to contain skyrocketing healthcare costs—offer health savings accounts (HSA) to go with them.

Healthcare experts say that by the end of 2006, more than one-third of all Americans will participate in a CDH plan. And the Center for Studying Health System Change expects HSAs to capture 15%–50% of the market by 2010. Therefore, you must take a critical look at how these arrangements may affect you and your patients and how you can prevent potential problems.

If you struggle to collect even a \$10–\$20 copayment from patients, the prospect of collecting hundreds of dollars at a time may seem daunting, says Gil Weber, MBA, a Florida-based practice/managed care consultant. Although it's too early to tell whether you will experience significant collection problems with HDHP patients, the potential for trouble is certainly there.

Prepare for changing patient preferences

Because CDH forces patients to pay a greater portion of healthcare costs themselves, they may refrain from visiting the doctor unless it is absolutely necessary, says the Georgia-based consultant Reiboldt. Patients will be much more reticent to spend money that comes directly out of their accounts. Therefore, take a multipronged approach to get your payment.

First, make it a point to educate patients about the importance of preventive care and well visits. Becoming more diligent in carrying out the following best practices may help:

- Schedule follow-up visits before the patient leaves the office

- Document and remind staff about what types of acute complaints require an office visit/follow up (e.g., prescription refills, rashes, infections, tick bites, etc.)

- Schedule well visits proactively

- Distribute patient-education materials that explain when it is and isn't necessary to make an appointment

• Confirm scheduled appointments

• Train staff to look for opportunities to market to patients (e.g., ancillary services) with a high level of ethics and professionalism

Second, plan how to handle an inevitable increase in call volume. As this trend unfolds, expect to have more patients calling to ask questions in lieu of making an appointment. Therefore, consider updating your first-answer protocols to include more thorough training on answering, triaging, and transferring calls appropriately.

Enhance financial counseling services

Not only will you have to cope with patients' reluctance to spend their own money on healthcare, but you'll also be responsible for collecting significantly larger amounts when they do receive services. As mentioned in Chapter 2, excellent financial counseling services will greatly improve your practice's chances of success with CDH.

Assign adequate staff to perform this counseling and set aside a private area to hold discussions with patients. To succeed, financial counselors will need a mix of public relations know-how, customer service skills, sensitivity, and financial knowledge. Specialized knowledge of local payers and entitlement programs is also essential.

HSA holders will generally be cost-savvy patients who will want to know more about the practice and its pricing mechanisms. They will also want providers to anticipate the amount of their final bills. That means your counselors must be able to discuss predicted costs and payment methods (e.g., credit cards, payment plans, etc.) with patients.

Counselors will often be in a position to negotiate fees with patients, so staff must possess significant knowledge about what deals your practice can make with patients that will not violate your contracts with managed-care plans connected to HSAs or HDHPs. Most HSA/HDHP products are still going to be under some level of managed-care contracting. There may be some opportunity for you to negotiate fees with patients, but in many cases, they'll be tied to a preferred provider organization network that has negotiated deals with physicians, hospitals, etc.

It will be crucial for staff to understand how these plans work, so consider inviting to your office a provider representative from each plan to educate everyone in the practice and answer questions. Set aside a time when staff are not distracted so they can benefit fully from the opportunity. The meeting may take away from clinical time, but it will cost you less in the long run if you understand the nuances of CDH-related plans.

One of the most important questions to ask plan representatives is whether your practice will be allowed to collect copays and deductibles up front. As you know, the best time to collect these amounts is when the patient is in the office prior to delivery of care that day. However, some plans ask practices to send claims to the payer for adjudication before they collect copays and deductibles.

Practice management consultants highly recommend against this. Remember, all insurance contracts are negotiable. Request that you be allowed to collect high deductibles before the patient leaves your office. Assuming that you receive the green light to do this, you will need to tighten your upfront collection policies as outlined in Chapter 5.

Under CDH plans—which require more of your payment stream to come from individuals—billing, collection, and follow-up issues will likely ensue. It's a good time to get all of your collection policies and procedures together to confront problems such as managing bad debt and outsourcing with collection agencies. If you work with collection agencies that charge a percentage of balances collected, consider negotiating lower rates in connection with larger amounts.

Chapter 8

Alternative revenue streams

Ironically, although patients may be more reluctant to spend their own money on routine care, noninsured or ancillary services are increasing in popularity. Today more practices provide these services to boost the quality of patient care and their bottom lines. These services make sense from a patient-care standpoint and add the potential for increasing revenue and capturing an additional share of the reimbursement dollar, says attorney Bruce A. Johnson.

You may appreciate being able to offer patients the services they need and to provide everything within the scope of your abilities, says William Caplan, MD, whose practice has offered ancillary services for more than 30 years. It also gives you the chance to maintain the quality of care by watching over these services, as opposed to sending patients elsewhere to get them done.

Make the move to ancillaries

If you decide to try adding an ancillary service to your practice, start with an ancillary-services committee that includes physicians, the practice administrtor, legal counsel, and someone who has business experience (e.g., an outside consultant). The group should do the following:

Evaluate your patient demographics

Determine which services you most commonly refer to other facilities. Look at those services first as potential ancillaries because you know that you have patients who require those services and could benefit from having them performed in-house.

For example, if you're a cardiologist, it makes sense for your practice to provide electrocardiograms and echocardiology because nearly every patient you see needs these tests. On the other hand, you may not have enough patient volume to cover the expense of nuclear echocardiology or other less common services. If you don't do the homework to find ancillaries that fit your practice, you can get hurt. Most ancillaries aren't profitable in the beginning, and you must carry them until they are.

Examine financial, operational, and legal aspects

Once you determine that you have the need and patient volume to bring these services to your practice, consider how much you'll get paid and how much the initial set-up and delivery of the services will cost. Decide where you will perform the new services, who will deliver them, and whether you'll need additional staff.

Most importantly, research the legal implications of adding the new service. With so many restrictions and regulations, you don't want to step into an area where you will expose yourself to an infraction that you weren't even aware existed. Pay close attention to the Stark laws and any state self-referral statutes.

Estimate best- and worst-case scenarios

You may initially feel overly optimistic about reimbursement and arrive at glowing financial projections for a new ancillary service. But Johnson warns that you must be realistic and realize that an ancillary service may initially cost you money.

Implement and monitor new services

Prioritize the list of ancillaries you're considering, and narrow it to two or three viable options. For your first venture, select the services that you believe will most benefit your practice. Once you begin offering the new service, monitor its progress. After six months, evaluate whether you need to change the system. Caplan says some of his ventures turned a profit within the first six months, whereas others took almost two years. Even with thorough planning, obstacles still arise.

Be aware

Some insurance companies will not pay for certain ancillary services or will take several months to accept them as medically necessary. Caplan says it took one insurance company nearly 18 months to pay for new endoscopy services. For the most part, if the services are within the scope of your normal routine, it makes sense to bring them to your practice, even with a delay in payment. You order these tests everyday, so why not perform them yourself?

Test the waters with noninsured services

As with ancillary services, you may want to consider offering noninsured services (e.g., complementary and alternative medicine [CAM]) at your practice instead of referring patients to other providers. This also can increase your bottom line, improve patient care, and offer practice diversification.

Most physicians at your practice will need to be on board. You don't need unanimous acceptance, but you'll have trouble profiting from CAM services if you're the only one who wants to add them, Johnson says. The longer you wait to have other physicians weigh in, the more time, energy, and money you might waste.

Adding these services to your practice can be simple, as long as you answer the following questions before you begin:

What do you consider complementary and alternative services?

This definition may vary by practice size, location, number of physicians, or specialty. CAM includes services such as nutritional counseling, massage and therapy, exercise therapy, and acupuncture. When defining these terms for your practice, consider how the extra services relate to what your practice already does and what the services will add.

What services will you provide?

As with ancillary services, you need to select services that make the most sense for you. Stay as close to your practice's original business model as possible. For example, a rehab and physical medicine practice may want to add massage therapy to its services, but it wouldn't make sense for that practice to start selling herbs.

How will you get paid for these services?

Some services have corresponding HCPCS or CPT codes. This means that you could potentially get paid for these procedures. However, few insurance companies will reimburse for them, meaning your patients may have to pay for them out of pocket.

Tie the amount you charge to the type of service and its average price in the community, Johnson says. If you're selling a product such as a vitamin, base your price on the price suggested by the manufacturer. For a service such as a massage, set a price close to the average charge in the community. You can also turn to nonhealthcare settings for additional help in determining an appropriate charge (e.g., the amount a salon or spa charges for an hour-long massage).

Does adding this service make business sense?

Evaluate both the short- and long-term profitability of offering these services. Is this just an idea or will it make money for your practice? If you're unsure how to determine these numbers or don't feel comfortable making this determination, bring in an outside expert and look at market research.

What legal requirements or prohibitions are associated with providing these services?

Legal rules vary by service and state. For example, practices cannot offer certain skin-care services unless a licensed aesthetician provides them. Certain states will not allow acupuncture and traditional medicine to take place in the same organization. Your state corporate practice of medicine doctrines can provide these rules and requirements.

How can you efficiently and effectively add these services?

You've done research and decided to offer CAM at your practice. Now you must determine how to add these services without disrupting your current practice or spending too much money.

Consider offering the services minimally in the beginning. For example, you can add physical therapy to your practice without hiring a full-time specialist by scheduling all patients for the therapist on the same day or close together in the week. Your patients never received these services before, so you have some scheduling flexibility.

Check your rearview mirror

Adding CAM or ancillary services can provide wonderful benefits for your patients. But don't allow these additions to divert energy from your core business model. For example, rethink using an exam room for complementary or alternative therapies if the dollar amount you generate from those services is less than what you'd make using that room for regular patient visits.

Check your bottom line six to nine months after you first add these services and then every six months thereafter. Even if the idea was a sound one originally, determine whether it makes money or detracts from the practice so much that it doesn't make sense. If you find that these services don't benefit your patients or bring in extra revenue, stop offering them. The financial loss to stop providing the services will be minimal, and you'll have flexibility to consider other alternative revenue streams or options such as updating your fee schedule, discussed in Chapter 9.

Figure 8.1: Do's and don'ts of adding an ancillary service

When considering this addition to your practice . . .

DO
Take risks.

Choose ancillaries that will help you control the flow of managed-care dollars. If you have enough volume to make money with an ancillary, control costs by preventing price increases.

Choose ancillaries in which your group already has a large referral volume.

Invest in joint ventures if finances or regulations prevent you from investing alone.

DON'T
Rely on a business plan alone and ignore physician experience. Physicians can sometimes predict outcomes better than a business plan can.

Plan on launching your ancillary services without completing due diligence.

Expect an initial return.

Invest in an ancillary you cannot afford to carry initially.

Improving collections from third-party payers

Chapter 9

Fee schedule updates

If you're like most practices, most of your collections come from third-party payers. Traditional indemnity formats (i.e., the 80/20 plans in which patients controlled which doctors they went to see) have all but disappeared, and contractual arrangements with HMOs, PPOs, and similar managed-care organizations dominate your billers' activities.

Contract arrangements may seem as though they should make it easy to collect amounts due. That's not always the case. You may have difficulty negotiating the best rates with your payers or appealing denied claims. You also need to keep your own internal fee schedule updated to ensure you know how much payers should pay for each procedure and when you should attempt to negotiate better rates.

It's tempting to not bother updating your fee schedules. With all of the different discounted fees from payers, it seems to make no difference what you charge. But that's just not true: If you neglect to keep your prices up-to-date, you will miss out on revenue that you earned.

Payers used to rely on your individual and regional billing history to determine allowable fees. Explanations of benefits used to commonly include "over UCR (usual, customary, and reasonable)"—the portion of the total charges greater than the allowed charges based on the contractual agreement between the insurance company and the provider. Although this generally no longer occurs, payers still track pricing to determine what the market will bear when formulating a discounted fee schedule.

The dollar amounts on your insurance bills do make a difference. Not only will undercharging put you at risk of missing contracted fees, but it also negatively influences the market price for your services—albeit subtly. Effective practice management includes properly setting and maintaining your fees.

Here are four important reasons to stay on top of your fees:

1. Discount contracts obligate the payer to pay the lower of the agreed-upon fees or the provider's usual charge

2. You still have some nondiscounted fee-for-service business for which you can receive a fair price

3. Keeping your fee schedule in tune with inflation provides a better benchmark for tracking your practice's performance yearly

4. When payers or patients want to negotiate, reasonable and up-to-date rates remind them how deeply you already discount fees

Updating fee schedules appropriately

Knowing the importance of updating your rates is only half the battle. Now you must actually take care of your fee schedule. If you still feel uncomfortable raising prices and setting new rates, try the following strategies to ease the process and fend off critics:

- Use objective standards to set fair prices. The Consumer Price Index, relative value scales, cost-based accounting, and regional "usual and customary" charge rates provide impartial data to help you create sensible fees.

- Budget time and resources to provide care for those who can't afford it. One radiologist sets aside one day out of every 10 to provide free care, calling it his medical tithe.

Objective measures and comparisons help you approach fee setting with a proper businesslike attitude. And purposefully helping patients who can't afford your services may help provide you with the courage to ask for fair payment from those who can.

Setting new fees

Medicare's Resource-Based Relative Value Scale continues to dominate fee structures, so rework your fee schedule to reflect those relative values. However, don't use Medicare's conversion rate. Build your own fee-analyzing spreadsheet such as the one in Figure 9.1 on p. 78.

Once you analyze your current fees, you have data that can help you decide on your new fees. First, search your existing schedule to determine whether any prices undercut Medicare's fee schedule. Especially note their effective conversion factors—and make sure your new factor is higher.

Figure 9.1: Sample fee analyzer

1	2	3	4	5	6	7	8	9	10
Code	Procedure	Existing fee	Total RVUs	Effective conversion factor	Proposed fee	Current Medicare fee	Plan 1	Plan 2	Plan 3
99201	Office visit new, level 3	$75.00	$2.19	Column 3 divided by column 4	Column 4 multiplied by column 5	$72.84	$59.00	$64.00	$68.00

Instructions for updating a fee schedule:

Columns 1–2: List every procedure in your fee schedule and its CPT code. Save time by importing the list from your billing system.

Column 3: Enter the current fee for each procedure. You may be able to import these with the procedures and the codes.

Column 4: Using the Medicare fee schedule, enter the total nonfacility RVUs for each procedure listed. For ancillary procedures with split professional and technical components, post global RVUs if that's how you normally bill. Geographical adjustments are irrelevant to this number.

Column 5: Divide your existing fee by its total RVUs. The resulting number is your effective conversion factor (dollars per RVU) for each procedure.

Column 6: Calculate your new fee.

Column 7: Enter the current Medicare fee for each procedure.

Columns 8–10: Enter the fee from as many contracted payers as you can.

Next, test a higher conversion factor—usually 50% above Medicare's fee schedule is about average. Create a formula to multiply each procedure's total RVUs by the new conversion factor; the result is the proposed new fee. Compare each new fee with its old fee to determine the price increase. Make sure your new fee schedule is within your community average for charges. If the fee adjustment is large, consider phasing it in over time. You may find that you need to adjust fees downward with your new conversion factor.

Handling reactions

Higher fees can elevate blood pressure throughout the practice. Patients, especially self-pay or those with traditional insurance, may react negatively. Your partners may be uncomfortable with raising prices, and your staff may take the patients' side when complaints arise.

Take a top-down approach to handling these challenges. Start by helping your partners understand the need to revise a neglected fee schedule and the practical advantage of relative-value pricing. Although physicians sometimes prefer multiple fee schedules to avoid overstating accounts receivable, a single schedule allows accurate comparisons between plans. Try instilling this simple fee-setting philosophy:

Your actual costs + a reasonable profit margin = your fee

Once you arrive at a new fee schedule, typically best timed with the annual release of the new Medicare fee schedule, hold a short orientation with your staff. Explain briefly the need to update the fees and prepare staff to handle patient inquiries. Encourage them to use a sympathetic tone when explaining to patients the reasons why practice costs continue to rise.

Chapter 10

Accounts receivable

Once you set your fees and set out to collect them, it's essential that you keep tabs on your accounts receivable (A/R). For example, do you know what it means when your practice's 120-day-old receivables are 50% higher than the national average for your specialty? Do you know what to do? In a nutshell, it means that you had better find out why.

Use aged national receivable statistics (e.g., from associations such as the Medical Group Management Association) as a starting point toward understanding what's happening with your billing and collection procedures. Use these numbers to start your analysis, but don't use them as your only benchmarks. Develop your own targets. Pay attention to your practice history; less-than-optimal A/R numbers aren't always a result of poor management of collections.

For example, one radiology practice carried what looked like an exorbitant amount of old receivables. However, the group handled many workers' compensation injuries that took at least one full year to generate payment. This expanded the practice's receivables, but ultimately, the physicians received 100% of their fees. Although the radiologists suffered while the initial claims worked their way through the system, after performing the work for more than a year, they passed the cash crunch. The group now appreciates the real value of those bad receivables.

However, more often than not, bad numbers signal problems that you must identify and fix. That requires starting fresh every month to understand the data in your receivables. Once you analyze the data, file the results for future comparison. Measuring against your practice's past is the best way to evaluate your financial performance.

As you examine your receivables, look for these common trouble areas:

Are your aged accounts consistent by payer?

If your third-party payers collectively average payment in 35 days, but one carrier takes significantly longer, determine why. Perhaps it recently altered its processing procedures, and you must update your staff. Maybe the provider is slow, and you need to turn up the heat.

Are your aged receivables distributed evenly among the group's doctors?

If one physician has markedly older receivables than the rest of the group, dig deeper. Does his or her payer mix differ significantly? Perhaps the doctor has a large concentration of slower-paying Medicaid patients.

How do self-pay receivables compare to other categories?

Poor receivables from self-pay patients often indicate problems with your collection staff. Maybe you need to push them to focus on their collections work. If so, start with the patients who owe the largest amounts.

If you practice at several locations, you should see similar aging results among sites, particularly if you centralize claims filing. If you notice site-to-site differences, perhaps staff in one branch don't follow billing procedures. Conversely, if you identify superior performance, look into it. You may find ways to improve procedures throughout all of your sites.

Try payer mapping to track A/R

In addition to tracking staff and practice sites, you need to pay attention to A/R by payer. Vetting your aged receivables may show that most of your problems stem from payer slowness and not inefficiency, understaffing, or lack of training at your practice. An ongoing payer-mapping process may help you identify problem payers.

Here's how to map payers:

- Set up a complete record for each payer, including contract specifications and filing requirements

- For each payer, list your top 25–50 procedures by CPT code and the expected reimbursement based on your contract

- Keep a running tally of consistently denied or underpaid procedures

- Identify which payers habitually deny or downgrade legitimate claims, as well as those who pay late (from the information you recorded in the tally)

- Target payers who have poor reimbursement records

The mapping process may take time to develop, but once it's done, it becomes an extremely valuable reimbursement tool. It helps you identify where to concentrate greater collection efforts and becomes particularly handy when dealing with payers who are slow to update their systems with current coding changes. Some payers routinely deny new CPT codes during this process. If you keep track of this information, you'll understand the reason for the denial.

Watch for indicators of serious payer problems

Uncovering a payer pattern of repeated denials for proper procedures or consistently late payments may signal trouble that requires more than cleaning up your internal claims-processing procedures.

If you continually encounter any of the following problems, beware. Healthcare attorney Dennis Hursh and practice administrator Ed Howley agree that constant problems with what should be normal reimbursements may signal that a plan is about to make significant changes that could eventually affect your continued payments.

Increased denials

If a plan suddenly begins rejecting services that it formerly covered or questioning every claim you submit, investigate. You might find a new medical director introducing different policies, strictly enforcing previously loose guidelines, or reinterpreting contract requirements.

Growing payment delays

Continual late-payment excuses or attempts to alter allowable payment-period deadlines can indicate serious financial trouble at the corporate level. Know your contracts' and state's payment time frames, and, if necessary, enlist your state insurance commissioner's intervention.

New procedural roadblocks

When a payer seems to create unnecessary difficulties where none existed before, be on guard. Don't automatically assume the worst when such problems arise, but instead, ask your provider relations representative for an explanation. Most importantly, pay attention to increasing staff complaints about dealing with a particular plan. Your staff form the front line for payer interactions and can alert you to the first rumbles of real problems with a payer.

Chapter 11

Relationships with payers

Regardless of how you submit claims, at some point you will rely on personal contact with your payer account representative. It's always better to form a working relationship with a specific person at these large, sometimes impersonal organizations.

To start, for each major carrier, find out who specifically handles your account. Have the billing coordinator at your practice call to make introductions. This is a good opportunity to determine whether the systems in place now work and whether you could do anything to make them run more smoothly. Review the relationship with the account representative periodically, and always call him or her directly with problems or questions.

Personal contact removes the ambiguity of being "just another number" to a big payer and makes the interactions familiar, moving from impersonal to a one-on-one handling of mutually important matters. It helps ensure that you represent your patients fairly to the payer, that the payer will answer questions and pay you more promptly, and that interactions regarding plan requirements are as smooth as possible.

Avoid conflict

Knowing your account representative well often lessens the chance of conflict with the payer. Taking an adversarial tone with a third-party payer when it denies, downgrades, or delays payment can prove tantamount to biting the hand that feeds you. But when you know the payer representative personally, try a good-natured approach before squaring off for battle.

When you discover a pattern of inappropriate denials, go to your new-found friend on the inside. That friend is responsible for training your office about insurance verification, copays, and billing procedures, and for answering your questions. A payer who is serious about provider relations will have that representative visit your office periodically.

Treat payer representatives with respect and heed their advice about how to submit claims. If you do, you may find someone who will take your list of problem claims and personally walk them through the system. Trying the peaceful tactic first will likely prevent you from ever having to go over your representative's head. The key to gaining such an inside advocate is having an unassuming attitude. Success in building productive relationships means making friends out of your opponents.

Unfortunately, neither provider-service representatives nor any other helpful payer clerks can solve every problem. Sometimes company policy or contract interpretation leads to claim denials. When you hit a policy wall, take your case up the corporate ladder. The less threatening you seem, the more help you will likely receive.

You may have to appeal to someone with more authority, perhaps even the medical director. A friend on the inside can help you arrange a meeting with the appropriate decision-maker, raising your chances of success.

Don't be fooled by a good relationship with a payer

Your friendly relations with your payer representative, although critical to a good working relationship, may not help you escape denied claims. Payers deny or downgrade about half of all submitted claims for no apparent reason. Too many medical practices accept the lower reimbursement and slow turnaround without argument. Payers delay payments to hold onto reimbursement dollars for as long as they can, frequently reinvesting the money rightfully owed to providers.

One medical practice administrator tells of the following informal conversation with an executive from a large managed-care organization:

"If you're a nonparticipating physician, the first check we would cut is for 50% of your charge," the executive said. "If you file an inquiry, we send an additional 25%. If you file a second inquiry, we'll pay the 25% balance."

Don't get caught in a situation in which you don't receive appropriate reimbursement simply because you don't know precisely how the payer thinks. If you've built a relationship with the payer, contact it directly. But don't do this lightly. Make sure you can demonstrate a clear pattern of denials, downgrades, and delays. Emphasize that you are finding it difficult to provide quality care for patients without increasing their out-of-pocket costs.

Before involving patients directly, check your contract to make sure that this tactic doesn't breach a gag clause. If it doesn't, you may want patients to step in and complain to their employers. Don't be afraid to educate patients about their consumer rights or encourage them to file valid complaints with the insurance commissioner.

Your staff can prepare the complaint for the patient's approval and signature, so keep on hand a form such as the one in Figure 11.1 on p. 91. Aligning yourself with patients increases your chances of obtaining results, particularly when a payer has been abusive or obstructive.

As a last resort, voice your own complaint to your state's insurance commissioner, particularly if you're experiencing chronic or complex reimbursement troubles. The commissioners generally have full authority to arbitrate cases. Because less than 2% of reimbursement issues ever make it to the insurance commissioner, a batch of complaints can get a difficult payer's attention fast.

However, it remains true that patients and their employers typically have far more clout with the commission than you do. Working with patients and employers, providing them information to take to the commission, and encouraging them to follow through may produce better—and faster—results than filing your own grievance as a provider.

In the long run, you'll collect best by building strong relationships with all the key players: patients, employers, and payers. That way, you can turn potential adversaries into allies in your fight to provide quality, cost-effective care.

Figure 11.1: Sample patient complaint form

To:
State insurance commissioner
Address
City, State, ZIP

Your name: _____
Agent or company complaint against: _____
Address: _____
Policy number: _____
Day telephone: _____ Evening telephone: _____
Date of treatment: _____ Insured: _____
Claim or file number: _____

Is this the only complaint you have filed with the insurance commissioner con-
cerning this matter? If no, please explain.
    ☐ Yes
    ☐ No

Have you taken up this problem with an official of the company, agent, or bro-
ker? If yes, give his or her name, address, and title.
    ☐ Yes
    ☐ No

Please provide a brief statement about what the agent or company has done or
has failed to do:

_____   _____
Signature   Date

Attached are the following:
    ☐ Copy of original insurance claim
    ☐ Copy of previous written correspondence to agent or insurance company
    ☐ Copy of insurance policy
    ☐ Copy of any correspondence from insurance company regarding claim

Chapter 12

Denied claims appeals

Did you know that most of the time, your billing clerks accept write-offs of denied claims without filing an inquiry? Unless your staff know to check each third-party payment and to inquire or resubmit each one that appears underpaid, you are losing important revenue. That's why it behooves you to have a well-trained insurance coordinator and to set strict rules for handling reimbursement.

Unfortunately, if you're like many of your colleagues, you may not know what reimbursement you should receive, so most of your unwarranted reductions or denials will not get appealed. The more you appeal downgrades and denials, the fewer the claims that will require appeals. It's not cost-effective for the payer to expend clerical hours addressing appeals of legitimate claims.

Streamline your appeals process

Because third-party payers routinely reduce what they owe you, defend yourself with your own routine appeal. For a carrier to even consider reversing a denial, you must provide concrete proof that you're entitled to the payment.

Before entering the fray, make sure that your billing house is in order, meaning your initial insurance submissions are complete and error-free. Verify your ICD-9 and CPT codes. Check all designated submission data fields. If you anticipate that the payer will require chart notes or other documentation, be sure you have documentation that substantiates what you billed.

A denial that you appeal should be based on a misinterpretation or another decision-making factor from the payer, not a mistake on your end. In other words, you shouldn't appeal a claim that was denied because your practice miscoded a procedure or because when you submitted the claim, you believed a service was medically necessary only to find out later that it wasn't.

Research the background of the denial before making a decision, says healthcare attorney Todd Rodriguez. Don't appeal when it's clear that the payer will not cover the service, and make sure that going through the appeal process will be valuable to you in the long run. Use discretion when determining which claims to appeal, and try to avoid those that are not financially significant to your bottom line.

Recognize that many initially denied procedures are typically either not "generally authorized" or fall into the vast gray area of individual circumstances. Acknowledge this endemic fuzziness up front and you'll save yourself, your staff, and the payer's staff a great deal of anxiety and generalized ill will by avoiding the entire question.

How? This simple combination frequently does the trick: Instead of passing appeals through several physicians (even with threats of legal action), try submitting substantiating medical documentation (e.g., the medical record for the service and a copy from the CPT book of the CPT definition for the code used) along with claims for such procedures, whether medical or surgical. Such substantiation makes it far more likely that you'll prevail on appeal.

Send a succinct appeals letter

Even sending medical literature along with your claims will not prevent all denials. That means you will need to put in place an appeals process. It doesn't have to be complicated. In fact, keeping it simple encourages your staff to wait it out until the claim is properly paid. A solid, well-written letter of appeal, along with back-up documentation, can help you convince a payer to rethink a denied claim and pay you the money you deserve.

The appeal letter gives you a chance to explain every piece of information in the original claim and sets the tone for the rest of the process, says healthcare attorney William Sarraille. Often, it's your only means of presenting your case to third-party payers.

The right person for the job

Once you decide to appeal a claim, assign the task of writing the appeal letter to the appropriate person. The type of denial will determine the primary author of the appeal letter, says Sarraille. If the payer denies a claim because of incorrect or questionable coding, ask someone who understands the codes to write the letter.

Don't pass off the job to low-level administrative staff. They often don't have the same standing to address certain problems as clinicians do, are not as sensitive to the issues, and won't be as effective. Also, lower-level staff may not know the appeals process as well as someone who is higher up. In using less knowledge-able people, you run the risk of creating other problems inadvertently.

Essentials of an appeal letter

Your appeal letter must tell the payer exactly what you want to say and paint you in the correct light. Start your letter with an introductory section that stresses your practice's qualifications, your commitment to compliance and providing appropriate services, and, if applicable, the importance of your practice to the payer, Sarraille suggests.

Then offer a detailed account of the treatment provided to the patient in question. Cross-reference the medical record. Use this as your opportunity to walk the reviewer through the parts of the medical record that you want to emphasize or that you think he or she might miss.

The rest of the letter should address the following:

- The patient's medical history

- Complaints on the date of the visit

- Necessity of the treatment and its relation to the historical problems and chief complaint

- Compliance of the treatment with accepted treatment patterns

- Benefits of the treatment to the patient

Include back-up documentation to support your argument (e.g., journal articles, excerpts or letters, or materials from appropriate medical societies). Check that the information that you include does not give the payer any material to use against you. If you find any information that could potentially hurt you—even if it seems insignificant to you—it's better not to submit the material at all.

Include with the appeal letter and back-up documents a tool to confirm that the payer received the information that you sent. Verification (e.g., a certified return receipt or signature on a Federal Express receipt) can provide confirmation that the appeal letter and accompanying documentation reached their destination, Rodriguez says.

Most importantly, remember the following five considerations when writing your letter:

1. **Make the process easy for the reviewer.** The more accessible you make the pertinent information, the more likely it is that the reviewer will see it and take the time to look through it. The reviewer shouldn't have to search for the important information.

2. **Keep the tone of your appeal letter upbeat.** Anger and frustration turn people off. Assume good will, even if it wasn't there, Sarraille says. Make a substantive argument rather than attacking the payer.

   During the review, you often deal with the colleagues of those people who made the original decision to deny your claim. Discussing the stupidity of the denial decision or policy will not be effective. Refrain from bad-mouthing the reviewer's colleagues and company and you'll get much further in the process.

3. **Double-check your back-up documentation.** If even the slightest possibility exists that the reviewer could use information against you, do not submit it. You don't want to give the reviewer any information to justify the original decision.

4. Involve credible outside parties. Neutral third parties can help in the appeal process, Sarraille says. Choose your resources based on the reason for the denial. Many resources exist: coding consultants, attorneys, state and national associations, and even members of your carrier's advisory committee.

5. Place the information in the broader context of your practice. Explain the benefits of what you do at your practice and how the service on the denied claim benefited the patient.

Follow up with the payer

If you don't hear anything but have evidence that the carrier received your appeal information, or if four or more weeks have passed since you sent the letter, follow up with a phone call. If you still do not receive word or payment after the phone call, send a second appeal letter. Make another copy for your pending-claims file.

If the form letter appeals don't resolve the denial after two cycles, try finding help further up the payer ladder. Carefully record the name of each representative with whom you speak, the date and time you spoke, and any notes from the conversation. Ask for everything in writing.

If you don't obtain the information you want from your account representative, ask to speak to his or her supervisor. If you're still not satisfied, go directly to the district manager. Management has greater authority to approve payment, so be prepared to take your case up the line. Managers and executives also are generally more responsive if they believe you'll damage their company's reputation.

Remember that the appeal process can be long and tedious. In most cases, the payer will not reverse the original denial decision unless the case moves past the review stage—also known as reconsideration—and past the fair hearing stage to the administrative law judge level. Even then, it could take several months to a year to set a hearing date.

But if you believe that your payer wrongly denied a claim and you want to appeal it, present your information in a clear, professional manner, provide proper proof to support your argument, and be ready to explain your reasons for the appeal. The payer isn't always correct. Carriers interpret federal regulations and guidance just as you do, Rodriguez says. Guidance from the national office isn't always clear, and payers also can make mistakes in interpreting it.

Chapter 13

Contract negotiations

Having a good relationship with payers and correctly appealing denied claims do not diminish the importance of how and when you renegotiate your contracts with them and what rates come from those negotiations. That's why instead of allowing your contracts to carry over from year to year, look at how they perform and determine whether you need to or can renegotiate them to bring in more money.

Look at contracts yearly and renegotiate them every two or three years, says consultant Lynn Steffes, PT. Don't avoid renegotiating contracts because you believe it's going to be a hassle or you won't receive the rates you want. That's a surefire way to miss collecting money you earned.

Look closely at the conditions of contracts

Before attempting any renegotiations, analyze your practice and your contracts to

- determine your own cost per visit for delivering the service

- calculate whether you make or lose money or break even on each contract

- look at the percentage of reimbursement that each individual contract brings in

- update your own fees as needed

Steffes says some practices never or rarely increase their fees because they assume that no one pays what they actually charge. However, costs increase all the time, and when payers see that your fees don't change, they don't see a reason to change their rates. Keeping static rates may have been fine when you originally negotiated your contracts. Maybe you didn't know quite what types of patients would make up the majority of your patient population or what kinds of treatment they would need. But after just one year, you should have a much better idea of the answers to those uncertainties.

Head to the negotiation table

If your payers will not work with you on the contracts, and your patients will not agree to pay for services with their own money, you will have to renegotiate with your payers. Keep in mind that this interaction shouldn't be the first time since you signed the initial contract that you speak to your representative. Check in with your contact fairly regularly, even if it's just to ask a quick question or say thank you for resolving a difficult account.

That said, if you get past that point and still need to renegotiate your rates, keep the following tactics in mind:

Know your reimbursement needs

Before sitting down with a payer, determine which rates will make the contract profitable for you yet still worthwhile for the payer. Figure out which procedures you perform the most—those that make up at least 80% of your business—and determine the minimum amount you need to be paid for those procedures.

Put all of this information into a spreadsheet that calculates the cost of your top CPT codes and your highest-cost procedures. For each procedure, identify all costs, including staff, overhead, supplies, and medicine.

Be prepared with benchmarks from other practices

Determine what changes other providers are making and the market for rate increases. Associations such as the Medical Group Management Association, the American Medical Association, or your specialty association may have these numbers handy. With them, you'll have a better starting point in negotiations. The bottom line: Keep your rates in line with inflation and other increases in the cost of treating patients.

Ask to review contracts electronically

Electronic versions of the contracts may help you determine whether the problem relates to the contract or the patient. Most plans have electronic versions of the contract available and will comply with your request if you ask. This wasn't always the case.

Until recently, most payers either wouldn't share electronic versions of their contracts or would send them in "read-only" format because they worried that providers would make changes and then bury them in the electronic version,

according to attorney Charles M. Key. But as payers have become more com-
puter-savvy and familiar with the software available, they have become less concerned about undetectable changes.

Working from an electronic version of a contract can make the review process
easier and speed up negotiations. You can more easily plug the numbers into rev-
enue-projection software to assess the fairness and profitability of the contract.
In addition, using electronic copies of the contracts allows much quicker transfer
back and forth between parties. However, beware of multiple versions of the
contracts floating around in cyberspace—not working from the newest version
could slow the process rather than speed it up.

Prove your value to the payer

Although it won't necessarily affect the rates to which payers agree, knowing the
value of your practice and showing that to payers can go a long way in negotiations, according to consultant Caryl Serbin, RN, BSN, LHRM.

You can highlight

- the qualifications of the physicians at your practice

- good patient outcomes

- your low nurse-to-patient ratios

- your enhanced services (e.g., state-of-the-art technology)

- your high patient-satisfaction rates

- any specialized services that your practice offers

Giving the payer representative a tour is a great way to show off your facility,
Serbin says. The rep will see firsthand how your practice operates. This gesture

also may improve your relationship with the payer, which will help in your negotiations.

Enlist help from patients

Plan members have a certain power over the payers, according to administrator Lisa Ferriss. If you're having trouble joining a particular payer or negotiating appropriate rates, ask your patients to explain to the payer that they want your practice in the plan. This can go a long way toward improving your odds for success.

Be creative

Consider incorporating a tiered system that gives patients an incentive to select you as their provider or gives the payer an incentive to recommend you. For example, hospitals often charge more money than your practice might for services such as evaluations, yet the patient pays the same copay at the hospital and at your practice. In such a case, renegotiate the contract to reduce the copay at your facility.

Also try to create an incentive plan for the network in which you provide rebates if the network sends a certain number of referrals your way. For example, if you normally see 100 patients under a contract but instead receive 125, you'll discount the plan. Clinical outcomes often work well to show payers that their enrollees are satisfied with your services. Payers want to see numbers that prove that yours is a cost-effective option.

Stay flexible, watch for unfavorable contract terms

Everything is negotiable, even if the representative says certain aspects cannot change. But remember, it is a negotiation. Be willing to give in some areas and hold firm on those that are more critical to your facility.

Don't just focus on your reimbursement rates. Also negotiate out of the contract any terms or language that might hurt your reimbursement. For example, make sure the contract does not have a cancellation clause that only allows you to cancel it for cause (i.e., if the payer violates the contract). A clause such as this can trap you into staying with an unprofitable contract. Instead, try to include a clause that allows you to end the contract with 90 days' notice, without regard to the reason.

Also, make sure that the contract contains reasonable claims-submission and payment deadlines. For example, a contract that stipulates that if you do not submit claims within five days of service you will not get paid may not be reasonable for your practice. Go through your negotiated contract line by line and have people such as the business office manager, the other physicians at the practice, and your attorney look at it before signing on the dotted line.

Chapter 14

Contract termination

Even after negotiations and renegotiations, some contracts still are not profitable for your practice. For example, maybe the payer's reimbursements for procedures that you perform no longer adequately cover your costs or measure up to the average payment that similar practices in your area obtain. Or maybe a payer doesn't reimburse you according to contract provisions, causing your staff to spend too much time chasing reimbursement. Or you may not serve enough of the plan's patients to make the contract worthwhile.

Nonfinancial reasons also may play a part. For example, frustrations related to the administrative burden of having the contract (e.g., systematic denials for no apparent reason or retroactive denials related to medical necessity) may give you cause to terminate a contract. Whatever your reason, terminate any contract that causes your practice grief.

Many facilities believe a simple phone call or letter will suffice for terminating the contract. However, successfully terminating a contract is a multistep procedure.

Step one: Analyze your leverage

First, get a sense of how much leverage your group has with the payer. How important are you to the plan? For example, if you are a big fish with substantial market share in that provider's pond you may be more likely to get results with negotiation.

Also assess what that contract really means to your group (e.g., the percent of your business that the payer represents and the potential consequences should you terminate). Also, look at the major employers in your community and determine whether they offer alternative health plans.

Weigh these factors collectively to determine whether you can truly afford to walk away, and only consider terminating the contract as a last resort. Determine what the payer would have to change for you to keep the contract. Then arm yourself with data to support your grievances.

For example, with a fee-for-service payment arrangement, compare the maximum allowable fee schedule for frequently performed services to what comparably sized health plans pay in the marketplace. If the payment you receive falls well below average or the payer reimburses you less than the amount in your contract, proceed to step two.

Don't get hung up on the plan's fee for one procedure or service. Focus on the weighted average, and pay attention to payer compliance. More sophisticated practice-management systems have a module in which you input the fee schedule for any major health plan, and then the system flags claims that are paid at a lower-than-negotiated rate. If you don't have a system like this, audit for substandard payments regularly, even if just by sampling frequently performed procedures.

Step two: Check your contract

At this stage, determine what steps you must take to terminate the contract. If you are unsure, it's always a good idea to have your attorney help you figure out what your contract requires. You may see one of the following types of termination clauses:

Termination without cause

A termination-without-cause clause allows either you or the payer to terminate the contract for any reason. These contracts generally require the terminating party to give written notice of termination to the other party. Take note of how many days' notice your contract requires, and adhere to the schedule strictly to ensure that your termination is effective.

Many contracts with termination-without-cause clauses also have minimum-term clauses. A minimum-term clause sets a certain period of time that the contract must be in operation before either party can initiate a termination (e.g., 120 days of honoring the contract before terminating it).

Termination with cause

A termination-with-cause contract requires a valid reason for termination. For example, you would have cause if the payer didn't comply with contract terms (e.g., by not paying claims in a timely manner or repeatedly making inaccurate reimbursements).

Most of these contracts require a written notice to the breaching party, which then has a period of time to fix the breach before the termination can take effect. If the breaching party doesn't fix the breach, the other party may terminate the contract immediately upon written notice.

Step three: Negotiate, express intent to terminate

Before moving to termination, try negotiating with the payer to get your demands met (discussed in detail in Chapter 13). If the plan won't budge or doesn't keep promised changes after the first negotiation attempt, consider terminating the contract. The type of termination clause in the contract (i.e., with or without cause) will determine what type of information you must provide.

Don't threaten to terminate the contract unless and until you're prepared to follow through with that threat. Most health plans will cede to your demands (or a significant portion of them) at the eleventh hour, but that doesn't change the fact that when a plan believes that your group is serious, you shouldn't bluff.

A better approach is to give the payer a strong warning. Send the payer a certified notice of your intent to terminate the contract (e.g., the notice in Figure 14.1 on p. 111) if the plan does not meet your demands within a certain time frame (e.g., 30 days).

Figure 14.1: Termination letter

Date

Payer
Payer representative
Payer address

Dear payer representative:

The purpose of this letter is to advise you that the Group Board of Directors will consider termination of our contractual relationship at its next meeting. Unfortunately, we and [*payer*] have apparently reached an impasse in our efforts to insert cause.

We consider contract termination a serious event and regret having to take this action. Specifically, we are looking for [*insert request*].

Our intent is to follow the terms of the contract and applicable government regulations relating to the termination. We also intend to notify our patients, local independent insurance brokers, and major employers of our decision. Our objective is to minimize the potential adverse effect to our patients by providing ample time to find an alternate physician or new health insurance coverage.

The Board meeting will be held on [*date*], and I will advise you of the Board's decision.

I would be happy to meet with you prior to our Board meeting to discuss ways to avoid contract cancellation.

Sincerely,

Physician signature

Source: Jeff Milburn, Colorado Springs Health Partners, PC. Adapted with permission.

Send the letter by certified mail with a return receipt requested. This way, you will know the precise moment at which the payer received the letter. With a signed return receipt in hand, you have proof of when and how the payer received the letter.

Step four: Influence other stakeholders

While waiting for the plan's response to your written warning, gather other community stakeholders to fight for your cause. For example, if you're a specialty group, go to the primary care physicians who routinely refer their patients to you, and explain that you may lose the contract. If many of their patients carry that plan and they refer to you often, they may try to influence the payer to comply with your requests.

Also approach independent health insurance brokers in town who sell that payer's product. Once the brokers learn they may lose several doctors from the plan's panel, they may alert the payer's marketing department. The marketing department may in turn pressure the contracting department to find a way to not lose your business. However, resort to this strategy sparingly—it's not likely to elicit this chain reaction more than once.

Your community's major employers may be some of the most important stakeholders who come to your aid. Inform their human resources departments that you may no longer be on the payer's panel. If the employers consider your group critical to providing care to their employees, they may call the payer's marketing department as well.

Step five: Proceed with termination

Despite your efforts, sometimes you will have no alternative but to end a relationship with a payer. Time this step so that it takes effect when you will lose the
fewest patients. Provide at least three months between notification to the payer
and patients and actual termination. This window allows for follow-up negotiations—and possible reconciliation—and gives patients plenty of time to make
alternate arrangements.

Consider making the termination effective during community employers' open-
enrollment periods (i.e., the time of year during which employees are allowed to
elect new insurance coverage). In addition, check your contract for pre- and posttermination requirements. For example, some contracts require that you give
payers 60, 90, or 120 days' notice prior to the annual renewal date.

Posttermination provisions may require that you continue treating patients until
their annual benefit-renewal period—another reason to have termination coincide
with open enrollment. But if it's July and most of your patients' open enrollment
begins January 1, don't despair. You can sometimes influence employers to hold
an open-enrollment period earlier by explaining the situation.

Once the termination takes effect, follow up with a telephone call to the payer
representative who received the notice. Make sure that the payer updates its computer system to show your facility as nonparticipating; this will help you avoid
billing problems that may arise.

Step six: Communicate continually with patients

If the termination process affects a large percentage of your patients, consider posting an "open letter" in the local newspaper—and maybe post it in your waiting room—that explains that your group could not successfully reach an agreement with the plan and that you will no longer be part of its network. Avoid any negative language that may elicit a response from the payer.

Describe the consequences should a patient visit your office on an out-of-network basis (e.g., a higher copay/deductible or bill for the balance that the insurer doesn't pay), and list the health plans that you will continue to accept.

But posting a letter on your waiting room wall is not enough. Notify patients individually. Identify affected patients via your practice-management system, and send them tailored letters signed by their physician—not the administrator—with the above information.

Some patients, especially those who come in infrequently, may not pay attention to your notices, so you need to continue the communication process. When patients who carry that insurance call your office, remind them that the visit will be out of network, and explain what that means before you book the appointment.

Finally, stay in touch with the patients who switch healthcare providers. If you have a practice newsletter, continue mailing it to those patients unless they specifically request otherwise. Also mail out gentle reminders that list the health plans you do accept and state that you would be happy to have the patients back should they change insurers.

Collecting from patients after they leave the office

Chapter 15

Collection process for pursuing delinquent balances

Even with the most efficient billing and collecting procedures, you will likely still have outstanding patient balances. Although patient accounts are generally smaller and less enticing than insurance accounts, not managing them correctly can create headaches and plenty of lost revenue. In addition, mismanagement of patient accounts can be construed as fraud, particularly in Medicare coverage situations.

A well-defined process with written policies can help you salvage significant revenue and reduce the amounts that you turn over to a collection agency or write off as uncollectible. Track the money from patients who come in to your practice each day and outline the entire process of collecting revenue, from spelling out the physicians' role and selecting outstanding balances on which to focus, to delineating the steps to try to obtain the cash. Do not send an account to collections until you have sent three statements to the patient and have exhausted all other means.

Track the cash

To address patient balances, you must know precisely what amount patients have already paid. This is especially vital if you see a high volume of patients who have large copays—numbers that likely will increase as consumer-directed healthcare becomes more prevalent.

Look at the cash receipts and the corresponding bank deposit slip every day. Make sure that your staff record cash and checks separately, so you can clearly see that the cash that comes in over the counter equals the daily cash deposit.

Depending on your office hours, the deposit slip might lag a day behind your cash receipts journal. That's fine as long as you keep a running record that compares the deposit slip to the previous day's cash receipts total recorded in the journal. Performing these checks regularly and comparing the results against your own prior performance will go a long way toward keeping you abreast of the funds that come into your practice.

Clarify physician role

Involve the physicians in your practice in this process. However, you have the ability to determine their level of involvement. Maybe you give the delinquent account information to the responsible physician before sending the account out for collection, so the physician can review the medical record to ensure that there is no overriding reason (e.g., a potential malpractice problem) for handling an account outside of your normal process.

Or perhaps you give physicians veto power. In other words, billing staff handle the claim up until it will go to a collection agency. At that point, they give you or the responsible physician the records related to the claim with a note that states that the overdue accounts will go to the collection agency on a specified date—typically a week after you receive the notice—unless you instruct staff not to do so. Build that time into your collection routine so accounts will move to collection on schedule unless you say otherwise.

Select appropriate balances to go after

In all likelihood, you will have a range of overdue balances from various time periods. Decide which money to go after and how to do so. To start, don't target accounts that are fewer than 30 days outstanding. Including claims within the 30-day net would bog down your system and create more backup. Plus, a system that flagged every patient who owes any amount would likely become overburdened—as would the person handling the balances.

Create a system to go after balances

Set up a timetable for handling account balances as they reach certain ages. For example, at 35 days, send a letter that asks patients to pay the remainder of the balance within 10 days. At 45 days, call the patients as a reminder of the debt and to offer a payment plan. At 55 days, take more extreme measures (e.g., involving a collection agency).

Once you determine which aged balances to tackle, you must go about obtaining them in the appropriate manner. This could mean taking steps internally (e.g., making collections calls, sending letters, or offering discounts) or externally (e.g., enlisting a collection agency or collecting through bankruptcy court or the deceased patient's estate). The appropriate method will vary from practice to practice. Subsequent chapters explain each of these methods.

Chapter 16

Internal means
to secure
patient payment

Collection calls, collection letters, and discounts are all internal means to secure patient payment.

Collection calls

Generally, collection calls effectively urge patients to pay their delinquent accounts. Personal contact by phone tends to accomplish more than mailing repeat statements. However, the calls are only as effective as the caller who makes them. A caller who has the proper polite, positive, businesslike attitude will have far greater success than someone who is pushy, rude, or angry-sounding.

Collecting by phone is a tough job, but the caller can smooth the process by going through these steps:

1. Ensuring that he or she is talking to the debtor and not identifying him or herself or the reason for calling without being certain that the correct person is on the other end of the line.

2. Identifying him or herself by first name and the name of the practice.

3. Specifying the purpose of the call and asking for payment.

4. Pausing and listening.

5. Suggesting solutions for a patient who cannot pay the balance and working out a reasonable payment plan. There is usually at least one plan that will benefit both the patient and the practice.

6. Agreeing to specific details of the payment plan (e.g., exactly how much you expect the patient to pay, exactly when and how the patient will make payments, etc.)

7. Closing the call with a positive statement. (e.g., "I'm so glad we were able to wrap up this concern for you").

It's essential that the caller be specific on the phone with the patient. Otherwise, it's a waste of time. Also, ask that he or she write down explicit details about the call for the scheduled follow-up and in case of a lawsuit.

If the caller makes 15 collection calls per day, time may not allow for such detailed accounts of the calls. Using a uniform set of abbreviations (e.g., those found in the list in Figure 16.1) can help the assistant keep track of the action while staying calm and professional with the patient.

Figure 16.1: Standard abbreviations

Note	Meaning	Note	Meaning
BLG	Belligerent	OOW	Out of work
EOM	End of month	PhDsc or PD	Phone disconnected
EOW	End of week	POW	Payment on way
FN	Final notice	PP	Promise to pay
HHCO	Have husband call office	RC	Returned call from patient
HWCO	Have wife call office	SEP	Separated
LB	Line busy	SK	Skipped
LMCO	Left message, call office	SOS	Same old story
NA	No answer	T	Telephoned
NFA	No forwarding address	TB	Telephoned business
NI	Not in	TO	Telephoned office
NLE	No longer employed	TR	Telephoned residence
NR	No record	UEmp or UE	Unemployed
NSF	No sufficient funds check	Vfd I or VI	Verified insurance
NSN	No such number	Vfd E or VE	Verified employment
OOT	Out of town		

Each staff member may want to set up his or her own abbreviations. That's okay as long as everyone understands each other's personal shorthand. Whatever your staff adopt, keep and distribute a master list of the abbreviations and their meanings.

As important as it is to establish clear procedures for effective collections calls, it's equally important to train staff about principles to keep in mind when scheduling and placing collections calls:

Always work big accounts first

Don't call in alphabetical order. Begin the process with the accounts that involve the most dollars and work down the list to the smallest accounts. If your computer system cannot print out by dollar amount all accounts that are older than 90 days, highlight on your regular printout all accounts that have balances more than $300. Highlight in a different color those that have more than $200, and so on.

This approach ensures that your collection efforts will concentrate first on the accounts that are most important to your bottom line. You need a precise routine to pursue all delinquents, but this "biggest first" priority makes the best fiscal sense.

Avoid going into detail on a phone message

A patient who knows exactly who you are and why your office is calling may not take the call or phone you back. Your objective is to get patients on the phone, not to get an answering machine. And the more private a message stays (i.e., no one knows about the patient's debt but you and the patient), the more likely it is that the patient will call you back.

Call as close as possible to the time of service

Collection specialists say calling closer to the service results in greater payoffs, so move your schedule forward as much as possible. Avoid making collections calls randomly. If your schedule prescribes a first call 45 days after initial billing, be sure that's when the call occurs.

Collection letters

Letters are the second line of defense when trying to obtain patient payment. Simple collection letters most often produce the best results. Unnecessarily formal explanations and lawyerly phrases allow patients to plead confusion about how much they owe, for which visit, and when you expect payment.

So be direct. State your point clearly and succinctly. Design collections letters according to these four simple principles:

1. Use no more than two sentences per paragraph

2. Limit sentences to a maximum of 22 words, and use fewer if possible

3. Avoid words that exceed three syllables

4. Rework paragraphs that begin with first-person pronouns or possessives (e.g., we, I, my, or our)

The following five characteristics often motivate the patient to pay (you may want to play them up in the letter):

1. **Pride.** "It took many years of hard work to build up a good payment record. We're sure you don't want to jeopardize it now."

2. **Self-interest.** "We want to treat your account in a way that will be in your best interest, but that is impossible unless you respond to our requests for payment."

3. **Fairness.** "We must collect our accounts promptly so we can continue to provide you with our services."

4. **Goodwill.** "You have always had a good doctor-patient relationship with Dr. Smith, and we're relying on that to discuss this matter with you now."

5. **Fear.** "You need the protection of being able to get credit when emergency expenses come up. If you have a poor payment record, you may not get what you desperately need."

Prompt-pay discounts

Some facilities use prompt-pay discounts as an incentive to get patients to pay up front. Here's how it works: You offer a set discount (e.g., 20%) for any patient who pays in full at the time of the visit. For example, if a patient owed $100 and wanted to pay that in its entirety, he or she would only owe $80.

But this method can also work to entice patients who have outstanding balances to pay. Offer a discount—smaller than the discount you offer to patients who pay up front—for any patient who pays in full after receiving one bill. This will not cost you any more money than you would lose waiting for payment from patients. In the long run, it reduces the number of phone calls you make and letters you send.

Set specific guidelines for offering these discounts and stick to them (e.g., early birds and self-pay patients are the only patients who receive these discounts). Also, before setting up a system such as this, review your current

- contracts. Do they prevent you from discounting services? If even one contract includes this stipulation, do not implement such a program.

- billing system capabilities. You must know whether your system can include the discounts on the bills and how you will enter this information.

- staff training and materials.

- advertising content.

Chapter 17

External means
to collect payment

If in-house collection methods don't work for getting patients to pay delinquent balances, take more extreme measures such as using a collection agency or enlisting help from a collector (e.g., the Internal Revenue Service, bankruptcy court, or local credit bureaus).

Collection agencies

There are pros and cons to using collection agencies. They generally have more experience obtaining payment, and they remove from your office the burden of these accounts. The less time you spend tracking down small amounts of money, the better.

However, you lose some of the account balance because you have to pay the agency, and not all collection agencies are created equal. The characteristics of an ideal agency for your practice will vary based on the size of your practice and the number of accounts you plan to refer.

Regardless of which type of agency (i.e., traditional versus light, explained later in this chapter) you choose, you need one that is responsible. How can you be reasonably sure that the bill collector you hire will act responsibly? Basic agency law makes you liable for the action the company takes on your behalf, so this question is more important than you may believe. If you decide to use a collection agency, do the following before making a final selection:

Determine the appropriate agency type

Traditional collection agencies collect the debt and receive a portion—usually about one third—of the recovered money. Light collection agencies buy accounts from practices, paying a flat rate (usually a percentage of the account's value, based on the age of the account). A smaller practice that has a lower collection volume may look into a flat-rate agency because it will cost less than those that take a percentage. Larger practices that have more volume will likely receive more of a discount from percentage-based agencies.

Check out the agency

Ask other practices that use the agency for feedback. Follow up with references the agency provides to check its business record. Also, review a sample of the letter that your agency will send to patients. Some agencies are far more hard-nosed than others, and you have a right to approve the tone and wording of your letters. If the agency refuses to make changes to your request, move on to one that will use language with which you feel comfortable.

Out of concern about the possibility of a malpractice suit, particularly for sensitive specialties such as anesthesia and OB/GYN, take this one step further and append the approved collection letters to the agency contracts—legally obligating the agents not to stray from the agreed format.

Use multiple agencies

Employing more than one agency at once will keep them on their toes. This also allows you to compare companies and have them compete for your business, which quite often results in better net returns for your practice.

Monitor performance and success rate

Discussions in advance of signing on with agencies may not show you how the agency will actually pursue your patients. If you worry that an agency may use tactics that are too aggressive for your taste, make up one or two fictitious accounts for patients in arrears, and have staff pose as the indebted patients. The collection agency shouldn't recognize the accounts as dummies, so it will presumably use its normal procedures and language to collect them.

Once you select an agency to work with your practice, track its success rate. A normal success rate ranges between 15%–26%, according to consultant Margaret Hoban. A below-average rate means the agency must work harder; an above-average rate means you may need to do a better job collecting the account balance before sending it to the collection agency. Review your success monthly.

You are ultimately in charge of this process. Some agencies are more heavy-handed than others, but you retain the right to specify how the agency collects for you. You may need to switch agencies if the one with which you work won't agree to your terms.

Other collectors

You may decide not to use a collection agency but still need help from outside resources. Try the following:

Local credit bureaus

This strategy is most effective in smaller, rural areas. Some credit bureaus are also registered collection agencies. The advantage of using these over a typical collection agency is that credit bureaus have more personal contact and pull with the patient. Also, those who have outstanding debts will be unable to obtain loans or other credit until they settle up with you.

Bankruptcy court

The reasons why individuals file for personal bankruptcy vary, but attorneys who specialize in consumer bankruptcy say that common reasons for filing include unemployment, marital problems, ballooning credit card debt, and large medical expenses. That means that your patients may join the ranks of the close to 1.5 million people who, according to the Administrative Office of the United States Courts, filed nonbusiness-related bankruptcies in 2005.

If you discover that a patient who owes you money has filed for bankruptcy, immediately stop your normal collection efforts. There is little chance that the patient can pay, plus you risk sanctions that could include punitive damages. But this doesn't mean you can't collect for the treatment you provided this patient, you just might collect less.

By filing a petition of bankruptcy in a federal court, a patient stops debt collection and sets in motion a process that will end with a settlement or discharge of most outstanding debts, usually in exchange for paying creditors just cents on the dollar. That may sound to you like a raw deal, but consider the alternative: Collecting nothing from an unwilling or unable person.

The bankruptcy process gets you what it can and relieves you of an all-too-often wasted effort. Once your patient files for bankruptcy, collection is stayed. All debts, including yours, are processed under court supervision. The patient will list for the court all creditors and the amounts that he or she owes to each. A few weeks after the filing, the court should send you a notice that lists the debts and assets available to pay the debts. Even if the list correctly shows your outstanding balance, you must complete and return to the court a proof of claim. Otherwise, you lose your right to stand in line with the other creditors.

A proof of claim simply states how much you are owed and why. It's easy to complete, and a blank copy of the standard form usually accompanies the notice. If you don't receive a copy, request it from the court. The notice will tell you who to call. You shouldn't need your lawyer's help to complete the claim form.

About three months after your patient files, a meeting of creditors will take place. There often is no actual meeting; this is just a formality. Even when an actual meeting occurs, you usually don't need to attend. Only in rare instances should you engage your lawyer. Then you wait for the court to pay. You likely won't receive the amount you are due, and if your patient files under Chapter 13, you'll have to accept installment payments, but getting paid is far simpler and more assured than doing nothing.

Your bankrupt patient may need to see you again for further medical care. Unless you have properly terminated the doctor-patient relationship, you are obligated to continue care. Even beyond the legal obligation, it's good customer service and patient relations to continue care. And the bankruptcy only applies to amounts the patient owed you on the date of the filing. You may bill and collect the full amount for later services—that is, if you can collect them this time around. Serve such a patient on an advance payment (i.e., cash-only) basis.

Deceased patient's estate

When you discover that a patient with an outstanding balance has died, pursue the balance as if the patient were still alive, trying the same approaches. After you've exhausted those resources, you'll have to work through the legal probate system.

Sending a bill does not make a legal claim for payment. Instead, properly file a claim with the executor or administrator of the deceased patient's estate. Each state has a time limit for doing so—ranging from one to nine months after death—so check with your attorney for the deadline in your state. If you miss the time limitation, your bill will be rejected.

Shortly after your patient's death, the will is admitted to probate to determine its validity. The executor named in the will takes possession of the deceased's assets and pays the proper expenses and claims before distributing the balance according to the will. If there is no will or no executor, the court appoints an administrator to perform these tasks.

The law requires that the executor or administrator notify those who may have claims and advertise generally in the county where the patient last resided. If you know about the death and haven't received such information, have your manager or your lawyer's office obtain it from the probate court. File your claim by sending copies of your itemized bill to the executor/administrator and to the probate court.

The probate process in the area where your patient last maintained residence handles the claim, and the address of that residence may not necessarily be his or her last address in your records. You may have to investigate if you cannot locate the probate court or if your patient's legal residence is unclear.

If you receive no response to your claim within 10 days, contact the executor/administrator or the county probate clerk for the forms for filing a legal claim in that jurisdiction. Usually, the executor/administrator will notify you as to whether the claim is accepted or rejected. If it is accepted, you don't need to do anything more. Although it may take months—and occasionally years—to get paid, if funds exist, payment must be made or provided before they are distributed to the heirs.

If the estate's representative rejects your claim, submit it directly to the probate court. It's best to involve your attorney at this stage, as you must show proof of your claim when the court audit or hearing actually occurs.

Conclusion

The more money you collect up front from patients, the less you will have to worry about outstanding balances and the use of outside resources to collect on delinquent accounts. By employing strategies to collect from patients while they are still at your practice, fostering strong relationships with payers, and using effective means to ask patients for money once they leave your office, you can improve your bottom line and make your practice more effective.

Acknowledgements

Special thanks to Marge McQuade, CMM, CMSCS, for her hard work on this project.

The following individuals provided source material for this book:

William Caplan, MD, medical director of Hawthorn Medical Associates, Dartmouth, MA, *wcaplan@partners.org*

Brad Engel, national health and welfare product leader, Mellon Financial Corporation

Lynn Ferriss, administrator, Urology Specialty and Surgery Center, Urology Center of Southwest Louisiana, Lake Charles, LA, *lferriss@ucswla.com*

Margaret Hoban, consultant

Ed Howley, practice administrator, Advanced Cardiology, Inc., Poland, OH, *www.advancedcardiology.com*

Dennis Hursh, healthcare attorney, Hursh & Hursh, Harrisburg, PA, *dennis@pahealthlaw.com*

Bruce A. Johnson, attorney, Faegre & Benson, Denver, consultant with the Medical Group Management Association, *bajohnson@faegre.com*

Charles M. Key, attorney, The Bogatin Law Firm, PLC, Memphis, TN, *ckey@bogatin.com*

Max Reiboldt, CPA, managing partner/CEO, The Coker Group, Atlanta, *www.cokergroup.com*

Todd Rodriguez, healthcare attorney, Alice G. Gosfield & Associates, PC, Philadelphia

William Sarraille, partner, Sidley Austin Brown & Wood, LLP, Washington, DC, *wsarraille@sidley.com*

Caryl Serbin, president and founder, Surgery Consultants of American, Surgery Center Billing, LLC, *cas@surgecon.com*

Lynn Steffes, PT, president of Steffes & Associates, New Berlin, WI

James Tripp, practice management consultant, Schenck & Associates Health Services Group, Appleton, WI, *trippj@schenckcpa.com*

Gil Weber, MBA, practice management/managed care consultant, Davie, FL, *gil@gilweber.com*

How to use the files on your CD-ROM

The following file names correspond with files in the CD-ROM accompanying the book, *Improve Billing and Collections: Get the Money You Deserve Now*.

File name	Document
Insurance agreement.doc	Customized financial agreement for insurance patients
Noninsurance agreement.doc	Customized financial agreement for noninsurance patients
Adding ancillaries.doc	Dos and don'ts of adding an ancillary service
Noncovered services.doc	Noncovered services authorization and payment agreement
Fee analyzer.doc	Sample fee analyzer
Insurance form.doc	Sample insurance information form
Patient complaint form.doc	Sample patient complaint form
Referral card.doc	Sample referral consultation card
Preauthorization form.doc	Sample telephone preauthorization form
Standard abbreviations.doc	Standard abbreviations
Termination letter.doc	Termination letter

To adapt any of the files to your own facility, simply follow the instructions below to open the CD.

If you have trouble reading the forms, click on "View," and then "Normal." To adapt the forms, save them first to your own hard drive or disk (by clicking "File," then "Save as," and changing the system to your own). Then change the information enclosed in brackets to fit your facility, and add or delete any items that you wish to change.

Installation instructions

This product was designed for the Windows operating system and includes Word files that will run under Windows 95/98 or greater. The CD will work on all PCs and most Macintosh systems. To run the files on the CD-ROM, take the following steps:

1. Insert the CD into your CD-ROM drive.

2. Double-click on the "My Computer" icon, next double-click on the CD drive icon.

3. Double-click on the files you wish to open.

4. Adapt the files by moving the cursor over the areas you wish to change, highlighting them, and typing in the new information using Microsoft Word.

5. To save a file to your facility's system, click on "File" and then click on "Save As." Select the location where you wish to save the file and then click on "Save."

6. To print a document, click on "File" and then click on "Print."